THE OLD BREED OF MARINE

THE OLD BREED OF MARINE

A World War II Diary

Abraham Felber
with Franklin S. Felber
and William H. Bartsch

McFarland & Company, Inc., Publishers
Jefferson, North Carolina, and London

Library of Congress Cataloguing-in-Publication Data

Felber, Abraham, 1906–
    The old breed of marine : a World War II diary / Abraham
Felber, with Franklin S. Felber and William H. Bartsch.
        p.   cm.
    Includes bibliographical references and index.

    ISBN 0-7864-1410-3 (softcover : 50# alkaline paper)

    1. Felber, Abraham, 1906– — Diaries.   2. United States. Marine
Corps— Biography.   3. World War, 1939–1945 — Personal
narratives, American.   4. World War, 1939–1945 — Campaigns—
Solomon Islands— Guadalcanal.   5. Marines— United States—
Diaries.   I. Felber, Franklin S., 1950–   II. Bartsch, William H.,
1933–   III. Title.
    D767.98.F45   2003
    940.54'8173 — dc21   2002011904

British Library cataloguing data are available

Front cover: Marine First Sergeant Abraham Felber, August 17, 1943;
Official USMC photograph (Hdqtrs. No. 60338), distributed by the
Division of Public Relations in Washington, D.C.
Back cover: December 28, 1943; 75mm pack howitzers of D. Battery, 11th
Marines, in action, against the Japanese, Cape Gloucester, New Britain.
(Official USMC photograph, Neg. No. 12203.)

Manufactured in the United States of America

McFarland & Company, Inc., Publishers
  Box 611, Jefferson, North Carolina 28640
  www.mcfarlandpub.com

Contents

Preface by Franklin S. Felber   1

Historical Note by William H. Bartsch   5

Felber's Timeline   7

1 — Preparing for War
  January 7, 1941–August 6, 1942   11

2 — Guadalcanal
  August 7, 1942–December 15, 1942   69

3 — Australia and Cape Gloucester
  December 16, 1942–February 7, 1944   160

4 — Return and Rebuilding
  June 2, 1944–December 31, 1945   197

Afterword   213

Annotations by William H. Bartsch   215

Bibliography   239

Military Index   243

General Index   247

Preface

by Franklin S. Felber

You are about to read the remarkable wartime diary of a remarkable person. What makes the author remarkable, though, is not that he is uncommon.

Today, the life of Abraham Felber may seem uncommon. He held one job with the post office in Newark, New Jersey, for 46 years, until his retirement. He remains married to his wife of over 55 years. He helped her raise their three children and put them through college and beyond, even though he never finished high school himself. He dropped out of high school so that he could work full time supporting his family. When the war came, he went out to fight for the simple reason that he owed it to his country. But this life, these deeds, did not make him uncommon for his generation.

With his embrace of responsibility and deeply held values, he typifies the American men and women of his generation. It is his generation that is uncommon. His is the generation that carried our country through the Great Depression. His is the generation that stood up to global tyrants and defeated them. His is the generation that built our country into what it is today — indisputably the leading nation in the world.

Like so many others of his generation, Felber was born to immigrants in the cauldron of poverty. His parents rented a one-bedroom tenement apartment on the Lower East Side of New York, where he was delivered by a midwife in 1906. Only Yiddish was spoken at home and on the streets. He doesn't remember how he picked up English.

In his second year of high school, Felber worked as a pin boy in the bowling alley of a saloon from seven until midnight. He had difficulty

Undated portrait of Felber in dress uniform.

staying awake in school on only six or seven hours of sleep, and he was too ashamed to admit that he couldn't see the blackboard without eyeglasses. His teachers called him a dummy. He dropped out of school on his 16th birthday, on May 21st, one month before the end of the school year, to work full time for a razor-blade maker.

Later, Felber passed his high school equivalency test with top grades. He scored in the 99th percentile on national standardized intelligence tests, and he is the oldest living member in New Jersey of Mensa, the high-IQ society. Felber was always a voracious reader. Mainly self-taught, he developed his appreciation for literature by starting at the A's in the library and working his way through the shelves to the Z's. Like many of his generation, Felber understood and appreciated the power of formal education, even though he couldn't afford it for himself.

At least we, the readers of his diary, reap the benefits of Felber's self-immersion in books and literature. Some readers will detect echoes of such great authors as Hemingway, whose simple declarative style in "For Whom the Bell Tolls" impressed Felber near the start of this diary in May 1941.

What makes this diary remarkable, however, is not the style, but the substance. Felber was a keen observer of all there was to see and hear around him. And he had a passion for recording events. For much of the war, it was his job to keep records for his unit. Felber wrote his diary contemporaneously in shorthand. Most of it is recorded in government-issued hardbound notebooks with drab-green covers appropriately imprinted, "Record of Events." After the war, he transcribed his shorthand into a typewritten volume of a quarter-million words.

Felber's passion for recording events extended to pictures, as well as words. Throughout his life, photography was his main hobby. He served, sometimes officially, sometimes unofficially, as photographer for his unit.

His photographs are in the National Archives and Records Administration (NARA II) in College Park, Maryland. His thousands of photographs spanning more than half a century are all numbered, dated, and captioned in neat files. The photographs in this book were chosen from among many hundreds in his collection from 1941 through 1945. (Except as otherwise noted, the photographs in this book are from Felber's collection. The others are official Marine photographs, National Archives photographs, or were graciously contributed by William H. Bartsch from his own collection.)

Felber's passion for recording events gives us a diary rich in historical detail of all kinds—social, political, economic—not just military. The historical details of military significance are greatly enhanced by the fully referenced annotations of William H. Bartsch, a prize-winning military historian specializing in Marine history.

As editor, I have had to make painful choices in cutting the diary to a more manageable one-third of its original length. I have made the tactical decision to eliminate many hundreds of daily diary entries in whole, but to preserve every word, every abbreviation, every punctuation of every daily entry that is retained in this book. Within each diary entry that was retained, I refused to tamper with the real-life mixture of the mundane with the terrifying, or the insignificant with the significant.

To be retained, each diary entry had to carry its own weight, either by historical significance or by demonstrating the author's values. I am grateful to William Bartsch for successfully advocating the re-insertion into the manuscript of dozens of daily entries, mostly of pre-war preparations, the military historical significance of which I had not fully appreciated. Nevertheless, in my approach to editing, I have lost much historical meat with the fat. What I have attempted to preserve fully is this: all significant military history, including all combat; the story of Felber's love for his wife, Bess; and the abiding values of Felber as an Old Breed Marine.

It was not Felber's age alone that made him an Old Breed Marine. True, at 35 when war broke out, Sgt. Felber must have seemed a grizzled veteran, a generation removed from the young boots. But what made Felber an Old Breed Marine was his adherence to the code.

The code was not written down in any manual, but its tenets will become clear to you as you read this diary. The code has a long tradition, predating the Marines by centuries, with roots at least as far back as the code of chivalry of King Arthur's knights. To the Old Breed Marine, the code was harsh and unyielding in war and chivalrous in civilian life. The code of the Old Breed Marine was the embodiment, in its purest form, of the generation's embrace of responsibility for others.

You do what you must to support your family as you grow up. Then you get married and work hard to raise and support a family of your own.

You stand for a five-hour bus ride to give your seat to a poor Mexican mother holding her baby.

You don't hold a grudge against your fellow Marine, and you don't let anyone hold a grudge against you. You settle matters here and now. If words don't work, then with fists.

You take the responsibility, and you take the blame, even if it's not yours.

When war comes, you fight, because that's what you owe your country.

In war, you depend for your life on your fellow Marine, and he depends for his life on you.

If you kill your fellow Marine accidentally, you are transferred and eventually forgiven. If you kill your fellow Marine through weakness, panic or cowardice, your life may be forfeit. If you kill your fellow Marine intentionally during combat, your life is surely and abruptly ended.

You respect your own airmen and sailors doing battle for you. They are fighting and dying in the skies and on the seas to protect you. That's a service you can't return to them.

You respect your enemy. They are husbands, fathers, and sons who fight and die just as bravely as you do.

And when the warrior's day is done, and your nation seems quick to forget your sacrifice and your honor, you remain ever faithful, ever loyal.

Historical Note
by William H. Bartsch

On May 1, 1931, in the depths of the Great Depression, 24-year-old Abraham Felber, a postal clerk in Newark, New Jersey, joined the U.S. Marine Corps Reserve, a component of the Marine Corps. It was the beginning of an association with the Marines that would last for almost 21 years. Like others who joined the Marine Reserves, he would be gaining the training needed in drills and at summer camp to prepare himself for the eventuality of defending his country — and, most importantly, in the service of his own choice.

Felber was assigned to the 2nd Battalion, 19th Reserve Marines, based at Newark and Elizabeth, New Jersey. In 1935, following a reorganization of the Marine Reserves, it became the 4th Battalion, Fleet Marine Corps Reserve (FMCR), one of thirteen battalions of the FMCR established at various locations in the United States, which at that time included only 407 officers and 3,054 enlisted men in its ranks.[1]

The Reserves constituted a pool of manpower available to report for duty in the event of a national emergency. For Felber and the others, this occasion arose when President Roosevelt declared a Limited National Emergency under Executive Order 8244 of September 8, 1939. In October 1940, all the Marine Reserve Battalions were called into active service to help meet the new authorized strength of 36,000 for the Marine Corps, almost double that of 1939.[2] Felber was called to active duty on November 26, 1940, with the others of his 4th Battalion, an infantry unit, and was subsequently ordered to the Parris Island, South Carolina, recruitment depot, where he would spend just two weeks before shipping out to the Marine base at Guantanamo Bay, Cuba. During this period, his 4th Battalion was merged with the 7th Battalion, which had been based in Philadelphia before being sent to Parris Island, to form an artillery unit.

Earlier, on September 1, 1940, the 11th Marine Regiment, an artillery unit that had been disbanded in 1929, was re-organized at Quantico, Virginia, with the formation of its 1st Battalion and assignment to the 1st Marine Brigade. On January 1, 1941, its 2nd Battalion was formed at Guantanamo Bay. On Felber's arrival there on the USS *Wharton* on January 23, 1941, a 3rd Battalion was organized, to which Felber's battery was assigned the following day as Battery H, 3rd Battalion, 1st Marine Brigade.[3]

On February 1, 1941, the 1st Marine Brigade was re-designated the 1st Marine Division, under the command of Major General Holland M. "Howlin' Mad" Smith. The 1st Marine Division was destined to become one of the most highly honored units of World War II. Felber's 11th Marines constituted its artillery regiment. As was the case for the rest of the Division, it was understrength at that time, with only three battalions assigned. Not until June 1942, just prior to overseas departure, was it brought up to full strength with the addition of its 4th and 5th Battalions.[4]

Notes

1. Public Affairs Unit, U.S. Marine Corps, *The Marine Corps Reserve: A History* (Headquarters, U.S. Marine Corps, Washington, D.C., 1966), p. 44.

2. *Ibid.*, pp. 25, 59–60.

3. Robert Emmet, USMCR, *A Brief History of the 11th Marines* (Headquarters, U.S. Marine Corps, Washington, D.C., 1968), p. 7; A. Felber, diary entry of January 24, 1941. Felber was reassigned to E Battery, 2nd Battalion, on March 1, 1941, and to H&S Battery of Regimental Headquarters on January 7, 1942 (diary entries of March 1, 1941, and January 6, 1942).

4. Emmet, *Brief History*, p. 7.

Felber's Timeline,
1941–1945

1941

Jan. 1–Jan. 2	Newark, N.J. (furlough)
Jan. 3	Newark, N.J. to Parris Island, S.C.
Jan. 4–Jan. 17	Parris Island, S.C.
Jan. 18–Jan. 19	abd USS *Wharton*—Charleston, S.C.
Jan. 20–Jan. 22	abd USS *Wharton*—at sea, en route to Guantanamo Bay, Cuba
Jan. 23	abd USS *Wharton*—Guantanamo Bay, Cuba
Jan. 24–Feb. 17	Caravela Point, Guantanamo Bay, Cuba
Feb. 18–Feb. 28	Grenadilla Point, Guantanamo Bay, Cuba
March 1–April 13	Castle Hill Point, Guantanamo Bay, Cuba
April 14	abd USS *McCawley*—Main Station, Guantanamo Bay, Cuba
April 15–April 17	abd USS *McCawley*—at sea
April 18	abd USS *McCawley*—Charleston (S.C.) Navy Yard
April 19–April 23	"F" Barracks, Parris Island, S.C.
April 24–May 9	on leave—Miami Beach, Fla. and Newark, N.J.
May 10	Newark, N.J. To Parris Island, S.C., via rail
May 11–June 3	"F" Barracks, Parris Island, S.C.
June 4–July 5	"G" Barracks, Parris Island, S.C.
July 6–July 9	abd USS *McCawley*—Charleston, S.C.

July 10	abd USS *McCawley*—at sea
July 11–July 18	abd USS *McCawley*—offshore, Hurst Beach, N.C.
July 19–July 20	abd USS *McCawley*—Cape Lookout, N.C.
July 21–July 26	abd USS *McCawley*—Paper Mill Dock, Charleston, S.C.
July 27	abd USS *McCawley*—at sea
July 28–July 31	abd USS *McCawley*—Miami Beach, Fla.
Aug. 1–Aug. 2	abd USS *McCawley*—at sea
Aug. 3	abd USS *McCawley*—Hurst Beach, N.C.
Aug. 4–Aug. 9	ashore at Hurst Beach, N.C., on practice maneuvers
Aug. 10–Aug. 11	abd USS *McCawley*—off Hurst Beach, N.C.
Aug. 12	abd USS *McCawley*—at sea
Aug. 13	abd USS *McCawley*—at NOB, Norfolk, Va.
Aug. 14–Oct. 29	"G" Barracks, MB, Parris Island, S.C.
Oct. 30	Overland, en route to New River, N.C. (Camp Lejeune)
Oct. 31–Dec. 26	11th Regt. Area, New River, N.C.
Dec. 27	en route to Newark, N.J.
Dec. 28–Dec. 31	295 Avon Ave., Newark, N.J. (New Year's leave)

1942

Jan. 1–Jan. 2	295 Avon Ave., Newark, N.J. (New Year's leave)
Jan. 3	en route to 11th Regt. Area, New River, N.C., via bus
Jan. 4–April 7	11th Regt. Area, Verona, New River, N.C.
April 8–June 8	11th Regt. Area, Main Sta., Jacksonville, New River, N.C.
June 9–June 13	en route, Jacksonville, N.C. to San Francisco, Calif.
June 14–June 20	abd *John Ericsson*—San Francisco, Calif.
June 21	abd *John Ericsson*—San Francisco Bay
June 22–July 10	abd *John Ericsson*—at sea
July 1	crossed equator—155'10" West
July 9	crossed International Date Line—East to West
July 11	arr Wellington, N.Z.
July 12	transfer from *John Ericsson* to *Hunter Liggett*
July 12–July 20	abd *Hunter Liggett*—Wellington, N.Z.
July 21	abd *Hunter Liggett*—Wellington Bay
July 22–July 27	abd *Hunter Liggett*—at sea
July 28–July 30	abd *Hunter Liggett*—off Koro, Fiji Islands

July 31–Aug. 6	abd *Hunter Liggett*— at sea
Aug. 7–Dec. 14	Guadalcanal, B.S.I.
Dec. 15–Dec. 18	abd *Hunter Liggett*— at sea
Dec. 19	abd *Hunter Liggett*— in harbor, Brisbane, Australia
Dec. 20–Dec. 31	Camp Cable — Brisbane, Australia

1943

Jan. 1–Jan. 6	Camp Cable — Brisbane, Australia
Jan. 7	Camp Cable to dock, Brisbane, Australia
Jan. 8–Jan. 9	abd *West Point*— Brisbane Harbor
Jan. 10–Jan. 11	abd *West Point*— at sea
Jan. 12	arr Melbourne, Australia
Jan. 13–Oct. 4	Camp Victoria Park, Ballarat, Victoria, Australia
Oct. 5–Oct. 9	Camp Murphy, Melbourne, Australia
Oct. 10–Oct. 17	abd *John Carroll*— at sea
Oct. 18–Oct. 19	arr and lv Townsville, Australia
Oct. 20–Oct. 22	abd *John Carroll*— at sea
Oct. 23	arr Beli Beli, Goodenough Island
Oct. 23–Dec. 11	Goodenough Island, D'Entrescastreau Group
Dec. 12– Dec. 13	abd LST-470 — at sea
Dec. 14	arr Tare Beach, Cape Cretin, New Guinea
Dec. 14–Dec. 24	Cape Cretin, New Guinea
Dec. 25	abd LST-456 — at sea
Dec. 26–Dec. 31	Cape Gloucester, New Britain

1944

Jan. 1–April 23	Cape Gloucester, New Britain
April 24	abd USS *Elmore*, Cape Gloucester, New Britain
April 25–April 27	abd USS *Elmore*— at sea
April 28–June 1	Pavuvu, Russell Islands
June 2	abd USS *Robert L. Howze*— Pavuvu to Guadalcanal
June 3	abd USS *Robert L. Howze*— at Guadalcanal
June 4–June 18	abd USS *Robert L. Howze*— at sea

June 7	crossed International Date Line — West to East
June 12	crossed equator
June 19	arr San Francisco 0818; debark 1330; entrain 1500
June 20–July 5	Camp Pendleton, Oceanside, Calif.
July 6	Camp Pendleton to New York, N.Y., via air
July 7–Aug. 23	Furlough
July 7–July 15	Newark, N.J.
July 16–July 25	Station Hospital, AAB, NAAF (malaria)
July 26–Aug. 21	Newark, N.J.
Aug. 22	New York, N.Y. to Los Angeles, Calif., via air
Aug. 23	Los Angeles, Calif.
Aug. 24–Nov. 20	Camp Pendleton, Oceanside, Calif.
Nov. 21–Nov. 24	San Diego, Calif., to New York, N.Y., via rail
Nov. 25–Dec. 6	Newark, N.J.
Dec. 7–Dec. 8	Newark, N.Y., to Camp Pendleton, Oceanside, Calif., via air
Dec. 9–Dec. 31	Camp Pendleton, Oceanside, Calif.

1945

Jan. 1–March 30	Area 17-B-1, Camp Pendleton, Oceanside, Calif.
March 31–July 24	Area 16-B-3, Camp Pendleton, Oceanside, Calif.
July 25–July 28	en route, Camp Pendleton to MB, Quantico, Va., via rail
July 29–Dec. 16	Marine Barracks, Quantico, Va.
Dec. 17–Dec. 31	Furlough
Dec. 17	to Miami Beach, Fla., via air
Dec. 18–Dec. 22	Miami Beach, Fla.
Dec. 23–Dec. 26	Havana, Cuba
Dec. 27–Dec. 31	Miami Beach, Fla.

CHAPTER 1

Preparing for War

January 7, 1941–August 6, 1942

January 7, 1941 Tuesday
Parris Island, So. Car.

A rainy, chilly day. The 7th Bn. men (the former USMCRes. artillery unit called to active duty from Phila., Pa., and merged with our 4th Bn. infantrymen from the Newark, N.J. area to form an artillery unit) have been issued rifles, and I spent all day teaching their NCOs the nomenclature, care and cleaning of the '03 Springfield rifle. Wrote to the insurance agent and thanked him for his efforts in my behalf, and told him what I had done in attempting to secure the return of my camera; and that I had not yet heard from the Chief of Police of Richmond, Va., or from the bus company. The portable oil stove in my tent had been left lit at noontime when I went to chow, and when I returned I found that it had started smoking and had deposited a coat of oily soot over everything. Had a difficult time getting the stuff off my clothes and the bedding, and all my other gear.

January 8, 1941 Wednesday
Parris Island, So. Car.

Another day of the command not knowing what to do with us. It seems that everybody is just waiting until the day we sail for Guantanamo Bay, and there is no definite schedule. It appears as though the schedule for the day is made up each morning. Today there was a hike in the morning for the 4th Bn. men, who had no rifles. I was scheduled to go along on this hike, but an officer spoke to me and detained me until the men were out of sight. In the afternoon we had a "field day," cleaning our gear and sweeping the wooden floors of our tents. Have been notified that I am to be Sergeant of the Guard tomorrow, with a detail of 38 men under me. The guard has been increased to this strength due to the stealing that has been going on. Completed two more correspondence lessons for the Marine Corps Schools and mailed them off.

January 18, 1941 Saturday
Parris Island — Charleston, So. Car.

We were awakened at 4:15 a.m., had an early chow, and were packed by 7:30. We moved out by truck to Port Royal, and entrained there. We reached Charleston, So. Car., by noon, and boarded the USS *Wharton*. The Charleston Navy Yard had several naval vessels and fighting craft lying in the harbor. The Wharton is quite a large ship. We were fed 4 times today — at camp, sandwiches on the train, and twice on the ship. At 5:30 p.m. we were called out to assist in loading trucks, cannons, machine guns, tent poles, stores, and all manner of other equipment on board. I worked until 11:30 p.m., and there was stuff still to be loaded at that time. To my compartment to turn in. The living quarters are very crowded, and the bunks are three high.

January 19, 1941 Sunday
Aboard USS Wharton, *Charleston, So. Car.*

Up at 5:45 a.m. Have learned that the *Wharton* has just recently been commissioned as a naval vessel, and that formerly it was the *Southern Cross* of the Munson Line, and that this is its first trip carrying troops. The ceremony in connection with the commissioning was held in the Brooklyn Navy Yard on Dec. 7, 1940. The *Wharton* is about the largest troop transport in the service of the Navy now. There are about 1,200 Marines aboard. Colds and influenza are spreading. Several of the men in our compartment were transferred to the hospital, and will come to Cuba on a later transport. I felt OK except for a sore throat from supervising the loading last night. Bove had a fever, and went to the hospital on board. I took a bus to Charleston and walked about in the sun all day. Had supper in town. Was back aboard ship by 6:00 p.m., and was so tired that I lay down on my bunk and slept through until morning.

January 22, 1941 Wednesday
Abd USS Wharton— *at sea*

The sea much rougher today, and seasickness quite prevalent. Several of the men assigned to sentry duty had to be replaced because they were too ill to perform their duties. Thirty sentries, 3 corporals and myself as Sergeant of the Guard comprised the guard complement, plus 2 runners (messengers). We are stationed at the 5 holds on the ship. Four hours on and 8 hours off duty. It turned out to be a beautiful day. Saw flying fish for the first time. Many of the guards became seasick. After relieving 6 of them, I invoked the Navy rule — seasickness is not "sickness," and the sentry must continue to perform his duty. I was in one hold with a corporal of the guard and two privates of the guard and all three were vomiting until nothing more came up, but I was especially fortunate in that I didn't become sick myself. Toward evening it became very warm, and all Marines were ordered to change from green woolen uniforms to cotton khaki ones. It rained for a short while.

January 23, 1941 Thursday
Abd USS Wharton— *Guantanamo Bay, Cuba*

Got a couple of hours sleep during the night. At 0415, after the guard changed reliefs, I up and took a shower and changed into my khakis. At 0800 my guard was relieved by "C" Battery, and I ate and up on deck. We were in the harbor of Guantanamo Bay, Cuba. It was a hot, sunny day. There was another transport in the harbor, and we saw the *Squalus*, the submarine which sank off New London, Conn., with the loss of several lives. It was subsequently raised. It has been reconditioned and renamed the *Sailfish*, and it was in the harbor on a shakedown cruise. We stored our greens in our seabags, made up our packs, and at 1100 debarked from the *Wharton*. The ship was unloaded by stevedores. We were taken to our camp in trucks. We are living in 8-man pyramidal tents. There are 7 privates in the tent with me. No electric lights. There is a nice NCO mess, with crockery dishes. The countryside looks dark brown and barren. Two different movies at night. Part of the camp is quarantined with measles. Saw several old Marine friends here. Wrote to Bess; and to the insurance agent about my camera.

January 24, 1941 Friday
Caravela Point, Guantanamo Bay, Cuba

Crockery dishes for NCO mess discontinued — we now eat from our mess gear. It gets very hot during the day. The sun is very bright and there are many cloud formations in the sky. We are left to our own devices, as there seems to be no program for us. There are many members of the former Eighth Reserve Battalion in camp. The Battalion has been all broken up. Twenty were transferred to our Battery, giving us about 95 in the Battery. We have been redesignated as "H" Battery, 3rd Battalion, 11th Marines, 1st Brigade, FMF. The place we are stationed at is called Caravela Point.

January 29, 1941 Wednesday
Caravela Pt., Gtmo Bay, Cuba
    Had a hike in the morning. After we got out a ways, we stopped for a rest; and then I was assigned to give a lecture to the entire Battalion on the method of approaching a hostile force — the approach march, forming squad columns, extended order, etc. In the afternoon I was assigned as instructor to the "boot" group (raw recruits). Gave them manual of arms and a bit of basic marksmanship. Today they burned out the head (latrine), and there was an awful stench about. Forwarded to the insurance agent the letter I received from the Chief of Police of Richmond, Va. Intended to write post cards to Bess's relatives, but so many men came into the tent to talk that I was unable to accomplish this purpose.

January 31, 1941 Friday
Caravela Pt., Gtmo Bay, Cuba
    Our company came off guard at 8:00 a.m., and the sentries expected the morning off; but they were told that we were on an expedition, and therefore the guard rated no time off. If this is so, and the expedition lasts more than 6 months, we will rate an expeditionary bar. We spent the day in straightening out tent stakes and policing up the river bank. A general had been around and criticized the condition of the camp. Tomorrow is inspection, so there was lots of policing. We signed the payroll tonight. A notice had been posted on the bulletin board last night about Hebrew religious services tonight; so after supper Sgt. Coleman and I went to the Post Chapel to attend them. We arrived at 5:45 p.m., and we were the only two present. A Christian gave us a prayer book and said one of us would conduct the services. So Coleman looked up the index and chose the Sabbath Evening Prayers, and read the English version for about 20 minutes. Just before we adjourned, another Jew came in. We decided to try to drum up some more attendees for next Friday. Bed linen was issued to us for the first time tonight. I am growing a moustache.

February 3, 1941 Monday
Caravela Pt., Gtmo Bay, Cuba
    Up and collected my guard: 21 privates, 3 corporals, 1 sergeant of the guard (me), 1 field music (bugler), and 1 truck driver (for emergencies and as a messenger). Relieved the old guard at 8:00 a.m., and was given two prisoners who had been sentenced to 10 days confinement for being picked up in Caimanera, a nearby town which is restricted territory for certain grades of Marines. Due to the heat of the sun, the sentries are relieved every two hours (instead of the customary 4 hours). During the night hours they

are on guard for 4 hours and off 8 hours. Received a registered letter from the insurance agent enclosing a draft for $183 in settlement of my camera loss claim. At about 2:15 a.m., a Marine cook named Walker came in drunk and raised a considerable commotion. He could not be pacified, so I called the relief in the guard house to take him out. They clubbed him several times, dragged him to the guard tent, and called the Officer of the Day. He was ordered to go to his tent, and some of the sergeants of his battery took him away.

February 4, 1941 Tuesday
Caravela Pt., Gtmo Bay, Cuba
Relieved by the new guard at 8:00 a.m. We had had very little sleep for the past 24 hours, but were told that the guard had to fall out with the rest of the company for a field exercise hike. I didn't have to go, but I said that if the lower-rated Marines were required to go, I would go also. A very fast hike, with emphasis on the approach march in enemy territory. Back by 11 a.m. Was visited by the cook, Walker, who had been slugged last night and he said he wanted to see who had been the sergeant of the guard so he could remember him. I told him that I had been, and that I was solely responsible for what had happened to him — that the sentries were only obeying my orders; and that though I disliked doing it, he could consider himself lucky to have gotten off so easy, as I didn't turn him in for possible court-martial. He went off muttering vague threats. I guess I have made an enemy, and can expect some excitement at what will probably be an inopportune time. Infantry training in the afternoon. Wrote a letter to Bess and enclosed the $183 check. Didn't mail this letter. Wrote to Kay and gave her the news to spread to the family.

February 5, 1941 Wednesday
Caravela Point, Guantanamo Bay, Cuba
Slept well last night except for being awakened by one of the men who nearly had hysterics when a huge rat got in under his mosquito net at about 1:20 a.m. In the morning inspected the new equipment issued to the Battery detail. A new 6-drop switchboard BD-71, eight new EE-8 phones, leg irons for pole climbing, and much other new stuff. In the afternoon I was asked to draw up a new setup for the Battery detail to take care of vacancies created by illnesses, discharges, and contemplated losses of personnel. There is much bickering going on in the Battery between the 7th Bn. (Phil.) men and those of the 4th Bn. (Newark area) and the 8th Bn. (Toledo, Ohio). Most of it is occasioned by the poor handling of the men by Platoon Sergeant Butler. Have heard that there are riots in Havana,

Felber's family pictured in October 1940. Back row, left to right: Abraham, brother Jack, brother Pat; front row, left to right: mother Rose, father Joseph, sister Kay (Gross).

and that the mail is not getting through. I wrote a letter to Bess, but I am not mailing it as I do not know how to handle the draft sent to me by the insurance company. We were paid today.

February 9, 1941 Sunday
Caravela Point, Guantanamo Bay, Cuba
      Up at 7:00, and after breakfast dressed and with 4 others from my Battery on a liberty party to Guantanamo City itself. A dirty, primitive town, lots of cheap liquor and cheaper women. Indulged in the former, but shuddered when the latter even came near me. It made me sick to see some of the Marines kissing and caressing some of the awful dark, coarse native women. The town itself is quite picturesque, and I spent most of the day walking about and absorbing the strange and interesting sights and scenes. The natives were having a Roman Holiday with the Marines, peddling sleazy stuff to them and fleecing them right and left. Several of the peddlers who approached me were Jewish. Bought a few souvenirs for some of the fellows in camp, and nothing for myself but some eats and drinks. Left for camp on the 4:00 p.m. train.

February 15, 1941 Saturday
Caravela Pt., Gtmo Bay, Cuba

It was drizzling slightly when we awoke. The uniform for the guard was khaki with boondock shoes and ponchos. The Officer of the Day is 2nd Lt Dwyer. There were 33 privates of the guard, 3 corporals, 2 prisoner chasers, 2 runners, and a truck driver. There are 4 prisoners who have been tried by Summary Court Martial, and who are awaiting sentence. A fifth prisoner was placed in confinement today for insubordination to an NCO. 2ndLt Donald Love was ordered to return the seabags and personal effects of the prisoners, and when he attempted to do so, the prisoner chaser told him not to do so until permission had been received from the Officer of the Day or the Sergeant of the Guard. Lt Love insisted on returning the stuff, and I was called. I had the stuff placed in the brig until authorization could be secured from the O.D. for the prisoners to possess these items, and I entered a record in the Guard Book that Lt. Love had interfered with the proper safe-guarding of the prisoners. This officer (Lt Love) once turned in a guard detail from this company for general incompetence and this will show him how it feels to be put on report.

February 16, 1941 Sunday
Caravela Pt., Gtmo Bay, Cuba

Was relieved (as Sgt of the Guard) at 0800. Had very little sleep while on guard last night, so as soon as I got back I on my bunk in my clothes and to sleep. It was a very hot, sunny day. Was awakened again at suppertime to eat. One of the men in my tent came back from a liberty in Guantanamo, and he was slightly drunk and very voluble about his adventures in town and of his affair with one of the prostitutes. Felt disgusted when I thought of those horrible creatures. (A large number of men were acquiring venereal diseases, and the towns of Caimanera and Boqueron have been declared "off limits.") One of the messmen in the NCO's mess was sent to the hospital with a case of gonorrhea. He had been sneaking off to Boqueron, one of the restricted towns. Others who were caught have been court-martialed and sentenced to 20 days hard labor on bread and water, with full rations once every third day.

February 18, 1941 Tuesday
Grenadilla Point, Guantanamo Bay, Cuba

Was awakened extra early again today and "worked out" with the boxers. After breakfast we moved to the new area and spent the day squaring away. It looks like a much nicer place than our last camp site, and the view is quite beautiful. There is plenty of work and we were kept going all day. One of the men, Denver Cunningham, walked off a detail before he was dismissed, and I ordered him back to work. He refused unless I ordered others back, and demanded to see the Battery Commander. I went back to the job, and in a little while he returned without saying anything and worked until the detail was finished. I intend to run him up before the Battery Commander anyway, as I had a bit of trouble with this man before for the same reason. Lots of tarantulas, scorpions, lizards, and even snakes in the new area.

February 23, 1941 Sunday
Grenadilla Pt., Gtmo Bay, Cuba

Hooray!! Received a letter from Bess stating that she had received my registered letter with the $175 in it. Gosh, what a relief. There are persistent rumors that Guantanamo Bay has been condemned as a Marine Corps Base by the MGC, and that we are to move from here to Wilmington, No. Car., by April 1st. The rumors have it that condemnation was caused by the great amount of coral dust that is so prevalent here. The April 1st back to the U.S.A. story is so strong that there must be something to it. Washed my bed linen in the morning, and in the afternoon went on a swimming party. Started a long letter to Bess, but before I could finish it was inveigled into a game of poker that kept me busy until taps.

March 1, 1941 Saturday
Castle Hill Point, Guantanamo Bay, Cuba

Very windy and quite cold. We started moving right after breakfast. We turned in all our bed clothes, keeping only our blankets. All my movements to date have been further away from home. This is my first move in a retrograde direction. I finally wound up in "E" Battery of the 2nd Battalion (11th Marines, 1st Brigade, FMF). 1stSgt Bove has been assigned to Regimental Headquarters of the 11th Regiment, back at Caravela Point. "H" Battery has been split 3 ways, and each

Felber's friend, 1st Sgt Frederick Bove, pictured in early 1941 at Guantanamo Bay, Cuba.

third has been assigned to one of the batteries in the 2nd Battalion. Platoon Sgt. Butler and 1stSgt Karlage are with "F" Battery. I have been given a hint that I am to be made a Section Chief on the 75-mm guns. Fairly reliable rumors have it that there are a bit over 10,000 men on the station; the place is full of ammunition and explosives. A man from our Battery who came out the hospital stated that there were 62 cases of venereal disease reported from the last liberty party to Guantanamo City. In the evening walked to Caravela Point to visit with Bove.

March 9, 1941 Sunday
Castle Hill Pt., Gtmo Bay, Cuba

Up and dashed about getting ready for liberty. It started to rain just before reveille, and the sky looked very threatening. Left at 7:30 a.m. for the boat to Boqueron. Got there early, and it began to rain very hard. Got aboard the train, and the rain leaked in very badly, and the windows were all nailed open. Arrived at Guantanamo City and it was still raining. This didn't stop the Marines any, and they were running about, completely ignoring the rain and sloshing about in mud up to their ankles in places. Ran into Lt. Lane C. Kendall, a former officer of "D" Company, 4th Battalion, USMCR, in Newark. Also met Lt. Ellison in town. He was very drunk and abusive, and I spent about an hour trying to get him settled. Finally left him sleeping at the police station. Walked about town taking pictures, and bought some cocoanut-wood bracelets for Bess. At 3:00 p.m. I collected Lt Ellison and got him to the train at 4:00. It had rained all day. After we got back to Boqueron and boarded the boats that took us back to the camps, fist fights broke out on the boats. We were all jammed in tight on these boats, and pretty soon nearly everybody was involved in the fights. At one time 4 different groups were fighting at once. Got home finally, and found letters from Bess and from Max Gelfond, and a box of candy from Bill Kuntze. Had intended writing to Bess, but a poker game for heavy stakes was in progress in the tent, and my bunk was being occupied, so that I could not do this. Waited until taps, and then to bed very tired.

March 11, 1941 Tuesday
Castle Hill Pt., Gtmo Bay, Cuba

Fell right in after breakfast, and at 7:00 a.m. started moving off on an RSOP (Reconnaissance, Selection, Occupation of Position). Marched for about 1½ miles, and set up the guns. No firing was done. After the guns were set up and the signal communications established, the Battery Commander took the men around and explained the set-up. I examined the communication set-up myself. There was not much difference between the regular set-up and the set-up I developed while with "H" Battery, 3rd Battalion. They made their wire splices much more rapidly than we did, but they didn't use rubber tape. They laid their lines more carelessly than we did, failing to bury wire and failing to tie into a tree at the phones. In the afternoon we cleaned gear and practiced semaphore signaling, at which I am becoming proficient. In the evening our lamp was borrowed for a poker game, so I had to forego writing any letters. Made up a package of the bracelets I had bought in Guantanamo, and sent them to Bess. Visited Bove.

March 14, 1941 Friday
Castle Hill Point, Guantanamo Bay, Cuba
      Care and cleaning of equipment was scheduled for this morning. I left it up to Corp. Kennedy to take care of cleaning the Battery Detail equipment, as he is in charge of the detail. I spent the morning lying around and writing a letter to Max Gelfond. In the afternoon we had a field day. All the cots were set out in the sun to air. I cleaned up on some shoes, and did some fixing around the tents. Was awaiting the evening so that I could write to Bess, but the poker games started again. I had to pick up my stuff and get over to Bove's tent where I wrote Bess a long letter. I didn't have time to say all that I wished, as by the time that I got over there it was quite late and I had to allow myself time to get back to my own tent before taps. Will continue my remarks in a letter I will write tomorrow. An order was received that we are to be designated hereafter as the Atlantic Marine Force; and that we are to maintain ourselves in readiness to move to a new base at 12 hours notice.

March 26, 1941 Wednesday
Castle Hill Point, Guantanamo Bay, Cuba
      In the morning we all gathered and the Battery Commander read the Articles for the Government of the United States Navy. After explaining the various sections, he informed us that our Battery was to return to Parris Island on the 17th of April. This is extremely welcome news to me, as I am eager to see Bess again. There is a dearth of women here, and what there is, is very low class. Assisted in instruction on the .45 calibre automatic pistol. In the afternoon had a small RSOP. Wrote to Bess, telling her about the news of our return. The weather here is becoming quite hot. I am getting heavier and lazier here. We have been told that the uniform up north will be greens (woolens instead of cotton khaki) with pith helmets. Notices have been posted not to reveal troop or ship movements in our

conversation or correspondence. I have been recommended for examination for Platoon Sergeant, as have all the other sergeants in the Battery.

March 27, 1941 Thursday
Castle Hill Point, Guantanamo Bay, Cuba
Out at 6:55 a.m. on a Battalion maneuver. We were supposed to be the artillery in support of the 5th Regiment of infantry. I worked on the Battery Detail, and we laid about 5 miles of telephone wire. It was a defensive problem today, and we had plenty of time to install our lines. This is the first real work-out I have had since I joined the 2nd Battalion. We had chow in the field, and in the afternoon took in all the lines that we had laid the morning. Felt very good after all the work I had today. Received a letter from Bess tonight, the first in 4 days, and it was very welcome.

April 4, 1941 Friday
Castle Hill Point, Guantanamo Bay, Cuba
In the morning we serviced the Detail equipment, and had school on signal communication. In the afternoon we had a field day, and the officers and the NCOs out to the Fleet canteen field and practiced for a regimental review which will be held on Saturday. The maneuvers for the review are very simple. When we got back to camp I heard that there was an opening on the liberty party that was going to Guantanamo City on Saturday, and I applied for it. I was called into the office today and asked if I wanted to go into the firing battery for instructions, as there was an anticipated shortage in the ranks of the section of 155-mm howitzers to be formed. I said I would be glad of a chance to learn gunnery, and I felt that I could run a signal section with what I know now. Several dolphins appeared in our cove today and disported themselves lazily and gracefully in waters, to our admiration.

April 5, 1941 Saturday
Castle Hill Pt., Gtmo Bay, Cuba
A beautiful, hot, sunny day. After breakfast I dressed and found that the liberty party had already left; and I ran all the way to the 5th Marines dock to join them, arriving in a lather of sweat. So to Guantanamo City and had a wonderful time. The city looked much different this time. When I didn't know how long I was going to stay down here, the place looked small and filthy. But now that I am going home, Guantanamo city was quaint and interesting, and the people friendly and gay. One of the natives became especially friendly with me and showed me about. We ate in a small restaurant, dining on local dishes he recommended. Bought several

bracelets for Bess's friends, and all too soon had to go back to the boats which took us to our home camps. Took a couple of rolls of films, and left them to be developed, but I feel that they are not especially noteworthy. So home and heard that the parade put on by the Regiment was a success and quite an impressive spectacle. Received letters from my brother Jack and from Bess.

April 6, 1941 Sunday
Castle Hill Pt., Gtmo Bay, Cuba
    Spent the morning carving a swagger stick out of mahogany, getting several blisters, but not much results in the way of a snappy swagger stick. Got paid today. Did some laundry in the afternoon. Started writing a letter to my brother Jack in answer to his, and it ran on and on for 8 pages. Dropped over to Bove's tent, and kept on with Jack's letter. Didn't finish it. Wrote to Bess, sending her a very nice letter. Also wrote to Gus Troxler (my boxing instructor back in Newark). Did some studying. It is getting very hot. I am taking my last few looks at this place. Now that I am going home, I am able to appreciate the beauties of this place. I shall look back on my stay here with many pleasant memories. But I am glad to get back to see the states and Bess again.

April 10, 1941 Thursday
Castle Hill Pt., Gtmo Bay, Cuba
    Coached again today; in the morning on the .30 cal. rifle, and in the afternoon on the B.A.R. There were 4 men on my position on the firing line, and 3 of them qualified with the B.A.R. Among them was Corporal Letiziano of the former 7th Battalion reserves from Phila. He has just been broken from a sergeant for fighting with one of the sentries. It was another blazing hot day today, and I am taking my last looks around with a feeling of regret that I am to be able to view these scenes no more — at least for a while. As I look at these scenes I realize that soon their beauty will fade from my memory, as have so many other ravishingly lovely vistas of the past. I do not believe people who say that certain scenes will always be remembered by them — or else they are different from me. I always have to renew my acquaintance with these views, otherwise they slowly fade out of my mind.

April 14, 1941 Monday
Abd USS McCawley, *Main Station, Guantanamo Bay, Cuba*
    We were awakened at 5:00 a.m. and were ordered to pack our seabags, roll our bedding rolls, and get ready to strike tents. I was caught unawares,

and had to do some tall rushing to get ready. The bags and bedding rolls were set out, breakfast was served, the tents were struck, and then started the interminable "policing" of the area. The heads were burned out, covered with lime, and filled in. The breeze was pretty stiff today, and it was very dusty. I had an early lunch, and with a crew of 20 men rode to Main Station and worked until suppertime loading the ship by means of cargo nets. It was very hot and dry, and my lips were very sore. We were loaded by 5:00 p.m. The bunks on the *McCawley* are 4 tiers high, and the ship appears to be smaller than the USS *Wharton*.

April 15, 1941 Tuesday
Abd USS McCawley, en route to Charleston Navy Yard
We were awakened at 4:30 a.m. Had an early breakfast and at 6:00 a.m. we got under way. We rode in convoy all day, being led by a destroyer and followed by another troop transport, the USS *Elliot*. Anti-aircraft watch was maintained all day, and an anti-aircraft gun was kept stripped for action all day. A school of dolphins followed us for a time. The ship vibrates less than the USS *Wharton*. We seemed to be making less speed than on the trip down here. At about 4:00 p.m. the ship's engines developed some trouble, and the ship stopped. We had supper (the food is very good compared with that we have been getting). After supper, I up on deck and watched a young shark circle about the ship as we lay wallowing in the sea. The shark was about 5 feet long. The *Elliot* didn't wait for us, but the destroyer stood by. In the evening we were given orders to "darken ship," and all lights were put out, no smoking was permitted, and all portholes in my compartment were closed. The engines were still not fixed by the time I went to sleep.

April 18, 1941 Friday
Abd USS McCawley— at Charleston Navy Yard
Another calm day of sailing. Reports in the morning said that we would dock at 5:00 p.m. today. Wrote a long letter to Bess telling her I didn't know what decision she had made as to our vacation. I gave her the news since I last wrote, and included some tentative instructions for packing in case she had decided to travel. I also said I would telephone her if I got a chance. Wrote to Max Gelfond, enclosing a money order for $11 for the Federal Credit and for hospitalization. Spoke to the Battery Commander about taking an examination for promotion, and he said to remind him when we got to Parris Island, which I will surely do. In the afternoon the order came changing the uniform of the day from Khaki to greens (woolens). We all broke out our greens. A notice appeared stating that

about 25% of the Battery would go to Parris Island by train, and the rest of us by truck convoy. I am to ride aboard one of the trucks which pull the guns. Docked in Charleston at 6:00 p.m. After supper I was assigned to a detail for 20 men as a working party to go on duty at midnight. Got my green outfit ready and lay down to rest until midnight.

April 19, 1941 Saturday
Charleston Navy Yard — Parris Island, So. Car.

Awakened at midnight. Had not slept much. Had some coffee and 2 sandwiches, and out onto the dock and helped unload the *McCawley*. Others had been working since we docked, and we finished the job by 3:30 a.m. Back to my bunk until 5:00 a.m. reveille. Had breakfast, packed my seabag, rolled my bedding roll and made up my pack. Off the ship and onto the dock until 10:30 a.m., when we ate our noon meal. The order and been changed again, and our uniform was now khaki. After chow we donned our packs, mounted the trucks and started off in truck convoy to Parris Island, about 78 miles from Charleston. Those for whom room could not be found on the trucks rode in by train. At Parris Island we ran the guns onto the gun park and lined up the trucks. Half of us were assigned to tents and the other half to "F" barracks. We moved right in, and soon were shouting and reveling in the luxury of hot showers and plumbing. These barracks are brand new, completed since we left here in January. I to bed early. Only the bedding rolls and seabags were delivered today.

April 26, 1941 Saturday
Miami — Netherland Hotel, Miami Beach, Fla.

Awoke early. Straightened out my stuff. Out and did some shopping, getting a double socket for my electric razor, some elastic to enlarge my patent scarf (necktie), and some tetra-chloride cleaner. I left my camera at a store to be repaired, and 2 rolls of film to be processed. Stopped at the post office to see if Bess had written to me in care of General Delivery, but there was no mail. It being 11:00 a.m. by then, I back to the YMCA, got my stuff together, packed my bag and checked out shortly after 12:00 noon. Left my bag at the bus terminal and to a cheap movie to kill time until evening. At 3:00 p.m. I out and took a bus to the train station. At 4:25 p.m. the *Silver Meteor* came in and I met Bess. Took a cab to downtown, and we ate at the Seven Seas restaurant. After eating and catching up on the news, collected all our bags and out to Miami Beach just as it started to rain. After looking about a bit we took a very nice room at the Netherland Hotel for $21 per week.

Bess Panitch Felber, Wilson, N.C., March 1942.

April 27, 1941 Sunday
Hotel Netherland, Miami Beach, Fla.

Rose at 9:00 a.m. and had breakfast in the hotel. Bess brought down 3 bags, so I have all sorts of civilian clothes to wear. The weather is cold, and there is a stiff wind blowing. After breakfast we went shopping and looking around the business district, reviewing our memories of last summer. We lunched at a delicatessen and then back to the hotel, where we changed into bathing suits and out onto the beach to lay around for a while. I went in swimming for a bit, but the water was quite rough. In the evening we dressed (the first time I have had civilian clothes on in several months), and down to the cocktail bar and had a couple of Bacardi cocktails. We made inquiries as to what was a good place to eat, and the Park Avenue Restaurant was suggested. We took a cab to the place, and had a delicious meal. Feeling full, we walked back to our hotel; and before going to our room, sat in Lummus Park in the dark under the palm trees.

April 29, 1941 Tuesday
Hotel Netherland, Miami Beach, Fla.

It rained all day, and a strong wind kept blowing. Arose quite late again, and sauntered over to Washington Avenue for breakfast. After eating we walked up and down Washington Avenue and shopped for small items. Bought some fruit, and so back to our room. Rested a while, and then out for supper at an Italian restaurant, after which we did some window shopping on Lincoln Road. At 10:00 p.m. we to a movie. Out at midnight, and to our hotel and to bed. We had intended to visit my aunt, but the weather is so bad that we cannot get to Miami. We are not doing any swimming, nor can we shop for the trinkets which we would like to bring back to the folks at home. It is very good to be able to keep in touch with current events. The British are being chased out of Greece, and in this country it seems that the President is doing everything in his power to involve us in the war. In my opinion, the war is inevitable; and if so, it is best that we get in as soon as possible. If we do get in, it will immensely complicate my affairs.

April 30, 1941 Wednesday
Netherland Hotel, Miami Beach, Fla.

It was still pouring rain when we awoke, so we lay abed until 11:30, when we were routed out by the chambermaid who wished to make up the room. We down and were baffled how to get out in the rain to get something to eat, until the doorman gave us an umbrella to get to a nearby hotel that had a functioning dining room (the dining room in our hotel is being repaired). We sat around after eating, and finally dashed back to our place with a pack of playing cards. We played cards and listened to the radio, and in the evening the rain stopped. We took the bus to Miami, ate, and took a taxi out to the Max Abends' and spent a pleasant evening there. Pres. F. D. Roosevelt broadcast a speech over the radio, but I didn't listen as I figured I would read it in the newspapers the next day or hear a rebroadcast. It is wonderful how important speeches can now be preserved. How thrilling it would be if we could listen to the voices of Washington, Napoleon, Caesar, or others of the great Greek and Roman statesmen of the old days. Tonight's speech was about "defense stamps and bonds."

May 3, 1941 Saturday
"Silver Meteor"— 295 Avon Ave., Newark, N.J.

I up at 4:00 a.m. and to the washroom (which I had all to myself at that hour) washed and shaved. To the observation car and sat there reading and dozing, and watching day break. Bess joined me at about 7:00 a.m. We sat about for awhile, and then to breakfast. The train kept rolling along, and at 11:00 a.m. we reached Newark. We got off and were met by a group of girl friends of Bess, who were on the way to a show in New York. With them were Olga Schnee and Bess's mother. Olga went with the other girls, and Bess accompanied her mother to a hairdresser where she had her hair attended to, while I got my suit pressed. Two of our big bags were not in the baggage room, so we took a taxi home with what we had. Unpacked and rested up. We were visited by the Sweidels, who stayed for the night. Called Hannah (Gross) Emerson and gave her her mother's message. Several relatives of Bess called, and extended their greetings. In the evening we played poker, and to bed at 10:30 p.m.

May 21, 1941 Wednesday
"F" Barracks, Parris Island, So. Car.

My birthday today. Would have forgotten the fact, but I received a very pretty card from Bess containing a nice sentiment that was really appropriate to us. At first I was disappointed that there was no letter or news from her; but then I pictured her looking for the best card she could find for her husband, and I finally appreciated the thoughtfulness of the remembrance. Worked in the office again. In the morning I took time off to go to the post tailor and had my khaki and shirts altered to fit me. Bought some dye to stain my new leather holster, an indelible-ink pad for stamping my name on my clothes, and some soap powder. I hear that the 3rd Battalion is to go on maneuvers upon the return of the men on furlough — June 3. I think that these men are going to be in war before they return; this will be no ordinary maneuver. I could go along if I desire, but I will not go. Just before bedtime I received a very sprightly letter from Bess, full of news.

May 22, 1941 Thursday
"F" Barracks, Parris Island, So. Car.

In the office again. Have finally arranged for an allotment out of my salary to pay for my National Service Life Insurance. Received another letter from Bess. Her mother had been very ill. Bess wrote all about my cousin Morris Abend's engagement, and she tells me that my cousin Bertie Goldberg is to be engaged in two weeks. She also sent me news from my folks and other relatives. The new First Sergeant told me he spoke with the Battery Commander, asking that I be kept in the office in place of Sgt Haines; and that the B.C. had told him that if Haines wished to remain in the office, he had the preference before me. The war news looks more ominous every day, and I do not see how we can possibly keep out of war, pursuing the course that we are. Pres. Roosevelt is moving as rapidly as the people will permit to involve us in it. And awful as the prospect is, to me it appears the only solution. We must take a more active part in the war now, or it will be too late for us later.

May 25, 1941 Sunday
Savannah, Ga.

Up at 10:30. We were rather short of money, so we did not eat until we had ridden for quite some time trying to find a place called Morgan's Bridge. Had a picnic lunch there; and after sitting around a bit, went swimming in the river. I think it was the Okeechee River. In the evening we rode back to Savannah, finished our sandwiches, and sat around talking until

about 8:30 p.m. Then back to the barracks. It was a very pleasant weekend, and Savannah is a charming city. The southern style of talking is very
pleasant. Have just heard that the British battleship, the Hood, has been
sunk by a small German ship. England sure is taking a beating. She is being
hard pressed on the island of Crete, and it is just a question of time before
she is pushed out of there, leaving her Mediterranean lanes exposed. It
looks very bad for her if we do not get in — and to save ourselves from a
similar fate, we *should* get in. The sooner we do so, the less difficult the
task confronting us will be.

May 27, 1941 Tuesday
"F" Barracks, Parris Island, So. Car.

We had a conference of the sergeants, and we were informed that our
Battery was to participate in a maneuver. We were to board ship on June
5, probably the *Barnett*, and we were to operate off the coast of Virginia
and North Carolina; and that we were to return about June 28. Received
two letters from Bess. The first one told about an offer a friend made to
bring her down to Parris Island, on the Decoration Day weekend, and
asked whether she should accept. The second, written on Monday, told
about the receipt of my letter concerning my leave on the coming weekend, and it sounded very depressed because I was leaving the country; she
was under the impression that this maneuver was to take place in some
foreign country, and that I would be gone again for several months. After
work I sent her a reassuring letter giving her all the facts. Pres. Roosevelt
made an important speech tonight at 9:30, and I meant to stay awake to
listen to it, but I was so tired I fell asleep. Was told later that the President
spoke very forcefully and fearlessly, and that he declared that a state of
unlimited emergency existed.

May 28, 1941 Wednesday
"F" Barracks, Parris Island, So. Car.

Up this morning and most of the fellows were still talking about the
tough speech made by the President last night. Worked in the office. In
the morning received a letter from Bess giving me the address she will be
staying at in Atlantic City; but in my telegram of last night I told her to
stay home and that I would go home and meet her there. I hope she obeys
my telegram. Kept working until evening, and then with Bove while he
sent a telegram home that he was coming some time Friday. So to the
movies. During the day my Battery Commander asked if I would be ready
for an examination for platoon Sergeant aboard ship. I said that I would
be. He said that in view of the President's speech, it looks as though the

Marine Corps was to be expanded, and that he wanted to be ready to recommend some men who will have taken the examination.

June 1, 1941 Sunday
Raleigh, No. Car., en route to Parris Island, S.C.

Awoke at 8 a.m. Standard Time, and Bess and I lay in bed and talked for almost an hour, and it was very pleasant. Then up, and I dressed in my khaki uniform and had breakfast. Rushed my packing, making up a small bundle of the articles I was taking back with me. Had just time to say a few words to Bess's brother Bob and sister Olga when the horn on Bove's car sounded, and I had to leave at 10 a.m. We wasted at least an hour after we started in hunting around to pick up the other passengers in Elizabeth, N.J., and Philadelphia, Pa., and then off. It had rained in Newark during the night, and it continued to rain on and off all day. We rode along without incident, I doing plenty of resting in anticipation of staying awake all night to keep the driver awake. We made our first stop to eat at Fredericksburg, Va., at about 7:30 p.m., as we had brought along sandwiches which we ate during the day as we drove. After a delicious deviled crab supper we off again and rode until about 11:30 p.m., when we stopped again at Raleigh, N.C., for gas. Then I up to the front seat to keep Bove awake, and we off again.

July 6, 1941 Sunday
Parris Island, S.C.— abd USS McCawley, *Charleston, S.C.*

Up at 6:00 a.m. and had breakfast. Fixed up our packs for the last time before leaving. Lunch at 10:30 a.m. Then back and donned our packs and assembled outside. Boarded trucks, and at 11:30 shoved off. It started to rain as soon as we got under way; and it alternately cleared up and showered all the way to Charleston, which we reached at 2:30 p.m. We went to some docks on the Cooper River, on the street that the railroad station is on. The USS *McCawley* was there, and at 4:00 p.m. we were permitted aboard. It looks terribly dirty. We are very crowded, and there are other units of Marines besides our Regiment. There are also some soldiers. Working parties were organized; and when our train came in, we unloaded our seabags and bedding rolls and brought them aboard. It is very hot. I have a nice position in the hold assigned to my Battery. One of the funnels of the ship has been removed and replaced by a gun turret. A big staircase and some fancy woodwork has been replaced by ladders and welded steel plates. An Army transport is moored alongside us; also, about 9 Higgins boats, and power boats capable of carrying tractors or tanks.

July 10, 1941 Thursday
Abd USS McCawley, *en route to North Carolina*
　　After breakfast the Battery was mustered out on the dock. The C.O. gave us a talk on our lack of cooperation among the NCOs. He made it clear that certain ones were not included in his remarks, and I am one of these latter. We were called aboard ship, and we made ready to leave. At 10:10 a.m. the USS *Lee* passed us, on the way from the Navy Yard out to sea; followed at 15-minute intervals by the USS *Elliot*, the USS *Barnett*, and our ship. Soon lost sight of land. The day was bright and the sea smooth. The 4 ships stayed together, shifting positions and directions at intervals during the day. All hands were mustered on deck and given strict orders against giving out any information of a military nature; or of writing to anyone and including any information as to troop movements, morale, equipment, etc. No mail received by "E" Battery yet. At about 5:15 p.m. we saw flying fish, and I was surprised to see them so far north. It appears as though we are heading in a northeast direction. Our destination is unknown to us. The ship was "blacked-out" at 1924.

July 11, 1941 Friday
Abd USS McCawley— *offshore, Hurst Beach, N.C.*
　　We were mustered at 8:00 a.m., and by that time we were in sight of land on the port side. We had reached our destination, which was the coast of North Carolina, near Wilmington and our proposed base at New River. On our starboard side were the troopship *Neville* and the supply ship *Arcturus*. Off on the horizon were 6 destroyers. Nets were lowered over the side of the *McCawley*; all the Higgins boats, tank lighters, and other boats were hoisted over the side and into the water. The other troop ships were engaged in the same activity. Into the small boats were loaded machine gun units, 37mm outfits, soldiers and Marines. The boats circled about the ship for a time, and then returned to the ship. The men and the gear were hauled aboard. In the afternoon, the same drill activity took place. This time my unit was included. Two howitzers and carts were placed in a tank lighter, together with 5 men from the gun section, and we circled about the ship until recalled. The men go over the side into the boat via cargo nets; and guns are lowered by boom and tackle. No "black-out" tonight. I hear that the sailor who fell down the hold on Wednesday fractured his jaw, ribs, collar-bone and pelvis; but that he is in good condition and will live.

July 12, 1941 Saturday
Abd USS McCawley— *offshore, Hurst Beach, N.C.*
　　Reveille at 0430 today; and at 0530 had a working party from my gun section lowering boats for the Battery detail to go ashore. The destroyers

had closed in during the night; and as I looked about, there were 9 ships visible from ours. All during the day boats were hoisted and lowered, and the troop transports slowly shifted positions. Twenty men from our Battery were picked; and together with some sailors, started scraping down the newly tarred decks. The ship is beginning to spruce up a bit. There is much cleaning and painting going on. While one of the boats was being hoisted aboard, one of the supports for a block snapped loose and nearly hit a sailor. It had been welded defectively at the Charleston Navy Yard. Was told by a sailor that about 20 sailors had left the ship before it started, not liking to serve aboard ship. The crew is shorthanded. The weather continues very bright and hot. Everybody sweats profusely. It is so hot that the men do not have much ambition. The wavering in the writing of these shorthand notes is caused by the constant throbbing of the ship's engines; and the "bleeding" of the ink on these pages results from dampness spread by sweating hands.

July 13, 1941 Sunday
abd USS McCawley, *offshore near Hurst Beach, N.C.*

Was awakened at 0400 and told to get the boat lowering detail together again. Had a difficult time finding the men in the dark, as some of them are sleeping up on the decks. The boats that were lowered this morning went to some other ship that was having a landing exercise, leaving us without boats to take a church party to the *Neville*, where services were to be conducted. We were mustered at 0800, and then had the rest of the day for ourselves. Washed some clothes. The washing facilities are very poor — fresh water is available only in the drinking fountains (scuttlebutts); salt water in the showers and washrooms. The chow is improving; but there are many men aboard, besides some 200 sailors. The Army men number about 50 only. At about 1400 the *Neville* left this area, together with 4 destroyers. Have learned that we are lying off Hurst Beach, just south of Bear Inlet and north of the New River.

July 14, 1941 Monday
abd USS McCawley, *offshore near Hurst Beach, N.C.*

Reveille at 0415. Breakfast, and then the boats were put over the side. At 0700 we went over the side with packs and rifles, but the howitzers were not taken out of the hold. The boats pulled away from the ship for a short distance and circled around in the assembly area for about 15 minutes, and then headed for shore. The beach at this point is sandy, hard-packed, and slopes gradually out to sea. The boats were run close inshore, and we jumped into the water, which was about hip deep. Ran up onto the beach, and inland for about 50 yards, and came to rest in stacked arms, and were given permission to go swimming. After about half an hour we were called out, got dressed, and the boats were signaled in. We waded out to the boats carrying our rifles above our heads, climbed aboard, and back to the ship at 1030. Changed our clothes, cleaned our rifles, and to lunch. There was a rifle inspection scheduled for 1500, but it was called off when it began to rain very hard. Sat in my bunk reading, and to bed soon after supper, as we were scheduled to get up real early in the morning.

July 15, 1941 Tuesday
abd USS McCawley, *offshore near Hurst Beach, N.C.*

Reveille went at 0200. Up and we were served hot coffee in the mess hall, and I drew 43 rations for the men in my boat. While the boats were being lowered over the side, I issued the rations— 2 sandwiches and an apple. We ate these before entering the boats at 0400. This served as our breakfast. The boats went to the assembly area, where we circled about for more than half an hour. The sea was choppy, and one of the Marines became very seasick. Most of the others were slightly green looking. Another 5 minutes, and I think I would have been sick myself. We hit the beach and onto the shore, where we took cover alongside a road a short distance inland. We lay there about an hour. At 0715 we were assembled, ordered to stack our rifles, and permitted to go in for a swim. It had been raining during the night, and the morning was cloudy and cool, but I thoroughly enjoyed the swim of more than an hour. At 0930 we were called out. We dressed, waded out to the boats, and were taken back to the ship by 1100. Changed to dry clothes, and to chow. Rifles inspected after chow. Rest of the day to ourselves. Received the first letter in about 2 weeks from Bess, dated July 6, 1941. Very nice, and greatly appreciated.

July 21, 1941 Monday
abd USS McCawley *at sea— and at Paper Mill dock, Charleston, So. Car.*

Reveille at 0530. The ship had been moving all night long, and we are out of sight of land. There is only one troop ship along with us. We were mustered at 0800. At 1000 our ship stopped and lay to in sight of land just off the entrance to the Cooper River. After lunch I visited the prisoners. At 1400 we got under way again, and up the Cooper River. Passed the Navy Yard, and tied up at the West Virginia Pulp and Paper Co. dock, right near the Charleston Ordnance Depot. The place is very dirty, and has a horrible odor at times (from the eggs used in sizing the paper). We are far from the center of Charleston. Liberty went at 1700. Two men were given 72-hour passes to go to their families at Roanoke, Va. I tried to get 4 days off to go to Newark, and was intensely disappointed when I was refused. Made up a bundle of my dirty clothes and to Charleston and left it at a laundry. Had some ice cream and a good meal. The usual liberty sights evident — drunks and fights and vomiting and blood; and cheap, greedy women.

July 24, 1941 Thursday
abd USS McCawley, *Paper Mill dock, Charleston, S. C.*
Up and we were mustered at 0800. No new absences. Sat on deck reading for a while, and then fell asleep for a while. Visited Jasinski in the brig. He is due to be released today at noon. We made arrangements to go into town together. Notice was posted that there was liberty today, beginning at 1300 and expiring at 0130; and that we would have to clear out of Charleston by 2400. We are due to leave sometime tomorrow. After lunch, with Jasinski and Corporal Smack, to town. Spent most of our time eating. Had a delicious meal at a kosher restaurant. Did some shopping and got out my laundry. Swam for a while at the "Y"; and while there, wrote a letter to Bess and one to Bove, giving them the details of my schedule. The men are slowly losing their speed. They have been taken for an awful ride here. This is a very poor labor town. I am very tired and sleepy, and was glad to get back to the ship. I hope we leave here soon, that our maneuvers are quickly over, and that I get a chance to go home to see Bess.

July 31, 1941 Thursday
Cardozo Hotel — Netherland Hotel, Miami Beach, Fla.
Up at 0900 and had breakfast at the Cardozo. Out on the porch and sat around, conversing with a man from College Hill, No. Car. At noontime I gathered my stuff together and called for our bill, which came to $16.03, most of which was made up of $7.60 for my telephone of yesterday and $3.05 for my laundry. I took my stuff for both of us — Bess and myself. Jasinski and I were told that we would have to vacate our room at the Cardozo Hotel by 3:00 p.m., so Jasinski made up a bundle of his stuff and left it in my room. We borrowed a car and to the railroad station and met Bess. To the Netherland Hotel, where we had a drink with Jasinski, and then Bess and I to our room, of which she approved. At 2000 to Jack Dempsey's Restaurant for dinner, and had our picture taken there. Back to our room. Bess told me all the news of home. She intends to stay until Sunday morning. I made arrangements for her return trip. At about 2300 Jasinski called and I left Bess; and Jasinski and I took a taxi back to the ship, arriving about 5 minutes to midnight.

August 2, 1941 Saturday
abd USS McCawley *at sea, en route to Hurst Beach, No. Car.*

Up and have been sweating so much that I am beginning to feel uncomfortable. Spent most of this day also on deck, reading magazines. Our rifles were inspected, and the Section Chiefs were permitted to cosmolene theirs and pack them away, to my great relief. It is pretty difficult to keep a rifle clean in the salt, damp air, especially with the slight amount of care I give it. No news yet as to where we are going to. The weather is still extremely hot. Spent some time down in the hold retrieving some of my clothes. There are all sorts of garments down there, together with about a hundred pair of shoes. Washed it and hung it to dry. This lack of knowledge as to where we are going is irritating. No preparations or plans can be made. If I were single, this lack would be adventuresome; but in my present state it is merely annoying. I am becoming very dissatisfied with my service, and would not mind getting back to my civilian life. It appears to me that much of my time is being wasted, and that I could do much more for my country if I were back at home.

August 3, 1941 Sunday
Abd USS McCawley, *Hurst Beach, No. Car.*

Up and dashed immediately for the showers. Took a salt water shower, rinsing with a bucket of fresh water, and felt much better. My lips and face are cracked and sore from the sun in Miami. Church call went at 0920. There are now 3 more destroyers following in our rear, making a total of 9 accompanying destroyers. I went below deck for a while, and came up again at 1030. On looking around, I found a good portion of the Atlantic Fleet stretched all about us. There were all sorts of naval vessels, including a hospital ship. I could count 31 navy ships. We had stopped in sight of land, and I was told that we were at the mouth of the New River, No. Car. In the afternoon, our ship got under way again. We were assembled and told that we would probably go ashore tomorrow or the next day. Emergency rations were issued. All the men began to pack their bags, fill their two canteens, and roll horseshoe rolls (containing blankets and sheets) that go around the outside of the full pack. I down into the hold and inspected the howitzer to see that all was in readiness for tomorrow. I taped up flashlights for night lighting devices. The ship was blacked out tonight. It is very hot, and the sweat just rolls off everybody. The time was moved one hour ahead.

August 4, 1941 Monday
New River, N.C.— Hurst Beach, N.C.

Reveille went at 0500, but it was still dark due to the time having been advanced an hour. The ship had been moving all night at quite a rate of speed. There were not so many vessels visible as yesterday, but there still were quite a few. They were stretched far out on the horizon. Yesterday's group of naval vessels was the largest I have ever seen at one time. I had breakfast and checked my pack and equipment again. Loaded water aboard my gun cart. We are the first wave to go over. The place looks like New River. We did nothing all morning. In the afternoon, at about 1500, the first gun went ashore. There are many ships off the coast of here and all are sending men ashore. One Marine fell off the deck into a boat. A couple of tanks were sent ashore in water too deep for them, and they had to be brought back. At 1900 the 2nd Section went ashore. At 2100 the 3rd and 4th Sections went over the side into a tank lighter with our guns, carts, and full crews. The guns were taken apart in the boat as we headed for shore. About 160 feet from the shoreline the ramp was dropped and the men started to carry the dismantled howitzer parts ashore, jumping from the ramp into the waist-high water, being handed a howitzer part, and wading ashore with it. The tide was coming in and it shoved the boat about, knocking the men around and causing several of them to fall in the surf. Once on shore, the gun parts were put together, the carts were hooked up, and we were guided about 400 yards along the beach and into some bushes. The guns were set up in firing position, aiming stakes with night lighting devices set up, and the guns were laid. The men then bedded down, and at about midnight I turned in. A 5-man guard was set up for night security.

August 5, 1941 Tuesday
Inland from Hurst Beach, N.C.

The mosquitoes were very bad. I slept on just a piece of canvas, and was nearly eaten up by them. At about 0600 it began to pour rain. I got my poncho out and covered my equipment and myself with it, and just lay there in the bushes until the shower stopped at about 0800. PFC Murphy, while operating a field telephone, was struck by lightning, and his right side is paralyzed. Chow was announced at 0800, and we gathered and ate. The rest of the morning was spent drying out our stuff in the trees back of our position, and in servicing our gun. We had to keep under cover, as all morning there was continued, extensive aerial activity with all types of planes participating. At noon we ate our emergency ration, consisting of a 15-oz. can of meat and vegetable stew; and a can containing 4.5 oz of biscuit, 0.5 oz. of sugar, and 0.3 oz. of soluble coffee. The afternoon was spent standing by. It was hot and sunny, and we were able to dry our most of our stuff. However, the ground remained muddy all day. The airplanes kept up a ceaseless activity, singly and in large groups—zooming, diving, and maneuvering. At 1900 we received "close station, march order." We had been awaiting this order, and had been all prepared. It took us but a short while to put the howitzer in travel position, hook up toggles for pulling it, and to get our cart set. We donned our packs and bedding rolls, and were moving in five minutes. We pulled out on the road, and then had to wait, as only one truck was available and our new position was some 4 miles away. A truck finally arrived for our 4th Section gun. It was loaded with water cans, however, so that only the gunner and myself had any room to accompany the gun. The rest of the crew would have to march to the new position. The truck started down the road for about a half mile, when we were stopped by a traffic line waiting for a ferry to take them across a river. A pontoon bridge which the Army Engineers had built was broken, and the ferry could accommodate only one vehicle at a time. We moved forward very slowly. While in this line, Lt. Hood came by and instructed me to proceed to a schoolhouse about 2 miles on the other side of the river, to unhook my gun there, and to wait until I was picked up. If I had any rations, I was to eat them, as he didn't know when he could get supper for us. We continued waiting for the ferry in the line of military vehicles containing guns, ammunition, water, troops, supplies, etc. I broke out my rations and shared them with my gunner, as he had none. Finally, at 2325, the pontoon bridge was repaired, after we had waited 4 hours. The line waiting for the ferry went to the repaired bridge instead. We rattled across and to the schoolhouse, where Lt. Hood was waiting with a truck. We unhooked from our truck and hooked onto the lieutenant's truck, and we were driven to the new gun position. The rest of the Battery marched in soon after. Some hardtack and jam was broken out for the men who had not had supper, and we were told to secure for the night. It was then 0100 in the morning. I to the edge of a patch of woods, laid out my roll, set up my mosquito net, and to sleep.

August 6, 1941 Wednesday
New River, N.C. area, inland from Hurst Beach.

A clear, hot day that left us all sweating. The place is full of insects—crawling and flying. Last night was one of the most miserable I ever spent. Had the mosquito netting up, but the place teems with gnats. They crawl right through the netting as though it were not there. They were so pestiferous that I had a headache when I awoke. We were issued canned rations again for breakfast. We laid (sighted in) the guns and spent the morning camouflaging and improving our position. The heat became intense. Our mess men caught up with us, and we had a hot lunch brought to us by truck. I rigged up a shelter and spent the afternoon in it, catching up on my rest. Some of the men put up quite elaborate tents and canopies. In the evening we set up our night lighting devices by means of which it becomes possible to aim the howitzer in the dark. I am suffering quite a bit from itchy, peeling skin. The mosquitoes bite terribly. I am very dirty and longing for a bath. In the evening we built smudge fires all along our position to keep the gnats and mosquitoes away. We set guards to keep the fires burning all night long. They kept the gnats away, but the mosquitoes still kept trying.

August 7, 1941 Thursday
New River, N.C. area, inland from Hurst Beach.
    Up, and a new torture has been added to my tribulations. I am now full of chiggers, as are all the men. We had hot food again today. In the morning my Section dug a new head (latrine) for the men. We cleaned our rifles, and also took down and regreased the howitzers. I hear that some 200 men have been brought back to the ship because of poisoning caused by the canned food. One of the men caught a black widow spider, placed it in a bottle, and exhibited it. We hear that this is one of the biggest maneuvers every pulled; but as far as the artillery are concerned, we had more activity back at Parris Island. The only indication we have of the activities is the constant droning and zooming of airplanes. At 1430 we received orders to secure our tents, and to pack our rolls and packs and stand by to displace forward. We did so, loading our car, filling in the newly-dug heads, and getting everything set. We just stayed around, doing nothing. At 1730 some hot chow came in. We ate, and reopened the head. Just before dark a practice problem on the guns was run off. We were then told to retrieve our rolls and bed down for the night; but to be ready to collect our stuff in the dark and move out at a moment's notice. Smudge fires were lit.

August 8, 1941 Friday
New River, N.C., area, inland from Hurst Beach.
    Spent another miserable night. I slept in the gun cart, fully dressed, and all cramped up, so that I would not have to sleep on the ground and get more chiggers. About 80% of the men are loaded with chiggers. They are beginning to drift back to the ship for medical attention for these chigger bites. I hear reports of 4 cases of snake bite, with one fatal case. We

had canned rations for breakfast. Something had been wrong with the food yesterday, and about half the Battery has diarrhea. The head had to be enlarged. I have a mild case myself. The mosquitoes are rapacious. Corporal Way, my gunner, went back to the ship today for treatment of his chiggers. Another man had to go back with diarrhea, and one with sore feet. My chiggers started festering. I hope they do not become infected. The itching from these chiggers is exquisite torture. We did some more gun drill in the evening. Guards were set, and fire watch organized. Smudge fires were lit. I to sleep in the cart again. Very uncomfortable and cramped. Had to sleep under a poncho to avoid being eaten by mosquitoes and gnats. I hear that the infantry is supposed to be retreating, and that we are covering their retreat.

August 9, 1941 Saturday
New River, N.C. area, inland from Hurst Beach.

Up and had a hot breakfast, with hot coffee. Back to the gun position, and we ran problems all morning. A truck came by and we in our section bought two watermelons. In the afternoon we ran two more simulated problems on the guns. The infantry is getting all the action in this "biggest maneuver ever," and we in the artillery don't even get to see most of this action. I got permission to leave, and with a couple of fellows to a nearby deserted farmhouse that had a well. Took one of the most refreshing baths I ever had, and shaved. At 1700 we had a hot meal that was very satisfactory. After supper we were given "close station, march order." We put the guns in travel position, made up our rolls and packs, got everything together, and awaited darkness. At dark we hooked up the guns and, without lights, to the main road. This road was packed with traffic and troops, but everything kept moving smoothly. We hit Hurst Beach and were told that we would have to await low tide at 0400 before getting boats for return to our ship. So we disposed our guns, carts and equipment along the shore and picked out places for ourselves to lay down and await the boats. The night was cool, and the mosquitoes were not as thick as further inland. My section was given a .50 calibre machine gun to get aboard, besides taking care of our howitzer.

August 10, 1941 Sunday
abd USS McCawley, off Hurst Beach, No. Car.

At about 0430 the first lighter arrived and we loaded 2 carts, 2 howitzers, and the 2 machine guns aboard. At 0510 the second lighter arrived and the rest of the stuff went aboard that. My section went with the second boat. The water was very rough, and I slightly ill. The ship looked very good to me. Up the side via cargo nets. The guns were hoisted aboard. We had breakfast, and then down into the hold and broke the guns down and cleaned them, thoroughly; then re-greased them. Nine of my newspapers caught up with me, and I spent some time reading the stale news, which was still new news to me. Also received an old letter from Bess, written before she came to Miami. I stowed some of my gear and then lay down for a while. It was good to stretch out after sleeping for 2 nights all cramped up in the cart. It was very hot aboard ship, and my chiggers itched unbearably. At 1800 I to the sick bay and had them painted with Scotts (?) solution. Had taken a salt water bath previously. It is good to get back to a mess hall and to have some variety in my meals. Those canned rations soon get tiresome.

August 16, 1941 Saturday
"G" Barracks, MB, Parris Island, S. C.
   Up sleepy, as lights go out at 2200 in these barracks. Right after breakfast to the gun shed and took apart No. 4 gun. I did very good with it, remembering quite well the procedure I watched yesterday. Cleaned up the gun, re-greased it, and put it together again. Wrote to Bess. Wrote to Studley and explained about the money order I had sent him. Received a lovely anniversary card from Bess, with a tender sentiment inscribed. She has been a good wife to me, and I have been more satisfied with married life than I had expected to be. In the evening I sent her an anniversary telegram, to be delivered tomorrow, the date of our wedding. Selected some pictures, pasted them up in a cheap album as a sample, and am going to sell duplicates of the set to the men. I have asked Bess to send me my camera. Lay around resting, as it was very hot. I am giving myself time off for the exhausting gun work I did in the gun shed this morning. Twenty volunteers were picked today and sent on a work party to Charleston, So. Car.

August 22, 1941 Friday
"G" Barracks, MB, Parris Island, So. Car.
   Soon after breakfast to the gun shed. Hitched up the guns and we out to a spot near the rifle range, set up the guns, and fired HE (high explosive) all morning. We had to get behind sandbag emplacements before each shot was fired. We stayed out there until 1130, and then back for chow. After lunch to the gun shed and we cleaned up the gun. I visited Bove and asked him to get a desk built for me. Made tentative arrangements to go home with him if we got some time off on Labor day, next week. The Battery had to attend a movie at which training films were shown. Back, and after supper I just sat around reading. I received some more old newspapers.

Time is hanging heavy on my hands. I am very disinterested in artillery, and heartily wish I could get out of the service. I hope that the provisions of the bill Pres. Roosevelt just signed, by which selectees over 28 years of age will be dismissed from service, will be extended to the Marine Corps Reserve.

August 26, 1941 Tuesday
"G" Barracks, MB, Parris Island, S. C.
Right after breakfast to the gun shed, hooked up the 2 howitzers that had the 37mms mounted on them, and out to the firing range. We had 11 shots per section to fire at a moving dummy tank. The other two Batteries had registered 3 hits out of 45 shots, and 6 hits out of 60 shots. As we had 45 shots to get off, we had a 3-hit mark to beat. The 1st Section got no hits; the 2nd Section failed to hit also; and the 3rd Section got 2 hits. I kept track of all changes in range and deflection, and had the "dope" down pretty well by the time my Section fired. We got our 11 shots off; and when the result of our firing came back, we had registered 4 hits on the target, and one on the frame, which didn't count. So our Battery had the highest percentage of hits; and the 4th Section won a case of beer, and several dollars inside bets. To lunch, and then cleaned the guns. To the post office and got the package of vitamin pills and toothbrush refills which Bess had sent me. Saw Bove and made tentative arrangements for going to Newark this weekend.

September 5, 1941 Friday
"G" Barracks, MB, Parris Island, So. Car.
Up at about 0430, and as we are on Daylight Saving Time, it was quite dark. We ate quickly and to the gun park. Hooked up our guns and off. Today's problem is a combined artillery and infantry maneuver. We passed many infantrymen on foot and on trucks. As usual, there was much waiting around; and it was several hours before we even went into our first firing site. Due to the size of the problem, there was some confusion and mingling of units. After setting up our guns in the first of our positions, we just stood around for a while. Got our guns hooked up again and to the Horse Island position. The first 3 guns went into position and fired several rounds, while my 4th Section just sat around. We had lunch there on the field. Then to the third position. This time our gun was set up for firing. It took over an hour before our first fire command came down. We fired about 3 shells in this position, and then came the order: "Close station, march order." Back to the barracks. Paid today. Received a letter from the Veterans Administration, which Bess forwarded to me, advising me that my insurance was in good order and the premiums paid.

September 10, 1941 Wednesday
"G" Barracks, MB, Parris Island, So. Car.

To the gun shed right after breakfast. All guns hooked up, and we off to the artillery position near the rifle range and set up our guns. There were 12 shells in the Battery, or 3 per gun. Our gun was first, firing against a moving tank target. The ammunition was HE, with 4 powder bags. We were ordered to fire at this target at 3 different ranges. When we fired last time, using 37mm cannons, we set the range for 1040 yards. Today we started at this range, but set the gun at 950 yards; but this was so far over that we lost it. All our estimation was over, and our gun didn't get any hits. The correct range was about 750 yards, with about 650 and 625 yards for the other 2 legs of this course. None of the other guns was able to register a direct hit on the target. We then went into a position a short ways from the original position, and our gun represented "A" Battery, while each of the others represented another Battery; and they fired the problem fired last Friday. Back for lunch after cleaning the guns. Lay around in the afternoon. Wrote to Bess. Received a letter from her.

September 11, 1941 Thursday
"G" Barracks, MB, Parris Island, So. Car.

Troop and inspection this morning. Back to the barracks for a short time. Then out for a Formal Guard Mount, which was a sorry exhibition. It was full of mistakes and lack of knowledge. After the guard mount we all to get two "shots" one for yellow fever and a "booster" inoculation for typhoid. I then to the post photo shop and got some of my processed photos. After lunch to the gun park, and we cleaned up the guns. Then to a training film, where the subject was infantry defense against air attack. Got back just in time for chow, and as it started to rain. After supper sat around the barracks reading. Pasted up some pictures in the album. At 2200 taps sounded. We turned out the lights, but turned on the radio and listened to the President speak. He notified the world that the American Navy had been given orders to attack any Axis submarine found in "Western Hemisphere Defense" waters. This, in my opinion, will soon lead to open hostilities.

September 27, 1941 Saturday
"G" Barracks, MB, Parris Island, So. Car.

A Battalion motorized review was scheduled this morning; but it had rained last night, leaving the field full of puddles, so the parade was called off. There was an inspection in the barracks by the Battalion Commander, after which we were free. Visited Bove, and he wanted to know if I cared to go to Savannah. I declined. After lunch I lay around for a while, then worked on another lesson of the M.C.I correspondence course, finishing it by nightfall. Was visited by several former Newarkers, members of the 1st Battalion, who are now back in Parris Island after having been stationed at Quantico. Large numbers of the men stationed on this post are being transferred to the New River base. Units from the 5th and 7th Marines are among those being shifted.

October 6, 1941 Monday
3-day maneuver by 2nd Battalion, BOQ Area
Reveille at 0445. Up and shaved hastily. To work and quickly rolled a heavy pack, had breakfast, drew a pistol, and out to the gun shed. Hooked up the gun and cleared the gun park at 0700. Rode a short distance to a position on the Island between Bachelor's Officers Quarters (BOQ) and Rifle Range, and put the gun into position. We are being required to wear steel helmets. After getting into position we fired a few concentrations. At noon we had 2 sandwiches and a cup of coffee for lunch. At about 1900, supper of stew, potatoes, canned peaches, and coffee was served. There was not enough to go around, and about 30 men had to wait until 2030 to eat scrambled eggs, fried baloney and coffee. We were given word that we were to stay for the night in that position; so the men started bedding down. Guards were established. The mosquitoes were terribly ferocious, and smudge fires were lit, but with little effect. All during the night concentrations of artillery shells were fired at intervals of 15 minutes, and I stayed up most of the night servicing the gun until 0400, when our ammo became expended.

October 9, 1941 Thursday
"G" Barracks, MB, Parris Island, So. Car.
Up at 0530, ate, and by 0600 was ready to go to the pistol range. I am coaching in the mornings this week. Things were very quiet, and the relays were pushed though quickly, so that at 0930 we were finished. I back to the barracks and to Main Station and had my hair cut. Bought a money order for $8 for Max Gelfond for Federal Credit and for hospitalization. In the afternoon to the gun shed, where several 155-mm guns of the latest model had been received. These have pneumatic tires and air brakes, and all the latest trimmings. I was able to get a couple of good shots of the old type 155a, with the solid tire wheels. Out to where we were digging dummy gun emplacements which are to serve as targets for our guns, and took several more pictures. Received another letter from Bess today, telling me that she had fixed my subscription to the newspaper. Received about 6 newspapers today. In the evening to the movies. Upon my return, I wrote a long letter to Bess and enclosed $13 for Building and Loan payment.

October 11, 1941 Saturday
"G" Barracks, MB, Parris Island, So. Car.

Up and had early chow again. It had turned cold during the night, necessitating the use of two blankets. Right after breakfast to the pistol range. The range is right on the shore of Parris Island, and I was dressed in khaki with no undershirt, and I was thoroughly chilled. Was glad when the sun came up, but a stiff wind persisted all morning. The shooters were firing for record over the short pistol course, consisting of 10 shots slow fire, 10 shots rapid fire, and 5 shots at the bobber target, all from the 25-yard line. Possible high score was 225, with a score of 135 to qualify for marksman, 162 for sharpshooter, and 180 for expert. There were five relays; and on my target 2 of the 5 men qualified. Back to the barracks, where I got into a sweatshirt to warm up. Got some pictures from the photo finisher, and they had done some very poor work. Sat around in the afternoon trying to comprehend one of the M.C.I. pamphlets. Fixed up my album a bit, and readied a new selection of pictures for the men to select for next payday. In the evening to movies.

October 19, 1941 Sunday
"G" Barracks, MB, Parris Island, No. Car.

New reveille time of 0630 on Sunday. Up, had a hearty breakfast, and then back to bed for an hour or so. Then up and started arranging the pictures which Jasinski had taken out for me yesterday. This took all morning and part of the afternoon. Word was received that Sgt. Mollenhauer was being detained in the Yemmassee jail under $50 bail for drunken driving. The Battery officers were notified, and one of the lieutenants went in and bailed him out. I stayed in all day reading and talking. In the evening wrote a letter to Bess, and early to bed. A list has been posted naming the ones who are to go to 4th Battalion, which is being organized. I am not among those selected for transfer, but Mollenhauer is. There is much talk about a 10-day maneuver to New River, which may develop into a permanent stay at that place. Rumor has it that the Colonel is to go up there, and if he finds the water supply adequate, we will most likely go up there to stay. I don't like the prospect of spending the coming winter in tents up there.

October 23, 1941 Thursday
"G" Barracks, MB, Parris Island, So. Car.

Attended the breakfast mess formation, and was relieved by the new guard at 0830. To the barracks. Some 20 new men have been added to the Battery. They are fresh out of boot camp. They are being assigned to the various gun sections. In the morning the firing batteries went out on the field and held gun drill. I was very tired from the guard duty, and didn't feel like explaining the gun to a new bunch of boots. So to the Main Station and took out some pictures. Then visited Bove and he told me of the nice time he had had in Savannah yesterday; and that he came back about 0500 this morning. In the afternoon we again had gun practice, but this time I attended. There were several new men, but no definite and final assignment of men has been made. At 1500 back to the gun shed, cleaned up the gun, boresighted it, and made it ready for tomorrow, when we will fire HE. Wrote a letter to Bess; and also one to Max Gelfond, in which I enclosed a money order for $10 to pay for Federal Credit deposits on November 1st and 16th.

October 30, 1941 Thursday
en route to New River, No. Car.

Reveille at 0500. Had breakfast, rolled our packs, and got set. The men were loaded aboard trucks. I rode in the 4th Section prime mover (the truck that hauled the howitzer on firing exercises). At 0700 we cleared the barracks. It was a cold damp day — sunless, and looking ready to rain at any moment. The convoy stretched for quite a ways. I was wearing my green woolen uniform, but became thoroughly chilled soon after starting. We rode along at 50-yard intervals at about 25 miles per hour. At 0900, nature called my driver and he stopped to relieve himself; for which I was grateful, as it gave me an opportunity to get my coat out and put it on. From then on the trip was a bit more comfortable. At 1000 the whole convoy stopped for a rest for about an hour, while arrangements were made for us to go through Charleston, S.C. At 1100 we rapidly through that city, across the Cooper River bridge, and on. Shortly after 1200 we were fed a cheese and jelly sandwich each. Then on, with but one more rest stop, to Myrtle Beach, S.C., which we reached shortly after 1500. Pitched pup tents. Canned rations were heated for the men. Jasinski invited me into town, and we had a good meal. I slept on the gun cart, not wishing to unroll my pack.

November 3, 1941 Monday
4-day maneuver by 1stMarDiv, near Haw Run, N.C.

Reveille at 0330. Very damp and chilly. Breakfast at 0400. Rolled my pack with 2 blankets, shelter half, and toilet articles. At 0530 sent all but 5 men on our truck to the assembly area, from where they will march on foot. The trucks came back and we loaded our gear on, and also one 50-cal. machine gun and its equipment. Twelve men rode on the truck, and it was very crowded. The trucks with the second load pulled out at 0745, and went to the assembly area. We are in support of infantry that is defending against red forces that are coming with an aircraft carrier and battleships to attack this country (represented by the New River shoreline). At about 1100 the trucks were stopped and the marchers got on the trucks while I and the other riders hit the road. At 1215 we stopped for a lunch of 2 cheese sandwiches, an apple, and water. Then back to steadily hike until 1530, when we reached our bivouac area. Had a big blister on my left toe. We hid the guns and trucks from the persistent aerial activity, selected a site for sleeping, and waited until after dark for a hot, coarse, substantial and very satisfactory meal. Then to bed on the ground, taking off only my shoes.

November 5, 1941 Wednesday
4-day maneuver by 1stMarDiv, near Haw Run, N.C.

I arose at 0530. Reveille at 0600. It started to rain, and it rained all morning. The chilliness of the air made everything miserable. There were a few simulated concentrations of artillery shells fired. The morning was spent mostly in trying to devise shelters from the rain. There was not much aerial activity today. The food is substantial, but not as plentiful as the men desire. In the afternoon the rain stopped, but it continued chilly. I lay down on a canvas for an hour or so until suppertime. We were told to put one man on watch on our guns for an hour, and to change this man every hour during the night. My men were tired, so I disregarded this order and told the men to go to sleep. I told my gunner to sleep right alongside the gun and I asked the regular sentries to keep an eye on the gun. About 2100 I was awakened and told that an officer had sneaked in and simulated being a parachute trooper and stolen the breechblock from the gun and the clothes of the gunner sleeping beside the gun. This left me in a very serious and embarrassing position. Grave charges could be brought against me. But nothing was done, and the breechblock was returned. I put men on watch for 2-hour intervals after that. It started to rain at 0100, so I rolled my pack and stood by the guns until morning.

November 9, 1941 Sunday
Guard tent

Up reluctantly and with much shivering had breakfast. Heated water and shaved. Got into my greens uniform and at 0815 fell out the guard. At 0830 presented ourselves at the guardhouse. Relieved the old guard and took over the 2 drafty tents that comprised the guardhouse. There is one 24-hour post, 1 daytime 12-hour post, and 3 nighttime 12-hour posts.

Nothing very exciting happened on this guard. At 1300 all the duty NCOs were called together, and an order from Major Buckley was published to the effect that all stoves must be extinguished after taps on penalty of losing them promptly. This order was issued because some of the Kerosene stoves had started fires; or had "sooted up" a tent because of defective wicks. The colors were lowered by our guard tent at sunset. After taps the OOD ordered that I check every tent in all nine Batteries to see that the stoves were extinguished, and to report the number of tents in which I found burning stoves. I found several, and I warned the occupants; but I reported only two, without giving their locations. The night turned very cold, and I was miserable. Had on my greens and my overcoat. I tried to sleep, but didn't get a wink. It was one of the coldest guards of which I was ever a member. Several auto radiators froze.

December 7, 1941 Sunday
11th Regiment area, New River, No. Car.
Up for breakfast, and then right back to bed again, as it was very cold and damp. Up again at 1030. In the afternoon just took things easy arranging my stuff. About 1630 word was passed from some of the fellows owning radios that Japan had attacked Americans at Honolulu. And after supper, the shocking news was confirmed by bulletin after bulletin on the radio. What an awful thing this is. When I think of all the effects this will have on all phases of my life, I am stunned. My mind is unable to cope with the many problems presented. This is the real, final thing. The days to come will be dark ones, and Lord knows how the course of my life is going to be affected by the misery and wretchedness of a prolonged war, which I think this is going to be. I thought of calling Bess on the telephone, but I wanted more time to think things out so I would know what to say to her, and what to tell her. I am sorry for what she must innocently suffer through me. And her case is probably multiplied thousands of times over in this country.

December 8, 1941 Monday
11th Regiment area, New River, No. Car.
Up, and Troop and Inspection was scheduled; but instead, the morning was spent in checking the clothing and equipment of the men in the Sections. After lunch we listened on all available radios to the speech of the President (Franklin Delano Roosevelt) announcing that a state of war exists between this country and Japan. In the afternoon we out on a small RSOP. All the men were notified that Court Martial offenses will now result in heavier penalties because of this country now being at war. All liberties

were cancelled, and nobody was permitted to leave the camp area. All sealed letters that the men had mailed were returned to them with instructions to mail them open (unsealed), so that they might be censored. I made out an allotment for $35 per month to Bess to pay my monthly accounts. This was done so that in the event I am taken prisoner, she will receive enough money to meet necessary payments. Sent Max Gelfound a short letter enclosing a money order for my Federal Credit and hospitalization. Another letter to the Essex County Building & Loan, enclosing payments for Nov. and Dec. And a 3rd letter to Bess, telling of the censorship and saying that the MC matter was off because of the conditions.

December 9, 1941 Tuesday
11th Regiment area, New River, No. Car.
At 0730 the guns were hooked up and we off about 3 miles on an RSOP. It was a very slow one, with much waiting until we got into position, and also between fire missions. Spent the entire morning out there, and then back to camp for lunch. In the afternoon we held school and cleaned up the guns. There is an NCO school every afternoon for an hour. The censorship has been lifted, and letters may be sent sealed. Received a package of pictures from Buddy Rutkin Photo. Also received a letter from Bess in which she describes the news broadcasts of Sunday concerning the attacks by Japan on this country's island possessions, and she seems also to realize that it would be futile to send that letter MC. She sounded shocked and depressed. I am really sorry for the poor girl. After supper I intend to go to the Main Station, as restrictions against liberty until 2200 have been lifted, but I was too tired. Instead, I sat around fixing the pictures I had received.

December 13, 1941 Saturday
11th Regiment area, New River, No. Car.
Slept late, and then up for breakfast. Wrote a long letter to Bess, and made up the order for Buddy Rutkin. Will mail them in town, first because it contains much personal matter, and second because it will get much faster service. In the afternoon the men began to be harassed by the officers, who were worried by the war news, and probably wanted to show that they were doing something for the protection of the camp. All the guns were run out into the field and scattered. We were told that during the night we would be awakened for gun drill, and that we were to establish an all-night watch of two men on each gun. They kept coming out with new ideas and changing the old ones until I was thoroughly disgusted. I called my second in command, gave him all the details, and told him I was

going on liberty. Shaved, took a shower, and got into fresh clothes. Bove came around at about 1930, and we off. The camp was completely "blacked out." To the Kennedy home outside of Kinston and spent a nice evening. Back to Kinston about midnight, and could find no hotel or tourist home that was not full. So we had to sleep in Bove's car in the street.

January 15, 1942 Thursday
11th Regiment area, New River, No. Car.

Up, and it is a bit warmer these days. The Communication personnel of the Battery out on a problem that lasted until 1600, they eating out in the field. I to the office and had things fairly easy all morning. The Marine Corps is being greatly expanded, and this Battery is making many recommendations for promotions. In the afternoon Platoon Sergeant O'Connor from "E" Battery came over to see me about a raincoat and a blanket belonging to that Battery. We settled about the blanket, but the raincoat seems to be missing. Received my newspapers, the first addressed to my new address. Also received 2 letters from Bess, which had been sent to my old Battery and forwarded. The newspapers carry word of a tanker being torpedoed off Long Island, N.Y.; and that submarines were infesting the east coast of the U.S. Our camp reacted by ordering anti-aircraft machine guns manned for 24-hours a day, and declaring a total blackout. Though all lights were turned off, the movies showed tonight. They are in a big circus tent, and can be concealed.

February 17, 1942 Tuesday
11th Regiment area, New River, No. Car.

It rained all day today, and the camp grounds are in terrible condition. Some of the spots that have to be crossed are ankle-deep in mud. All the men in the Battery have been issued arctics or galoshes for getting about the area. Today word was received that New River has been designated as the home base for the First Marine Division. Up to now we have been here on a 6-week maneuver which had been extended. Now this place is officially our base, and the first three pay grades can get the Government to ship their household effects here. The men are looking about for low-cost housing. To the movies at night. After the show I wrote a letter to Sam Marcus, asking him to check my accounts with Gelfound.

February 26, 1942 Thursday
11th Regiment area, New River, No. Car.

To the office. The sun was up all day, and the snow is practically all melted. The roads are a muddy mess, and only emergency trips are made

Maj. Gen. Thomas Holcomb, Commandant, USMC, addressing the troops of the 1st Marine Division at Marine Barracks at New River, N.C., on March 26, 1942. Seated in middle is Col. Pedro A. Del Valle, C.O., 11th Marines.

out of camp. We are practically marooned. Heard that Jasinski had been out one night, and had come in after Taps. He had been reported by the Officer of the Day, and was now restricted to camp for a couple of weeks, so I cannot get to town with his car. The Captain was told of the appointment of Bove, and after discussing the matter with Bove, he asked if I would consider acting as First Sergeant. I told him I would like to have a chance at it; and though nothing definite was said, I guess I will act. Things were rather mixed up, as I am trying to get the hang of everything. I had some uniforms cut down for me.

May 25, 1942 Monday
11th Regiment area, New River, No. Car.
　　Up, and had my warrant typed out. This promotion is going to mean a big increase in pay for me. I will now be able to claim quarters allowance for my wife, and this amounts to about $35 per month. The raise in base pay amounts to $12; and as of the fourth of this month, my Reserve service counts toward longevity pay. So I am going to get a big boost in pay. I have not written to Bess for a long time, so I sent her a telegram telling her of my promotion, and advising her that I was increasing her allotment $50. I was kept very busy all day. We are transferring all men who are ill, in the brig, or absent without leave. Preparations are being made for leaving this place, and I believe that we will not be here for another two weeks.

Abraham Felber and wife, Bess, at home in
Newark, N.J., early 1942.

June 5, 1942 Friday
11th Regiment area, New
River, No. Car.

Another very hot day. I
am right up with my work. I
am just awaiting the return of
the clerk, Murray, to get my
Muster Roll out, and I will be
set for a while. We were given
instructions as to the type of
pack to be taken when we
leave. I completed and mailed
a lesson to the Marine Corps
Schools today. Yesterday was
Bess's birthday, but I had been
unable to acknowledge it. So
today the first thing I did was
to send one of the men out
and had him wire her a dozen
roses, with a tender message.
Also wrote her a letter in the
evening. Received from her a
waterproof, shock-proof wrist
watch with a radium dial and
a sweep hand. This is one of
the things I figure I will need
overseas. Others that I have
are a cigarette lighter (should
there be no matches available)
and a hunting knife.

June 9, 1942 Tuesday
abd train, en route to San Francisco, Cal.

Up, and feeling good. At Roll Call gave the men the instructions for
today's movements. At 0730 all seabags and bedding rolls were placed out
in the street, and a detail came along and trucked them off. The man who
had been closed out as a deserter yesterday, showed up this morning. We
had to re-open his book and declare him AWOL, we had to rescind the
reward notices which we had mailed yesterday, and we had to get him his
stuff back from the Quartermaster. We ate lunch at 1100. The office had been
closed at 1000, and all the desks and chests shipped off. The office tent was

Top: The 11th Marines are lined up for regimental photo, March 30, 1942, Marine Barracks, New River, N.C. *Bottom:* March 1942, 75mm pack howitzer battery with wooden wheel mounts, Marine Barracks, New River, N.C.

taken down. My pack was all made. We ate again at 1500. At 1530 I had the men fall out with "field transport packs," and we marched about three blocks to the train. After a short wait we boarded the pullman cars, 26 to each car. The train headed past Camp Davis, through Wilmington, and on westward. No meal served today aboard the train — we ate fruit which we had brought along. The berths were made up at 2230, and I glad to get to bed.

June 14, 1942 Sunday
Pier 44, San Francisco, Calif. Aboard Motor Vessel, John Ericsson

Up, and found that we had passed through Reno, Nevada in the early morning. We were now in Truckee, Calif. It was considerably warm, and we rode along looking at the magnificent California scenery. We saw many places where the snow still lay on the ground. We were up rather high, and in some places we could look down and see snow beneath us. We received word that we were to arrive at our destination early in the afternoon, so the morning was spent in shaving and washing, in getting into clean clothes and in making up our packs. About 1600 we arrived at our destination, and walked about a quarter of a mile from the train to the waterfront. We boarded a large ship named the M/V *John Ericsson*, formerly the *Kungsholm* of the Swedish-American Line. The men were assigned to a compartment which was comparatively light and roomy. The Staff NCOs were assigned to staterooms, and I picked one of the less desirable ones. We got our stuff stowed away, and our seabags and bedding rolls were soon distributed. Made up our bunks, and I glad to get to bed.

June 22, 1942 Monday
Abd MV John Ericsson, *at sea*

We filled out another card today stating that we had been transferred to a foreign country, and that we had arrived safely. These will be sent ashore to be kept until notice of our arrival is received, when they will be mailed to the addressees. Had the clerks make out a new pay table, which raises my pay. Besides this, I will get 20% extra for foreign duty while we are under way and outside the continental limits of the U.S. There are more than 5,000 men aboard this ship, and the food situation is pretty bad. It takes almost 4 hours to feed everybody. At noon we had only a cup of soup and some crackers. It is going to work out so that we will get only 2 meals a day. At 1500 we had "abandon ship" drill, and lifeboat stations were assigned us. At 1615 the ship started slowly off, stood down the bay, and so out to sea. I to eat a wretched meal. The ship started to roll and pitch, and soon the men began getting ill. Some were very sick. I became sick for a while, and went to bed early.

June 24, 1942 Friday
Abd MV John Ericsson, at sea

Up at 0700, and feeling much better now that I am catching up on my sleep. Mustered the men at 0845. Checked in the last radio, which must be turned in for safe-keeping to prevent anybody playing them and disclosing our position. We had read to us a message of encouragement from the President of the United States. Also, a message from the Commanding General of the First Marine Division, telling us that we were going to New Zealand and admonishing us about our behavior. The work is fairly light now, and staying on the topside in the fresh air is pleasant. We must be travelling southward, because the weather is becoming warmer. I am making an effort to get permission to take pictures, and I have made a good start. The Colonel (Del Valle) has agreed that I may take pictures under the supervision of the R-2, the Intelligence Section. In the evening I closed the office early and spent a hot, uncomfortable 2 hours seeing a movie. The movie was funny. Down to my stateroom in time to take a shower, but all the water, including the salt water, was shut off. One of my roommates gave me a big helping of fruit salad.

June 30, 1942 Tuesday
Abd MV John Ericsson, *at sea*
      Up on deck after breakfast, and didn't hold muster, as nearly all of the Privates and PFCs are detailed on guard duty or working parties. Bothered all morning by men trying to get excused from their assignments. There was much to do about the business of initiating the "polliwogs" and making them "shellbacks," as we are due to cross the equator some time tonight. I spent most of the day working on pay cards, and I now have them in fairly good shape. I checked for the first time today, and counted 9 other ships in our convoy. Two of them are painted with camouflage markings, and the others are painted various shades of gray. One of them is the Matsonia, and is reputed to have 300 nurses aboard. The weather is quite warm, but not as hot as I expected it would be around the equator. In the evening they began posting all sorts of comic guards about, as "Davy Jones" was expected aboard with a message from King Neptune. The goings-on became so rough that the General who is aboard as commander of the troops ordered it to cease; but it was soon resumed. I to bed early.

July 1, 1942 Wednesday
Abd MV John Ericsson, *at sea*
      Up and prepared my camera and plenty of film. Secured a good position aft on "A" deck, and was able to get some good shots of King Neptune and his court coming aboard. The day was given over to the ceremonies of initiating the "polliwogs." The preparations for the ceremony were very elaborate. The court was most fancifully decorated to resemble some villainous characters, and they meted out punishment to all pollywogs, whether of high or low station. The men were looking for me, and soon ordered me to appear before the court. I was stripped down to my drawers, and

King Neptune's Royal Court, awaiting Davy Jones, at sea crossing the equator aboard the *John Ericsson*, on July 1, 1942, bound for Wellington, New Zealand.

led on hands and knees down a long double lane of men armed with paddles, which they laid on with much vigor and enthusiasm as I inched my way forward. I then mounted a platform on which the court was convened, and I answered to various scurrilous charges against me. I was then administered an electric shock, bedaubed with iodine and purple stuff, made to drink quinine and other vile-tasting mixtures, plastered with paste, made to kiss the Royal Baby's foot while my rear was smacked with a tremendous sword carried by the Royal Executioner. I was then seated on a bench on the edge of a tank of water and my face and hair were plastered with paste. The Royal Barber shaved me with an immense wooden razor. I was then dumped backward into the pool, where a group of Shellbacks began ducking me until I yelled "Shellback, shellback." I was then permitted to climb out of the tank, to be met by one of King Neptune's henchmen armed with a triton which had been wired with electricity. An application of this weapon made me leap in the air and started me off down another double lane of paddlers who took vicious swings at my rapidly retreating rear (with very few misses). This ended the initiation for me. I then climbed way up in the rigging of the ship, and proceeded to take about 20 pictures of the doings on the deck. Most of the initiations were similar to mine. Some they made swim on the deck, while they were being paddled.

July 1, 1942. Shellback initiation, the swimming course, at sea crossing the equator aboard the *John Ericsson*, bound for Wellington, New Zealand.

Those with moustaches had one side of this adornment shaved off. The officers, including the general, were not spared, but had to submit to the same treatment. Things were funny for a while, but soon there were many newly-made Shellbacks who were itching for revenge, and they took it upon themselves the task of assisting the older Shellbacks with grim enthusiasm. The air resounded with the whacking and thudding of paddles, and after about 3 hours the deck was covered with splinters from broken paddles. The deck became quite slippery with paste, and with water from the tank and from hoses played on the pollywogs. Some of the men dashing through the last lane of paddlers could not stop on reaching the end of the lane, and their feet flew out from under them and they fell very hard. I saw 2 of them carried off unconscious. They were finally forced to walk through the last lane of paddlers. At 1500 nearly all of the ship had been subjected to initiation, and the ceremonies were called off. I had been watching the proceedings dressed only in drawers, and I think I have received a good sunburn. This sunshine is unusual, as we have been having cloudy and muggy weather. But the sunshine was excellent for photo purposes. Spent the afternoon working at my desk. In the evening took a fresh water shower in the crew's quarters, and washed off all the paste and other accumulations from the initiation.

July 9, 1942 Thursday
Abd M/V John Ericsson, *at sea*

> Crossed the International Date Line from East to West during the night, thereby losing this date.

Last night we had been fed roast beef, and it had looked like very good meat. During the night nearly all of the men (including myself) developed diarrhea, as the meat must have been spoiled. The heads were so busy during the morning hours that several men found it necessary to relieve themselves right on the deck.

July 11, 1942 Saturday
Abd M/V John Ericsson, *Wellington, N.Z.*

After breakfast up on deck. We were very close to land. It was raining, and there was a strong wind blowing, so that it was uncomfortable to remain on deck. Couldn't open the office desk, as the rain blew in and wet the papers. At about 1300 we began to approach the harbor of Wellington. At 1405 we dropped anchor, and several men received tidy sums from betting pools as to the exact time this would take place. There was much scurrying about the ship. The men lined up on the rails and called to the natives, and threw money and cigarettes to them. The 2nd Battalion of our regiment is here since about a week. They were plied with questions as to where they were staying, what the liberty conditions were, and all other interests close to the heart of Marines. Liberty from 1900 to 0100 was granted to 25% of the men. Then orders were received to prepare to leave this ship by 0900 tomorrow, with only our field transport packs. We will leave our seabags and bedding rolls, and one man and one officer, and go aboard some other ship. No other instructions.

July 12, 1942 Sunday
abd U.S.A.T. Hunter Liggett, *Wellington, N.Z.*

Up, and the day was a very disordered one. We started packing right after breakfast; and soon cargo and seabags and bedding rolls began leaving the ship. The corridors were all jammed with men lugging equipment or huge field transport packs, and it was difficult to move. I had roster made up to take with me, and then I gave him his final instructions, and then to my stateroom and made up my pack. At 1530 we fell in on the dock, and I called the roll. We then marched with our field transport packs about ¾ of a mile to the *Hunter Ligget*. There was only one gang-plank, and cargo was going aboard ship on that, so with all our equipment we were made to climb up the side of the ship by way of a cargo net. The troop space seemed very much smaller than that aboard the *Ericsson*, but it is surprising how soon one becomes accustomed to almost any condition. The first three pay grades soon found a better space, and we moved in. Liberty was declared, and I decided to take some for myself. At 1900, with several other men, I went into town. The city is under blackout conditions, and we carried flashlights. There was not much to be seen in the gloom, but it was exciting to see the English people, stores and manners. There were so many Marines in town that all restaurants had their doors closed, and admitted people only when the others were finished and left. It being Sunday, most of the stores were closed. We finally found a confectionery store that lured us with the sign "Lounge Bar," but it was only an ice cream parlor. We sat down and had 3 malted milks each, plus a large sundae. We have had two meals aboard the *Liggett*, and they have been very satisfactory — and food of good, substantial quality. After the drinks we decided to go back to the ship, as there was very little else to do.

July 14, 1942 Tuesday
abd Hunter Liggett, *U.S.A.T. P-27 Queens Wharf, Wellington, N.Z. harbor*
     Lt. Harris went for the pay early in the morning. I got the rest of the signatures of the men in the Battery, and at 1330 we paid the Battery. It was raining all day again today, and it was noon before I was dried out from the soaking I had last night. We paid the last of the stragglers again at 1700. Then I went up and asked the Battery Commander for liberty. He granted it. As I was about to leave the ship, Capt. Mossburg told me he had a report to get out, and ordered me to get him a typist. I got one, but the Captain said he was not sufficiently adept. He ordered me to do the typing. I told him the typing was not a Battery matter, that I had furnished him with a typist, and that I had been granted liberty which I wished to take advantage of. He asked if I was going to do it, and I said I would rather not. He then ordered me to stand by to see the Colonel — that I was on report. I acknowledged the order and left. With Jasinski I went ashore, and the town was all blacked out. We had flashlights, and we picked our way to a "fish and chips" place, where we had some delicious "terekihi" fish. After paying our bill we started for the ship. We passed a large building, and several ladies and some New Zealand soldiers urged us to attend a dance for servicemen going on inside. We entered and found a well-filled hall with some lovely New Zealand girls. Jasinski and I sat down and soon were introduced to some girls and we had several dances and some saute wine (liquor is very hard to procure.) About 2300 the dance started breaking up. I was sitting alone for a moment when another Marine, Militano, came to my table and told me he had been abused by

me aboard the *John Ericsson* because I had been taking advantage of my
superior rank; but that we were now outside and away from Marine Corps
authority and he wanted satisfaction from me. I told him that if he felt
that way, it was best to get it over with right now. Calling Jasinski, we three
left. It was very dark outside in the blackout. I walked quite a distance away
from the dance hall, as there were several MPs present and I didn't want
to get caught by them as I was already on report on Capt. Mossburg's
charge; and it is a serious offense to be caught fighting. Finally I picked a
secluded corner and doffed my coat and tie. It was so dark I could barely
see the other fellow. We traded some mighty hard blows. He caught me
once on the cheekbone so hard that I was knocked right back on my butt.
He went down a couple of times also. We would rush for each other, swinging in the dark until we collided, then trading punches. I connected with
his nose, and he bled profusely, covering my shirt with blood and even
dripping on my trousers. He was getting the worst of it. He was getting
tired, and so was I. By this time a crowd had collected, and finally one of
the men stepped in and suggested that we quit then as the MPs might be
attracted by the size and noise of the crowd. Militano decided that he had
had enough and to take this advice. He picked up his coat and strode off.
I was glad that it was over before the MPs had arrived, so I also took my
coat and left. With Jasinski to the dance, and I had him go in and bring
out my hat, as my shirt was covered with Militano's blood. Jasinski stayed
at the dance, and I went back to the ship, took off my shirt, washed up,
and to bed.

July 15, 1942 Wednesday
abd Hunter Liggett, *U.S.A.T. P-27 Queens Wharf, Wellington, N.Z. harbor*
     Spent a very painful night, not being able to sleep comfortably in any
position. Up, and my lip puffed up, but I feeling good at having handed
out such a drubbing to Militano. Had breakfast and lay down again until
0840, when a man came down and told me Capt Mossburg wished me to
be ready to see the Colonel at 0850. I dressed and up, and was taken in at
0900. I was charged with refusing to obey an order; and after discussion
the Colonel, Pedro Del Valle, said my case merited a Summary Court Martial. However, in view of my good conduct, he would not decide at that
time, but would take until noon to think the matter over. I took things
easy all day. Made a trip to the Hotel Cecil in the afternoon to return the
SMR, and to find out about some new pay rulings. The rain stopped, and
it became very cold. By bedtime there was still no report about my court
martial. Three of the Communication Section NCOs who were supposed
to take out a working party failed to show up, and I had them paged over

the loud speaker. They were not on the ship, and I will run them up tomorrow.

July 17, 1942 Friday
abd Hunter Liggett, U.S.A.T. P-27 Queens Wharf, Wellington, N.Z. harbor
    Up, and was kept very busy all morning. At 1000 I was told that my case would be ready for trial at 1300, and that I should get counsel for myself. I approached Capt. Viall, and he heard my story. He told me I had a good case, and that he was willing to act as my counsel; but that he was loading ammunition aboard the ship at 1300. He suggested that I either get the case postponed, or that I secure other counsel if I didn't care to wait. I thought it over, and knowing the members of the court were favorable to me, I decided to get other counsel and asked Lt. Harris. He took the case, and the trial was held from 1300 to 1500. Capt. Mossburg, when called upon to testify, balled himself up and made out a poor case against me. Lt. Tatsch testified in my behalf, and furnished excellent testimony in my favor. The court was sympathetic to me, and acted amused at Capt. Mossburg. I requested permission to make a statement so as to be able to give my side of the story. I would have done better to keep my mouth shut. I made some stupid remarks that hurt more than they helped my case. The trial was finally finished, and I glad to get out again. After supper I dressed and into town. To the Kodak store and was able to buy one roll of Verichrome film, which was practically bootlegged to me. This sale disposed of the stock for that particular size of film for that week. At other stores, they do not get even that much film. I walked about town for a while, had some ice cream, and then back to the ship.

July 18, 1942 Saturday
abd Hunter Liggett, U.S.A.T. P-27 Queens Wharf, Wellington, N.Z. harbor
    Learned today that there had been an opening for First Sergeant, and that I had been passed up because of being under Capt. Mossburg's charges. Had it not been for that, I would now be a First Sergeant. In the morning to the warehouse where our seabags are stored and tried to find mine, so that I could get some fresh clothes out, but was unsuccessful. But I did get thoroughly drenched by the continuous rain. The saying is going around that when you can see the mountains, it is about to rain; and that when you cannot see the mountains, it is raining. Fussed around with working parties and other matters until evening. Had a light supper; and later in the evening felt so hungry that I out to town and bought 2 shillings of delicious fish and chips. Read a while, and then to bed at 2330.

July 21, 1942 Tuesday
abd Hunter Ligget, *U.S.A.T. P-27 Wellington, N.Z. harbor*

Up, and had breakfast. The fighting ships are still in the harbor. The loading was finished today. The men are being instructed in combat procedures. They are cleaning up their mess gear, and oiling up their weapons. Canteens are being filled. Meals are still excellent and substantial. New fiber identification tags were issued to those of us who had only paper ones. Ammunition is being issued to all hands, and anti-aircraft defenses are being set up. At noon word was passed that all hands were to be aboard by 1500. I had sent my clerk out to return some Service Record Books to the camp where Murray was staying (Camp Paikakeriki), and he returned just in time. At 1545 my Battery was inoculated with anti-tetanus and cholera shots. About 1600, lines were cast off and the ship stood out into the bay. We didn't go far — just out to join the others in the bay, and then we anchored. Watertight doors were closed, and the ship became very hot, and the various compartments became well-nigh inaccessible. I am going to have much difficulty getting to different ones.

July 22, 1942 Wednesday
abd Hunter Liggett, *U.S.A.T. P-27 — at sea*

Up and shaved. Had breakfast. Didn't hold muster today, as I had no instructions for the men. At 0745 the ship pulled up anchor, and at 0800 we stood out to sea. Through Cooks Straits, and turned north, with North Island on our port side and the great, bare mountains of South Island on our right for a time. There are many ships in our convoy — troop ships, destroyers, and cruisers. One can count 10 ships on either side of our ship. It makes a grand sight to see these vessels lift and plunge in the seas, but I would feel a whole lot safer if there were an aircraft carrier or two with us. I drew 2100 rounds of .50 cal. ammunition for our two machine guns, and 2000 rounds of .45 cal. ammunition for the rifles in the Battery. Saw a representative of the D-2 (Intelligence) Section today, and was given negative permission to continue taking pictures — I was not forbidden to take them. Besides the Navy guns, we have mounted ten 20mm guns for anti-aircraft protection.

July 23, 1942 Thursday
en route to Koro, Fiji Islands

Very uneventful day. Up at 0600; and at 0630 was on my way to chow when "General Quarters" was sounded. All hatches were battened down and all water-tight doors were closed. I was caught in between compartments, and I had to remain on deck until recall from General Quarters.

July 23, 1942. 20mm anti-aircraft gun and crew in aerial gunnery drill aboard the U.S. Navy Transport *Hunter Liggett* (AP-27), at sea in the southwest Pacific Ocean en route to Guadalcanal from New Zealand.

At this signal all men are supposed to go to their compartments and stay there, as during the time this alarm is given is the best time for submarine attack. I took a couple of pictures on deck today — one of the 20mm guns and one of 3 Australian cruisers off the starboard bow. There are well over 20 ships in this convoy. The *Liggett* was built at the Sparrows Point, Maryland yards of the Bethlehem Shipbuilding Company in 1922. Today I received 3000 rounds of .30 cal. ball ammunition, and 890 rounds of armor-piercing ammunition for the men in the Battery armed with rifles. The meals continue ample. I took my pistol apart and cleaned it today.

July 26, 1942 Sunday
abd Hunter Ligget, *U.S.A.T. P-27 — at sea en route to Koro, Fiji Islands*
　　Up, and the sea had subsided considerably, and the ship was much steadier. Shaved and out on deck. The sun was shining, and the fresh air was deliciously exhilarating. I took a chance and had a drink; and suffering no bad effects, I down to breakfast. I was feeling quite weak, so I back to my bunk and lay down. At 0900 I had Notaro, one of the corps men, brought up for office hours for AWOL, and he was awarded 30 days restriction. I back to my bunk and rested up. At noon, I down and had some very good chicken. I took my camera and snapped a couple of pictures on the deck.

At 1230 a group of war vessels hove in sight of the horizon. They joined our convoy. We are now a formidable group. In one section aft of our ship I counted 22 ships. There are all types of ship with us, including 2 aircraft carriers, cruisers, troopships, destroyers, etc. I feel much more secure. In the evening to the head, and worked hard washing some underwear and the shirt that had been bloodied in the fight at Wellington. I also washed myself a bit. (Have had no bath for over a week).

July 27, 1942 Monday
abd Hunter Ligget, *U.S.A.T. P-27 — at sea en route to Koro, Fiji Islands*
　　Up, and my stomach is settling down quite nicely. Had pancakes for breakfast, passing up the sausages that went with it. Heard today that yesterday, when the other ships joined us, they made a total of more than 52 ships in the fleet, and included the *Ranger* and the *Wasp*, aircraft carriers; and the battleship *North Carolina*, the newest battleship in the U.S. fleet. Most of these ships have left us, and we hear they will go ahead and will meet us where we are to stage some landing rehearsals. A dispatch was circulated, informing us that the "landing rehearsals this week involve landing through reefs on coral beaches on Koro Island." Most of the men are making up packs for landing, and getting themselves set. I have received no definite orders in the matter, and am still unprepared. Spent several hours today reading a book by Louis Bromfield, "It Takes All Kinds."

Servicing 105mm guns on deck aboard the *Hunter Liggett* en route to Guadalcanal, July 27, 1942.

July 28, 1942 Tuesday
offshore from Koro, Fiji Islands

Awakened at 0215 and held my watch upside-down in looking at the time, and thought it was past 0700 oclock. So up and to the head and shaved and took a leisurely and most pleasant bath, having the place to myself. Finally realized that it was only 0300, and back to bed. Up at 0730, and we were anchored off a mountainous island about 5 miles north, which I supposed to be Koro Island. I told the men in the Battery to make up their packs. At 1230 several units started to go over the side via cargo nets, into the Higgins boats which had been lowered during the morning. Some sections of my Battery went over, but I was not scheduled to do so. Had substantial lunch, which most of those going over missed. In the afternoon up on deck and watched the proceedings, taking 2 pictures. The landing boats suffered severely on the jagged coral beaches, several propellers being damaged. The

Boarding the *Hunter Liggett* from Higgins boats after practice landings off Koro, Fiji Islands, July 28, 1942.

practice was finally called off, and the men all returned to their ships. The whole affair had been a ragged, awkward exhibition. One of the officers in the stateroom shared by my Battery Commander was shot through the body today, but I am unable to get the full details. Early to bed.

July 29, 1942 Wednesday
abd Hunter Ligget, *U.S.A.T. P-27 offshore from Koro, Fiji Islands*

Up, and found the ship under way; but we were only shifting position. We were still of the island of Koro. Had a hearty breakfast, and then

July 29, 1942. Loading ramp boat with Jeep and supplies at practice landings off Koro, Fiji Islands, aboard USAT P-27 *Hunter Liggett*, en route from New Zealand to Guadalcanal.

up on deck. At 0830 the word was given to lower all boats, and they were lowered in 29 minutes, which is the record for this ship. The boats were lowered with men and equipment, and they cruised about near the ship. None of them landed on the beach, as it was too full of coral. We cannot afford to have any boats damaged, as it is expected that we are soon to go into combat. I did nothing all day but sit around on the gun deck looking for good pictures to snap. I found only one, as I am conserving my film. I hear (unofficially) that it was Lt. Tatsch who shot Lt. Jones. Anyway, Lt. Tatsch has been relieved as Battery Commander and as Adjutant. Lt. Harris is now the Battery Commander, and Marine Gunner Stuart is the Adjutant. The accident occurred when the officers were fooling around with their pistols. The shot passed through the victim from side to side, but missed all vital organs. I am very sorry to have this happen, as I was on excellent terms with Lt. Tatsch.

July 30, 1942 Thursday
abd Hunter Ligget, *U.S.A.T. P-27 offshore from Koro, Fiji Islands*

Learned today that the officer who had been shot — Lt. Jones — had died at 1500 yesterday; and that it was Lt. Tatsch who had done the shooting. The body was placed in a casket today and left on the deck, from where it is to be transported to a different ship. There was intense aerial activity during the morning, and bombers and fighter planes zoomed and

July 30, 1942. Bringing a ramp boat aboard the *Hunter Liggett* during practice landings off Koro, Fiji Islands.

roared. In the afternoon some cruisers and destroyers opened up with gunfire against the island of Koro. There was very little going over the side in Higgins boats. I had very little to do, and spent most of the day carrying my camera and waiting for pictures. In the evening we were gathered and told about the proposed operation which will take place in about a week against Jap installations on the island of Guadalcanal in the Solomon Island group. The enemy forces are estimated at 7,000, while we will have about 15,000 troops. We were shown maps and charts of the proposed action site, and were instructed in the Jap methods of fighting and their proneness to treachery. In the evening I played cards until midnight. Wrote a letter to Bess.

July 31, 1942 Friday
at sea

It is very hot and muggy hereabouts. The boats went over the side in landing practice right after breakfast; and troops, guns, equipment and trucks were lowered into them. They went to within about 200 yards of the beach, and then returned. At about noontime the landing exercises were called off and the afternoon was spent in quickly reloading the troops and equipment aboard. The body of Lt. Jones was transferred to a destroyer during the afternoon. By 1700 nearly all the boats and gear was aboard again. The ships in the convoy had assumed traveling formations, and at

A truck being hoisted over the side at practice landings off Koro, Fiji Islands, aboard USAT P-27 *Hunter Liggett*, en route from New Zealand to Guadalcanal on July 31, 1942.

1700 we stood out to sea again. Those boats which had not yet been taken aboard followed us and were lifted aboard while we were under way. We are now off to pit our forces against the Japanese. Even though it appears that we will likely be the victors, there will be much toil and bloodshed and death. There are reported to be about 7,000 Japs on the island we are going to, and the Japs do not permit themselves to become prisoners.

August 1, 1942 Saturday
at sea, en route to Solomon
Islands

When I arose for breakfast this morning, we were passing some of the Fiji Islands. We were under way in convoy formation. The weather is very hot, and water is turned on at certain short hours only, making it difficult to get a bath. Spent most of the day arranging boat assignments. The men are engaged in cleaning the machine guns and cannons. They are very confident, and seem to think only of the losses they will inflict on the Japs, and not at all of the possibility of becoming a casualty themselves. An investigation is going on in the case of the shooting of Lt. Jones. I read some of the books that are available, and played cards for several hours. The games are getting quite steep, as the men realize the lack of value of money in our circumstances. One of the men showed me a receipt for $800 which he had sent home after winning heavily in a crap game; and several of the men told me about one fellow refusing $20 for 4 ice cream cups that cost only $0.40. Change and bills of small denomination are scarce, and I have heard offers of a $10 bill for $8 in change for use in card games.

August 4, 1942 Tuesday
abd Hunter Liggett, *U.S.A.T. P-27 at sea, en route to Solomon Islands*

Destroyer 349 came alongside this morning, and was refueled from this ship while both vessels were moving ahead. This compelled me to use 2 of my precious films on the scene. A notice came out stating the Lt. Tatsch had been detached from this Battery and transferred to the 5th Battalion. After the destroyer *Dewey* (No. 349) had been refueled, destroyer No. 350, the *Hull*, was refueled. Today is the birthday of the Coast Guard, and the crew of this ship is composed of Coast Guardsmen. Messages of felicitation were received from the Task Commander and from Col. del Valle on this occasion. A message was also read to us, from the Commander of this whole movement, complimenting us and advising us that aircraft, surface vessels, submarines, Marines, Navy and Coast Guard, and Australian and New Zealand troops were all to participate in this common attack; and that he felt confident that we would acquit ourselves well. He named the date of the attack as August 7th. In the evening there was a meeting of the NCOs, at which the new Battery Commander, Lt. Harris, spoke and gave us some further details of the proposed action.

August 5, 1942 Wednesday
abd Hunter Liggett, *U.S.A.T. P-27 at sea, en route to Solomon Islands*

Made up the remarks on the Change Sheet in the case of Lt. Tatsch — he has been released from arrest and restored to duty pending review of the investigation held in the matter of his shooting Lt. Jones. The men were again gathered and had their pistols checked, as two of these weapons have been stolen. There is quite a bit of stealing going on, and among missing items are supplies of Quinine, two cases of hand grenades, a case of field glasses, and all sorts of other articles. In the afternoon I tied my dungaree trousers and one of my shirts to a line and hung it over the fantail of the ship and let the ship's wake slap the dirt and sweat loose. In the morning I had taken a bath out of the washbasin in the head. Spent some time playing blackjack, and finished reading the book "Cabbages and Kings," by Stevenson. I have been eating heartily these last few days, so that I will have a reserve in case of food shortages. I have been assigned a boat when it comes time to leave ship. The different units keep holding meetings and instructing the men (on the landing procedures).

August 6, 1942 Thursday
abd Hunter Liggett, *U.S.A.T. P-27 at sea, en route to Solomon Islands*

Up, and it had been raining last night. Checked on my boat assignment. There was a General Quarters signal around 1000, and the men acted twice as promptly as usual. The time is getting close. The day was cloudy, and in the afternoon it began to rain slightly. At 1400 ammunition was issued for the small arms. Passwords were published for the next 3 days. They will be in effect from noon of one day to the following noon. Orders were given that men going ashore were not to take any diaries or papers containing addresses or unit designation. I will have to place this diary in the part of my pack that will be left on the ship. After supper the men made final preparation for tomorrow's work. There was an air of almost festivity aboard ship. In the gloom of the decks they were singing sentimental songs and cracking jokes. I fixed up my pack, and then to bed. Had a queer feeling in the pit of my stomach.

CHAPTER 2

Guadalcanal
August 7, 1942–December 15, 1942

August 7, 1942 Friday
Beach Red, Guadalcanal, B.S.I.P., Coords: M675-335
No. coast Guadal. 3-sheet M square system map

Reveille went at 0245. At 0330 I rose and had breakfast. We were under way and it was dark. There was a bright half-moon out, and the stars were shining. I went back to my bunk for another couple of hours of sleep. At 0600 a furious cannonading started. I arose and took my shaving gear and to the head. From the deck I could see all the fighting vessels slamming salvo after salvo into the shores of an island about 5 miles off our starboard side. Planes were also active. I down and took a shave. Back to my compartment, made the final arrangement of my gear, and loaded my pistol. At 0650 the boats were lowered. Hatches began to be opened, and the men stood by. Zero hour was announced as 0910. Boats and gear were put over the side, and the men descended into the boats. The ships' cannons kept pounding away at the shore. Explosions were heard on shore, and at one place a great fire was started that sent up a billowing mass of smoke through which shot flames of great height. At the appointed hour the Higgins boats streaked for the shore. When they hit the beach, the shellfire ceased. Word was flashed back that a successful landing had been made. From then on, in accordance with a pre-arranged schedule, boats were lowered, filled with their designated men and equipment, and sent ashore. None of them had any difficulty. The only resistance I saw all morning was a small motorboat (possibly a torpedo boat) which came out and started firing a machine gun at a destroyer. The destroyer turned one of its guns on it, and with one shot blew it out of the water. A Jap plane which

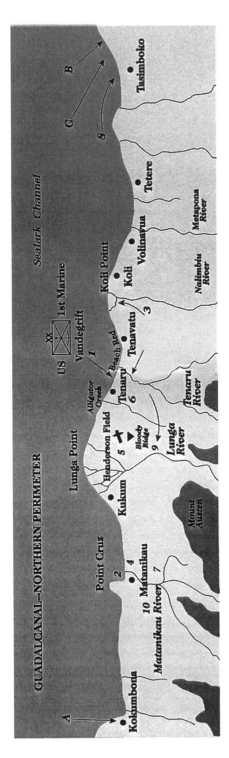

Operations in August and September 1942

1. 1st Marine Division lands August 7, 1942 and advance westward against minimal Japanese resistance to occupy Henderson Field.

2. Patrol led by Colonel B. Goettge, 1st Marine Division Intelligence Officer, wiped out August 12th.

3. Brush patrol encounters Japanese reconnaissance party near Koli Point, August 19th.

4. First battle of the Matanikau River; 3 U.S. companies destroy the small Japanese garrison, August 19th.

5. Henderson Field becomes operational, August 20th.

6. Battle of the Tenaru River; Ichiki's force destroyed, August 20/21st.

7. Second Battle of the Matanikau River, August 12th

8. Tasimboko Raid, September 8th

9. The Battle for "Bloody Ridge", Kawaguchi's Brigade repulsed, September 12-14th.

10. Third Battle of the Matanikau River, 3 U.S. battalions try to clear Matanikau area but are forced to withdraw, September 24-27th

A. Yokosuka's Fifth Special Landing Force arrives on August 18th.

B. Ichiki's battalion lands on August 18th.

C. Kawaguchi Brigade lands between August 29th and September 1st.

rose to meet us was quickly shot down. For the rest, it appeared as though we were practicing a landing against an unoccupied coast. My boat was not scheduled to leave the ship until after noontime. I went down to the galley for lunch, but only the crew was being fed — the Marines had secured their galley. I broke out some chocolate ration and ate that. About 1300 my boat pulled up and with four others from my Battery, together with about 15 others, got into it. As we pulled away, I took a shaky picture of the *Hunter Liggett*. We landed on a sandy beach that was swarming with Marines. Jumped ashore, and up on the beach. All sorts of ammunition, food and supplies kept coming ashore in the Higgins boats, where they were dumped on the beach by working parties, and the boats sent back for more. My party dropped our packs and rifles in a heap under a cocoanut tree. I left them there while I took one man and went searching for the Regimental Command Post. The Marines were spreading out all over the beach, setting up machine guns, 37mm guns, pack howitzers, etc., and running communication lines all over the place. The big amphibious tractors were churning about in the underbrush and across streams, carrying men and guns into the most difficult places. One of the tractors had slipped a tread, and was left stranded, half in and half out of the water on the beach. I did much walking before finally finding my outfit. The RCP had been established and communication set up. I secured a truck and went back and picked up my gear and the rest of the party, and we to our position. We selected cocoanut trees under which to spend the night. This whole beach front here, and about a hundred yards inland, consists of a cocoanut grove. I had some more of my canned rations. I then borrowed an axe and opened several more and drank the milk. All over the place those Marines who had established their positions were gathering cocoanuts. When they couldn't find any in the immediate vicinity, they shot them out of the trees with pistols and rifles. The Battery Commander had me set up a system of "internal guards," and arrange for their reliefs. I instructed the sentries in their duties, and then took them around and posted them. I opened my poncho on the ground and spread a blanket on it; and this served as my bunk for the night. It was quite warm. I slept with my pistol loaded and right at my side. Higgins boats kept coming in all night, and we furnished working parties to unload them and stack the stuff on the beach. I inspected the sentries twice during the night.

Opposite: Map adapted by Nancy King from P. D. Antill, T. Dugdale-Pointon, and Dr. J. Rickard, "Military History Encyclopedia on the Web," military history internet resource URL: http://www.rickard.karoo.net.

Top: Marines landing at Guadalcanal, August 7, 1942 (official U.S. Marine Corps. photograph 1-18). *Bottom:* An "Alligator" amphibian tractor of the 1st Amphibian Tractor Battalion coming ashore on Guadalcanal, August 7, 1942.

August 8, 1942 Saturday
Guadalcanal, B.S.I.P. Coords: 982-400 near mouth of Tenaru River
No. coast Guadal. 3-sheet M square system map

Up at dawn and rolled my gear in a compact bundle. Had some of my canned rations for breakfast, supplemented by juice of several cocoanuts. The ships in the harbor were still unloading gear and supplies; and working parties from our Battery had been on his detail all night. The unloading continued all day today, the beaches becoming piled high with equipment and food. Looting started, and the men stationed near the beaches took axes and broke open the cases of food and canned fruits and stole the contents. I came across a big 50-pound cheese which had been broken out of its case, one slab cut from it, and the rest left to waste on the sand. I found some cases of canned pineapple that had been broken into, and I salvaged a can for myself. That, together with a can of Viennese sausages, helped me pass a day of subsistence on canned rations. The RCP was moved about 2400 yards eastward along the beach. The movement started at 1000, and the last unit left at 1540. Communication was set up in the new position, and we settled down for the night. We were in another cocoanut grove. We were issued one meal of canned rations here. I set up an interior guard, then spread my poncho and lay down for the night.

August 9, 1942 Sunday
Guadalcanal, B.S.I.P. Coords: 482-400 near Lunga River bridge
No. Coast Guadal. 3-sheet M square system map

During the night it started to rain. I gathered all my equipment and piled it on a slight rise of ground at the base of a cocoanut tree, and covered it with my poncho. I then crept under the remaining portion of the poncho. There was only sufficient poncho remaining to cover me up to my knees—from my knees down I was exposed. Shortly after midnight shelling started in the harbor, and soon there was a furious thunder of cannonading as a big naval battle took place off shore. Airplanes were also involved in the battle, and it continued for quite some time, finally fading off toward the northwest. I felt very small and lonely, lying there on the ground, with my feet sopping wet and the rain teeming down in the midst of all the shooting. There was much running back and forth amongst officers as they gathered intelligence of the action in progress; but as they didn't call for me, I just lay under my poncho. The outfit to the west of us began firing out to sea with rifles and automatic rifles, and I began wondering whether we were going to be attacked by a landing party. At 0440 the Colonel called me and told me to arouse the Battery and for us to be on the alert for a possible attack. It was still raining heavily. I arose, leaving the poncho to protect my pack and equipment, and walked around in the dark arousing the men. No lights were permitted, as this would have disclosed our position. I was soon dripping wet. At 0510 Major Hughes told me to get all the available men and take them down on the beach. I was able to get about 30 men in a hurry, and we off to the beach. There we were told that some Higgins boats were trying to land, and we set up lights to guide them in. They had been trying to land for several hours, but every time they came near the shore, they had been fired upon by our sentries and men. A sailor in one of the boats had been hit. Finally one of the sailors had swum in and explained the situation to the men on the beach. The boats came in finally — 5 of them, and we were sent back to our bunks. This was at 0455. We had just about gotten settled again when Major Hughes told me to get them out again and we went down to the beach in the rain and unloaded the 5 Higgins boats. They were from the *Hunter Liggett*, and carried our equipment. Some men came ashore from these boats, including our galley force, who said they had been on the water about 6 hours trying to get in and getting shot at every time they approached the beach. They told us of a fierce air attack yesterday, in which many enemy planes had been downed by our own air force and by the anti-aircraft guns on the ships. In this battle, the transport ship *Elliot* had been hit and set afire, and she had to be beached and abandoned, a total loss. I had the galley force bed down, and set about arranging for breakfast. We were issued canned rations again. As it was getting light, small fires were permitted, over which the men heated water for their coffee. I drank mine cold. I was able to get some fruit and tomato juice from men who had picked these items from the broken cases on the beach, and also had some cocoanuts. At 0950 the rain stopped, to my great relief. We rearranged ourselves. At noon had some more canned rations. At 1310 we began moving further westward to a point about 5000 yards further along the beach. The new position is about a mile in from the beach, on the inside of a U-shaped ledge of rock. I left with the last unit at about 1620. While waiting to move, I saw many strange sights. Saw a wounded Korean brought in for treatment, saw Jap prisoners being marched around, saw the 1st Marines come back from some hard chasing after the enemy, and they were a hard and dirty looking lot. They had bicycles, blankets, wine, .25 cal. bullets, paper money and coins, and other Jap souvenirs. A truck finally came and brought me to the new position. It was getting dark, and I had to hustle to get the interior guard arranged for that night. Then I had to find a place and fix up a bunk in the dark. Before I could get to bed, I had to furnish a working party to haul food and ammunition from the beach all night.

August 10, 1942 Monday
Guadalcanal, B.S.I.P. Coords: 482-400 near Lunga River bridge
No. coast Guadal. 3-sheet M square system map

Up and looked around. My bunk is at the edge of a short road that leads down to where the galley is set up in a depression, a short distance from the Lunga River. Our men are scattered alongside a road which runs in a semi-circle around a grassy field. There is a low ridge to the south of the road, where some coral formation juts up about 50 feet. To the west, the land slopes away toward the river. The RCP is in the center of the semi-circle, and I am close to them on the western side. On the south side there is the remains of a Jap weather station, at which I found some "occupation" money, some wind current balloons, weather charts, and several other interesting things. There were several bottles of wine and beer, but these had been emptied. The Battery was busily engaged in digging foxholes and slit trenches for protection against air raids. All available trucks were employed in hauling ammunition, guns, and food only from the beaches, so that we could strengthen our position as much as possible should there be any counterattacks. The men were gathering little wooden platforms, left by the Japs, on which they spread their blankets for sleeping. These platforms are only about 5½ feet long, which makes them almost too short for the purpose. But it is better than sleeping on the damp ground. The Japs are a short people. The men are still eating canned rations, and are becoming a little tired of them. Later in the evening we sent a couple of men along with one of the trucks, and they located our kitchen gear and loaded the stuff aboard the truck. They covered this with boxes of ammunition, and thus were able to get it back to our position. It was set up, and we had hot coffee from the galley for the first time. We will be able to get hot meals from now on. There is much firing going on all day, and in greatly increased volume during the night. This firing is done by our men, who imagine they hear or see Japs moving about in the bushes. Lots of the shooting is done by Marines who fire to get the cocoanuts down from the trees. Several Marines have been killed by other Marines through being mistaken for Japs. It is not safe to move about after dark.

August 11, 1942 Tuesday
Guadalcanal, B.S.I.P. Coords: 482-400 near Lunga River bridge
No. coast Guadal. 3-sheet M square system map

The day was spent in strengthening our position, deepening the air raid shelters, and fixing up our bunks. The trucks were still busy hauling food and material only. In the evening an interior guard was established. The Motor Transport, Quartermaster, and Ordnance Sections are at the extreme northwest part of our position, separated from our galley by the Special Weapons Battery. They mount their own guard. Sgt. Casey, of Motor Transport, was acting as Sergeant of the Guard tonight. As usual, there was much promiscuous shooting going on. Casey had come in from an inspection of his sentries when Pvt. Leland W. Mattice was aroused by a burst of rifle fire. Mattice was confused and scared, and he thought some Japs had sneaked through; so when he saw the dark form of Casey moving about, he thought it was somebody who had come out of the woods, and he instinctively grasped his rifle, aimed it at the shape, and fired. He shot Casey right through the chest. This happened at 2245. A truck was quickly called, and Casey rushed to the sickbay. At 2310 Casey expired. He is our first casualty. But he is not the first to be shot by his own men. There have been several other such cases since landing on this island. There is a slight amount of sniping by Japs at night, but not enough to justify all the shooting that goes on every night. Most of the shots are at shadows or animals. Casey will be buried tomorrow.

August 12, 1942 Wednesday
Guadalcanal, B.S.I.P. Coords: 482-400 near Lunga River bridge
No. coast Guadal. 3-sheet M square system map
      At about 0500 an enemy submarine came in off-shore and shelled the island for about 10 minutes. We were all awakened by this gunfire. Early in the morning Kelly, Casey's friend, learned about Casey's death; and he was so upset that I had to take his pistol away from him for fear of what he might do to Mattice. The chaplain calmed Kelly down, and had him make a cross for Casey's grave. I was granted permission to go along to Casey's funeral. At 1500, Casey's body was placed in the ambulance, and we all got aboard and rode about a mile from camp to where the First Marine Division had established a cemetery. It was very recently established, and there were only two occupied graves. There were also three open graves. When we reached the field, there was another funeral party there with another body. We all waited for a while, as another body was expected, and all three bodies would be buried with one service. Finally, our chaplain told the one with the other body that he ought to go ahead with his service, as he had far to go to get back before dark, and it was already getting late. It was quite cloudy, and looking as though it might rain. There were great masses of clouds over the mountains to the south. The artillery was "registering" its guns, and they were firing over our heads and out to sea. Every few moments they would let go a salvo, and the noise came right at us, and a few seconds later we could hear the burst way to the rear. The other chaplain had the body which was in his care laid in one

of the open graves; and while we all uncovered, he pronounced the solemn services. It was a very impressive scene, with the banks of pearly clouds hanging low over the purple mountains, and the rumbling thud of artillery drowning out the intoning voice of the chaplain at his melancholy task. When he finished, the two men quickly filled in the grave, and the party mounted a truck and left. The other body had not yet arrived, so the chaplain decided to go ahead with Casey's services. We took him off the ambulance. He was wrapped up in a blanket, and around this was his poncho. We lifted him by the corners of the poncho and carried him to the third grave in the first row. We lowered him gently into the grave, but he didn't fit. The grave-digging detail had been in a hurry, and as they dug further down, the grave had become shorter and narrower. I asked the chaplain if we should dig the grave a bit longer. The chaplain directed us to shift the body about, and we did so; but still Casey was not lying flat — his head and feet were against the wall of the grave. I was afraid the chaplain would not let us straighten the grave. I would never have been easy again for thinking of poor Casey in his cramped position. At last, to my great relief, the chaplain told us to take the body out again, and one of the men jumped in and shoveled out more dirt, making the bottom of the grave longer. We placed Casey in again, and this time he lay straight and relaxed. The chaplain commenced his services, and commended Casey to his Maker. During the services the other body arrived. It was that of a very large man — over six feet, and heavy. He didn't have a poncho covering him, and his feet protruded beneath the blankets. He had on shoes, but was not wearing socks. As soon as Casey's services were over, they placed this big Marine in the next open grave, and Chaplain Dittmar said the services over him. Then we all turned to and covered both graves. On top of each grave was placed a long green cocoanut palm frond. The men with the big body made a cross on the field from a nearby tree, and placed it on the grave of their friend. Kelly stuck his cross in at the head of Casey's grave. The grave of the man who had been buried first was without a cross. His friends had gone, so we made one up, fastening the cross-piece with some barbed wire from a nearby fence. Then we gathered up the shovels and picks, got into the ambulance, and back to camp.

(No entries for the period of August 13 through August 19, 1942)

August 20, 1942 Thursday
Guadalcanal, P.S.I.P. Coords: 482-400 near Lunga River bridge
No. coast Guadal. 3-sheet M square system map
    At 0400 I awakened the Battery as word had been passed the night before that that was the hour for us to "stand to" in anticipation of an enemy

attack. We dressed, donned our gas masks and helmets, looked to our weapons and stood by until 0600, at which time the alert was secured. We lit the fires for coffee and breakfast. We do not light fires before daybreak. We have coffee at about 0645, a meal at 1000, and another meal at 1600. The orders from Division are that only two meals will be served; but we sneak in the coffee and crackers in the morning. Regular Battery routine continued for the rest of the day; but there was much activity in the Intelligence Section, which might mean that some action is impending. In the evening I to the river and shaved and bathed. A new map has been drawn that includes our Battery area; and it will be used in the future to designate our position in the Record of Events. I will also use it in my diary. It is called the "D-section map #101, dated 18 August 42, scale: 1/20,000."

August 21, 1942 Friday
Coords: 58.6-116.65. D-2 map #101, 18Aug42

At 0350 I was awakened by a large volume of small arms and cannon firing. At 0400 the Battery was aroused to "stand to." We dressed and armed ourselves, and stood alert. There was an active engagement going on about 2 or 3 miles east of our position, and in the dark we could see the flight of tracer bullets, hear the rattle of automatic weapons and the roar of artillery. At 0600 it began to get light, and we started our coffee going. We could not start before, as we were directly in the line of fire, it seemed to us. Our Battery was not affected by the firing, though it was evident that a fierce engagement was in progress. Our planes took off from the airfield shortly after daybreak, and probably assisted our men in the fighting. The din of heavy firing continued until approximately 1000, then dropped off to sporadic bursts. The artillery ceased firing. All sorts of rumors drifted in as to what was happening. The general run of stories is that a party of Japs had landed, and that our Marines were cleaning them out. Estimates of the Jap casualties varied from 150 to 300. I could learn of only two Jap prisoners having been taken all day.

August 22, 1942 Saturday
Coords: 58.6-116.65. D-2 map #101, 18Aug42

This Battery was again awakened at 0400. There was still intermittent firing going on in the east toward Beach Red, near the Tenaru River, about 2 or 3 miles away. It was reported to me that one of the sentries from my Battery had been found asleep on post by Col. del Valle, and had been recommended by him for a General Court Martial. I spent all day getting statements from him and from the other sentries who had been on watch with him; and in getting the guilty one examined to determine whether he was physically fit for retention in the service. All day reports came back from men who had been up to the battlefront, describing the scenes encountered and the number of Japs killed and the extent of their wounds. I was very eager to get there, but I had no means of transportation. The most reliable details I could get were these: About two days before the battle, two destroyers had landed about 700 or 800 Japs about 65 miles up the coast. The Japs had marched down the shore, traveling by night and resting by day. On Friday the 21st, they made contact with our men, and they had been wiped out. The official figures given to the press were 670 out of 700 killed. They had been crack troops, and seasoned veterans of several previous battles.

August 23, 1942 Sunday
Coords: 58.6-116.65. D-2 map #101, 18Aug42
It had rained all night, but after breakfast it cleared up. I induced Sandman, the Police Sergeant, to take me to the battlefield, and we left aboard a truck with a party of workers. As we approached the place, the stench became very strong. I showed my pass to take pictures (a pass signed by Col. del Valle, designating me as an "official photographer"), and was permitted to go anywhere on the place that I desired. A horrible odor hung over everything. A large pit had been dug, and the bodies of some 60 or 70 Japs were thrown therein, one on top of the other, like a bunch of discarded wax figures. They had been shot up terribly; and since two days had elapsed since the battle, they were all puffed up and bloated. About 50 Korean prisoners were collecting the bodies on stretchers and throwing them into the pit. Some of the bodies were so badly decomposed that it was necessary to bury them where they lay. The Japs had carried all sorts of equipment, including flame throwers, machine guns, grenade throwers, wire cutters, etc. It was sad to see the pictures of their families that were found among their possessions. Just two days ago they had been strong, virile sons, fathers, and husbands; and now they were putrid corpses in some far land. From the notebooks found on some of them, it was learned that these were the same men who had taken the island of Guam, and killed all the Marines there. Marine emblems and effects were found on some of these Japs. The sight and the odor was so overpowering that one of the Military Police (who were in charge of the body disposal) took sick as I was talking to him; and the men in our party had their faces all screwed up in horror and disgust. At 0930 we left the scene and back to the Battery. I washed up and had lunch at 1000. It rained a little, then cleared up. I got a lift in a truck back to the battlefield, and spent the next two hours in morbid fascination watching the collection and burial of the

Top: Korean prisoners used for a burial detail for Japanese dead on August 23, 1942, following Battle of the Tenaru on August 21, 1942. *Bottom:* August 23, 1942. Dead Japanese soldiers in a burial pit after the Battle of the Tenaru.

bodies, and the piling of their effects of what had so recently been brave and confident soldiers. These men never had a chance against the odds they faced. They had been told that there were only about a thousand Marines on this island. They were not lacking in courage. A wave of their men would be mowed down by machine gun fire, only to be followed by succeeding waves. They were hemmed in and greatly outnumbered (see Division Bulletin No. 32a-42)... At about 1500 it began to rain, so I started walking toward camp. It rained quite hard, and I was thoroughly soaked before I finally got to my bunk. It rained the rest of the day. I washed thoroughly, and got set for supper.

August 24, 1942 Monday
No. coast of Guadalcanal,
B.S.I.P. Coords: 58.6-116.65.
near Lunga River bridge
D-2 map #101, 18Aug42

Before going to bed last night we had been ordered to "stand to" at 0200. This morning, right at 0200, some enemy vessel — destroyer or submarine — began shelling this island. About 5 shots were fired, and they seemed to come from a gun of about 8-inch caliber. We sat around after that, but nothing further unusual happened. Most of the men lay down again, but I remained on watch until 0600, when I aroused the galley force and had them start breakfast. I made a trip to the beach near Kukum, where the supply ship *Normalhaut* was unloading supplies for the 1stMarDiv. I intended buying some chewing

"Glory's End": A dead Japanese soldier under a palm tree after the Battle of the Tenaru, August 23, 1942.

tobacco, cigarettes and other supplies for some of the men of our Battery; but when I got there, the ship had already left. During last night a Jap torpedo had been fired at the *Normalhaut*; but the torpedo had missed the ship and had continued on toward the beach. The torpedo had gone completely out of the water and had climbed up the sand on the beach several yards past the water line. I went down to the beach and took a picture of it. It is over 20 feet long, and is a wicked-looking instrument. It came to rest a scant 30 yards from a 37mm anti-tank gun emplacement... There is no trouble hitch-hiking here. Bathing is done in the river about 400 yards from my bunk, at a bridge crossing the Lunga River.

A Japanese torpedo fired from a submarine on August 23, 1942, at cargo ship *Fomalhaut* (AK-22) missed the ship and ran up on beach, Guadalcanal. This photo was made the next day.

August 25, 1942 Tuesday
No. coast of Guadalcanal, B.S.I.P. Coords: 58.6-116.65,
near Lunga River bridge D-2 map #101, 18Aug42

At about one minute after midnight a group of enemy destroyers began shelling this island. The gunfire was quite loud, and the shells were falling in the very near vicinity, because I could hear the fragments whistling through the branches as the shells burst. Every time a salvo came over, I would drop flat on my bunk and hug the boards most ardently, hoping fervently that none of the fragments would end up in my body. I was very scared. Finally got my clothes, helmet, pistol and gas mask together, and into the air raid shelter with the greatest relief. The shelling lasted only a short while, and we soon back to our bunks. The Battery arose at 0400 to "stand to" until 0600, when breakfast was started. As soon as it was light, a "dud" (unexploded shell) was reported about 45 yards from my bunk. Another shell had exploded about 10 feet from that one. The dud was from a 5-inch gun. Lt. Williams was along later in the day, placed dynamite under it, and blew it up. Sgt Rasmussen of Special Weapons Battery, who was sitting in the head about 150 yards away, was hit in the back with a piece of the blown-up shell, and wounded with sufficient severity so that he had to be evacuated on Sept. 1, 1942. This shelling is the closest I have been to fire during this war. In the afternoon I with Sandman to the beach to see if I could find a box for some of my belongings. While out there, we saw 21 bombers with a fighter plane escort come over and drop bombs on the airfield adjacent to our Battery position. There was some dog-fighting after our planes took off after them. Later, reports were circulating that 17 enemy planes (8 bombers and 9 fighters) had been downed by our planes; while we had lost 1 plane definitely, and 2 were still unaccounted for. I was called into the adjutant's office and asked how many men I needed to replace losses. I asked for four men to replace the following: Casey, killed by one of our men; Sideman, transferred to Division HQ; Mattice, who shot Casey and is to be tried by GCM; and Mason, caught sleeping on watch, to be tried by GCM. This request for replacements may mean an early involvement on our part; and it probably won't be back to Wilmington — it will probably be to further attacks. The "press news" is full of references to large movements of American soldiers arriving in the British Isles for the purpose of establishing a second front. It may be that a big push is about to start. I wish I could catch up with my seabag — we are all very low on clothes and supplies.

August 26, 1942 Wednesday
No. coast of Guadalcanal, B.S.I.P. Coords: 58.6-116.65,
near Lunga River bridge D-2 map #101, 18Aug42
We "stood to" at 0400, but no excitement. Breakfast at 0630. At 1205, 17 enemy bombers came over and dropped a load of bombs on the airfield, which is only about 1300 yards from my position. The 90mm guns didn't fire at all on the bombers today. Yesterday the bombers flew at an altitude of 26,400 feet, and I am told that this is beyond the range of the 90s. After the bombing today, there was a series of dog fights between the enemy fighters and ours. The final results of this raid, according to those who claim to get their information from D-2, was five enemy bombers and 8 or 9 Zero fighters lost; while we lost only 1 plane. At 1500 I to the Lunga River, where I shaved, bathed, and washed some clothes. There is no early reveille tomorrow, so I to my bunk to enjoy a good night's rest.

August 27, 1942 Thursday
No. coast of Guadalcanal, B.S.I.P. Coords: 58.6-116.65,
near Lunga River bridge D-2 map #101, 18Aug42
Had forgotten to wind my watch, and it stopped during the night. It was 0530 before I awoke and aroused the galley force and got breakfast started. At 0700 our cannons started firing, and the firing continued all morning. A party of our men left at 0600 to observe the fire. I am told

that the 5th Marines are going into the hills of this island to clean up the remaining Japs, and that our artillery is supporting them. Three men from the Communication Section have been recommended for appointment to the rank of Second Lieutenant. There was a protracted air raid, starting at 1045, that sent a number of planes up, but no bombing occurred in our vicinity. I tried to get to see the Colonel, but he was busy with artillery fire for the 5th Marines, who were mopping up the Japs in the hills to the south; they had made contact with the enemy at about 1300, and had met with some resistance. At 1500, the commander of the 5th Marines had sent back word that he wanted to come in. Gen. Vandergrift had told him to turn over the command to the second in command, that he was relieved, and he was to come in by himself — his men were to continue on their mission. The Colonel relieved was Maxwell. The 5th remained in the hills.

August 28, 1942 Friday
No. coast of Guadalcanal, B.S.I.P. Coords: 58.6-116.65,
  near Lunga River bridge D-2 map #101, 18Aug42
Sandman, the former Regimental Police Sergeant, was transferred to the Ordnance Section today. Also transferred were Battery Police and Property Sergeant Coffey, to the 2nd Battalions and Corp. Persinowski to the 3rd Battalion. There joined us SgtMaj Donald D. Nevin as Regimental Sergeant Major; and PFC Talmadge L. Miles; and Pvt. Peter A. Pardi. The Regimental Police job was abolished with the transfer of Sandman, and Sgt Sladovich was placed in charge of the Battery police sergeant's job. All the remaining men from Sandman's section were transferred to Sladovich. There were no air raids on our position, nor was our position shelled. Things are quieting down. We are beginning to get information as to why we were being awakened at those very early hours during the early part of the week. The "press news" dated August 27 contains the following paragraph:

> "Admiral Ghormley's headquarters announced that in the sea and air battle southeast of the Solomon Islands Tuesday night 6 to 9 or possibly 10 enemy ships were either sunk or damaged, 21 enemy planes were shot down. Among ships sunk or damaged were 2 cruisers, 2 destroyers, 2 transports, 1 aircraft carrier, and 1 battleship. No indication of the damage sustained by the American Navy or aircraft was revealed, except that minor damages were received."

There had been persistent rumors that a Jap task force was on the way to attack the island that we are on, but that it had been intercepted by our aircraft and by our naval forces. A battle had ensued, and the Japs were supposed to have taken a licking and to have dispersed. I didn't put much credence in these rumors, but this dispatch seems to verify them. It also accounts for all the security measures and for all the aerial activity of the last few days. In the evening to the river, shaved and bathed, and to a chow of Jap food. The Japs, besides equipment, have left large stores of food; and this is supplementing our rather meager supplies. Tonight's chow consisted of Jap spaghetti, Jap seaweed, whole hominy, Jap hardtack, American salmon, and coffee. For dessert we had American fruit salad and Jap candy. This was followed by Jap cigarettes. Our diet is very unbalanced.

August 29, 1942 Saturday
No. coast of Guadalcanal, B.S.I.P: Coords: 58.6-116.65,
near Lunga River bridge D-2 map #101, 18Aug42

At 0045 I was awakened from a sound sleep by the drone of planes overhead, followed by the dread whistling of falling bombs. That is a horrible sound. It was too late to do anything then, so I just hugged my bunk as flat as I could make myself, and hoped fervently that I would not be hit. About 10 bombs landed, but they were not near my position. After the explosions, I gave the alarm and dressed hastily. As there was no further indication of attack, I did not enter my shelter. I learned later that one man was killed and 3 seriously injured in the 5th Battalion. The bombs had landed on the eastern side of the airfield. I lay down again for a while; and at 0530 woke the galley force for breakfast. At 0945 we received another air raid alarm. The men hurried through the 1000 meal, and we stood by. Shortly after 1100 our planes went up, and there was considerable aerial activity. One enemy bomber was shot down directly across the ridge to our south, and one enemy bomber crashed directly into one of the four hangars on the airfield, setting it afire and starting one of our planes on fire, together with much gear. Some of the bombs dropped by the Japs landed on an ammunition dump about a mile or so to the east, and for quite a while there was the sound of exploding shells. About 300 shells were burnt up. Men were hastily recruited to fight this fire, and one of them was killed and several injured before the fire was brought under control. I took a trip out to the airfield to see the wreck of the burning hangar; and while there saw a plane being consumed by fire for lack of equipment to douse the flames. A cargo ship had come into the harbor to unload, so I to the beach. Got a ride on a Higgins boat whose coxswain said he was going to the supply ship (Burrows). He started for the Burrows, but turned and went to an English ship lying nearby. There he began taking on a load of 500-pound bombs. There was only a small working party on the boat, and the manner in which the bombs were swinging about and banging against the side of the ship made me jump to give them a hand in loading and stowing them before they exploded. We took 10 of them aboard before we pulled away. I spoke to the coxswain and asked him to deliver us to the Burrows. He did, and I was greatly relieved to leave him and his 5,000 pounds of explosives. Once on the deck of the Burrows, I made my way to the post exchange, intending to purchase about $25 worth of candy, tobacco, and toilet articles. But there was a long line of others with the same idea ahead of me. I got in the end of the line and after about 10 minutes the call sounded "All ashore that's going ashore." It was 1600 and the ships all put out to sea at night to avoid being caught in the harbor by submarines. I was able to get a hammock for our mess sergeant before dashing up to the ladder. About 60 Marines had been aboard this ship getting supplies, and we all crowded into a ramp boat and were taken ashore. Back to the Battery, and found that the Chaplain had been able to get soap, razor blades, tobacco, writing paper, etc. These were sold to the men at cost. He also disposed of a crate of apples, the first fresh fruit we have had since landing.

August 30, 1942 Sunday
No. coast of Guadalcanal, B.S.I.P. Coords: 58.6-116.65,
near Lunga River bridge D-2 map #101, 18Aug42

Awakened at 0045 by an air raid alert. I lay awake the rest of the night listening to our planes taking off and coming back, expecting each moment to hear the whistling of falling bombs. No bombs had fallen by 0530, so I awakened the galley force and had them start breakfast. At 0830 I hitched my way to the beach, intending to get aboard the Burrows early today so that I could get some supplies before night. But on the beach I learned that the Burrows had grounded on a sandbar out at sea last night, and was not able to get in. There was an English ship in the harbor with supplies, and there was an argument going on; the English people not wishing to unload on a Sunday, and the Marines with working parties insisting that this day be not wasted. The Marines won the argument. I back to the Battery in time for lunch. Lay down after lunch. At 1230 the air raid alert was given. At 1300 it began to rain. The rain stopped at about 1400. I to the river for a shave and a bath. As I was shaving, 2 heavy thuds were heard in the direction of the beach, and there were several of our planes in the air. All the bathers took to the woods in the nude, leaving their clothes on the bank. I stayed in and finished shaving, as I figured that the bridge under which I was was too minor a target for the enemy. Before I finished, it started raining again, and I dressed in the rain. I have no towel—I just put my clothes on and they dry on me in a few minutes. I saw our ambulance going past me toward the beach; and when I got back to our area, I was told that a fleet of about 15 Jap bombers had stolen in and bombed the ships in the harbor, hitting and sinking the American destroyer *Gregory*. The destroyer went down in about 3 minutes. A few minutes later a British destroyer in the harbor sunk an enemy submarine with depth charges. The enemy planes got away unscathed. It is reported that 32 dive bombers and 2 fighter squadrons of our planes were assigned to us, and were coming in when the enemy bombers attacked. The enemy was able to sneak in among the incoming planes. Several of the men have fevers, and there is quite a bit of gastro-intestinal disease. Today I noticed blood in the stools in the head. There are about 7 men during each of the last few days who were incapacitated from diarrhea. I have been very lucky so far. I am trying to get a raw onion to eat every day. I do not know who is suffering more from this practice — me or the germs.

August 31, 1942 Monday
No. coast of Guadalcanal, B.S.I.P. Coords: 58.6-116.65,
near Lunga River bridge D-2 map #101, 18Aug42

At 0030 I heard some heavy firing in the distance in the direction of the beach, as though a naval battle were in progress. At 0130 it began to rain, and it rained intermittently all night. There was much aerial activity, and I could hear our planes shuttling back and forth all night. There was no bombing or shelling of our position, however. At breakfast I learned that 3 cruisers and 2 destroyers had been sighted early last night. Some of our planes had sighted these enemy ships, and it appeared as though they were attempting a landing along the coast east of our position. The planes had come back for bombs and reinforcements but when they went out again, they had been able to sight only one destroyer, and they had been unsuccessful in sinking that. An order came out requiring the burying of all ammunition in dumps, and that the piles were not to be covered with palm leaves or other inflammable materials. Another order gave a list of the preventative measures for the control of gastro-intestinal disease. It is prevalent among the troops all over the island. We have a pit 8 feet by 2 feet in size, and 8 feet deep for our head. This is covered, but flies breed by the thousands. Among the new measures is provision for covering the heads with seats to act as fly-proofs. This is an excellent measure, and should be of much assistance in controlling the intestinal disorders prevalent in the whole Battery. An air raid alarm was given at 1130, and our planes took to the air in force, but no enemy planes were sighted, and I hear we succeeded only in damaging 3 of our own planes. No further word concerning the enemy that was supposed to have been landed, so I guess that was just a false rumor. Or else, we will hear from them very soon.

There was another air raid alarm at 1810, which lasted until 1845, but I saw no enemy planes and heard no bombings. Our planes must be intercepting them before they can get over the airfield. One of the ships in the harbor had unloaded some fresh meat, and we had steak for supper. This makes the first time we have had fresh meat since coming ashore.

September 1, 1942 Tuesday
No. coast of Guadalcanal, B.S.I.P. Coords: 58.6-116.65,
near Lunga River bridge D-2 map #101, 18Aug42

After breakfast I started on my daily reports. The diarrhea is decreasing. We are running out of toilet paper, a serious shortage. Yesterday we drew food enough for 2 weeks. The night before had been very peaceful, and I had been able to get an excellent night's rest. At 0830, Lt Appleton came around and said he was going out to some supply ship in the harbor. It was the *Betelgeuse*, K-28. I went with him; and though we were on board before 0900, others had been there before us and the post exchange was sold out. Back to the Battery for noon chow. At 1230 the air raid alarm was sounded, but I saw no enemy planes and heard no bombing. There are strong rumors that some mail had come in. If this is so, it will be the first mail this outfit has received since leaving New River June 9th. In the afternoon to the river and shaved and bathed. Back, and after supper there were delivered two pouches of 1st class mail. Found therein two letters from Bess, and one from Gladys. These letters were dated June and July, but they sure were nice to receive. I read them several times, and will answer them soon.

September 2, 1942 Wednesday
No. coast of Guadalcanal, B.S.I.P. Coords: 58.6-116.65,
near Lunga River bridge D-2 map #101, 18Aug42

There was aerial activity all night. At 0450 1 lay awake in my bunk listening to the droning of planes, when I heard the sound of bombs whistling in descent upon us. There had been no air raid alarm given, but I couldn't mistake that sound. I yelled "Air Raid!" and sat up. By that time the bombs began landing and exploding. I yelled "Air Raid!" once more and scrambled barefooted into the air raid shelter, clad only in my drawers. The raid was soon over, and I went back to bed. After breakfast I was called to the Adjutant's office and was shown a warrant for my promotion to the rank of First Sergeant. This warrant was direct from Headquarters, Washington, D.C., and was not a "spot promotion" (or "field promotion"). Col. Bemis called me in later and told me that Col. del Valle (commanding the 11th Regiment) had decided to let me accept this promotion despite the 6-months probationary restriction under which I am, because of the excellent job I was doing as First Sergeant of the 11th Regiment H&S Battery. He told me to keep up the good work. But the probation was still to be in effect. This promotion dates back to 8 August. At 1110 we received an air raid alarm. I prepared myself as usual, and stood in the entrance of the air raid shelter. Soon I heard the droning of the enemy planes; and looking out, I saw 18 bombers moving slowly across the sky from east to west. The enemy planes have been coming in from west to east, and our planes have been going out to the west to intercept them. But today the bombers sneaked in from the east, and had the place all to themselves—our planes were in the west. As soon as I had counted them, I went into my shelter and it was not long after that before the bombs began thudding and exploding. They came very close—the shelter shook, my eardrums ached from the concussion, and the air was filled with flying earth, dust and parts of trees. I was never so glad of the protection of the shelter. The planes passed on, and I looked out. I heard calls for the ambulance, and ran to the spot near the R-3 Section from whence the calls came. A runner from the Division Message Center had gone to the edge of the cliff, and a bomb fragment had struck him in the lower jaw. The doctor gave him emergency treatment, and bound up his face. They wiped the blood off him, and I noticed that he had another wound in his left arm, where a fragment had entered. He was placed on a stretcher, but he sat up and indicated that he was choking on blood in the prostrate position. He was unable to talk. I followed as they carried him along the edge of the cliff to where a path descended, and placed him in the ambulance at the base of the cliff. Just then a loud explosion in the vicinity shook the ground, and we were all ordered to take cover. They brought the wounded man into the nearby R-2 air raid shelter. In a few moments the "all clear" signal was given. The last explosion had been caused by a bursting of one of our airplane bombs. A dump of these bombs had been hit, and they continued exploding for quite a time. The wounded man was taken to the Division Field Hospital. I went back to my bunk and found two huge bomb craters, in either of which a truck could be contained, and caused probably by 500-pound bombs. They were about 15 feet across, and 9 feet deep. One was only 20 yards from the air raid shelter, and the other was about 25 yards away. My bunk was about 5 yards closer to these craters, and was covered with earth, twigs, and leaves. If this air raid would have caught me in my bunk, as this morning's raid did, I would have been killed. This is the closest I have come to death so far. I hope they keep being only close. The war has really been brought home to me. Before this, the units all about me have been doing the fighting and getting bombed; but this raid shook me up, and gave me a feeling of personal participation in the war. Altogether, about 15 bombs hit in our position. Most of them were 500-pounders, and there is a lane of craters across the field in front of our position. One of these big ones hit only about 15 feet from the entrance to the Colonel's quarters. A 100-pound "personnel bomb" exploded near the hospital tent, and fragments from this bomb pierced the tent, several 5-gallon cans, hit two trucks, a raincoat, and mess gear. But there was no injury to anyone who had been at a shelter, no matter how shallow. More mail is being distributed, and I received 3 letters from Bess, and one each from my brother Jack and from a Sarah Lewis, who sends gift packages to Marines.

September 3, 1942 Thursday
No. coast of Guadalcanal, B.S.I.P. Coords: 58.6-116.65,
near Lunga River bridge D-2 map #101, 18Aug42
　　At 0100 I was awakened by some shelling from an enemy vessel off shore. About six shells were fired. I yelled for the men to take cover, and in my bare feet dashed for the air raid shelter, clad only in my drawers. The sound of some shell fragments made me leap. It soon became quiet again, and I back and slept soundly the rest of the night. At 0420 I read my watch incorrectly, and rose and dressed, thinking it was later. I kept napping only all night, looking at my watch frequently, so that I would be able to awaken the galley force at 0520. At 0905 the air raid alarm was sounded. There was much activity by our planes, but I heard no bombing. At 2220 it began to rain. A strong wind blew the poncho (which I used as cover against the rain) off from part of my mosquito net, and my bunk and blankets were thoroughly drenched. I had some papers lying alongside of me in the bunk, and I spent a miserable night trying to keep them dry amid my sopping blankets. I would have preferred a bombing raid to this rain.

September 4, 1942 Friday
No. coast of Guadalcanal, B.S.I.P. Coords: 58.6-116.65,
near Lunga River bridge D-2 map #101, 18Aug42
　　The rain continued all night, until after breakfast. It then dried up a bit, but it rained again later in the afternoon. There was an air raid alarm about noon-time, but I heard no bombs. The new fly-proof head has been installed, and there are hundreds of flies crawling all over it. It is almost impossible to sit down, so numerous are the flies. The place is sprayed three times daily with creosote, but to no avail. It was finally decided to burn out the head every other day; and though there was not much fire, due to poor draft, the smoke had a very satisfactory effect. This may be the answer to the fly problem. The incidence of diarrhea is decreasing rapidly. We

have set up four pots of hot water in which to rinse mess gear after eating — the first containing a soapy solution, the next two being for rinsing, and the last being kept boiling hot for sterilization. Fever has disappeared from our Battery. PFC Miles of this Battery was caught asleep on watch last night by Col. del Valle, and has been charged with that offense and recommended for a General Court Martial. The following promotions were effected today: Maj. Hughes accepted appointment as a Lt.Col.; QmClk Dalglish accepted promotion to the rank of 2nd Lt.; and QmSgt Gibson was promoted to the warrant rank of QmClk. I had hung my blankets to dry, but as it rained again during the day, they were still wet; so I decided to sleep on the benches which had been constructed for the mess, as they were under canvas. I left my blankets on the line, and spent the night on the benches, fully dressed, but without covering.

September 5, 1942 Saturday
No. coast of Guadalcanal, B.S.I.P. Coords: 58.6-116.65,
near Lunga River bridge D-2 map #101, 18Aug42

At 0053 the Battery was aroused by some shelling against this island. More than 20 shells were fired, and there were a couple of casualties; but the shells didn't land in our position. A heavy cannonading could be heard offshore, and the sky was lit by the flashes of gunfire. I heard later that one or two enemy destroyers and a cruiser had shelled this island; and that two of our APDs (destroyers) had engaged them. Though the APDs had started fires on the enemy vessels, they were both sunk; and the fires on the enemy vessels were put under control. The action lasted about 45 minutes, during which I stayed in my air raid shelter. After the sound of the sea battle drifted off to the west, I back to the benches and slept the rest of the night. There was an air raid alarm at 0950 that interrupted our mess. It was in effect for about an hour, during which I heard fighting between our planes and enemy planes, but no bombs fell in our position. There is much talk of our position being moved further back into the hills, to escape the dampness of the rainy season, and to secure better protection from shelling from the sea and from air raids.

September 6, 1942 Sunday
No. coast of Guadalcanal, B.S.I.P. Coords: 58.6-116.65,
near Lunga River bridge D-2 map #101, 18Aug42

Cloudy and rainy all day. This hampers bombing raids and shelling from the sea. I have fixed up my bunk so that the rain does not pour into it. I slept in it tonight, instead of on the benches under the mess fly. The amphibian tractor unit has moved into position across the river from us;

and during the night they imagined they saw or heard something, and there was a great racket as they blazed away into the woods with rifles and automatic weapons. Pvt. Mattice, who shot Sgt. Casey, was sleeping on the mess benches, and he became frightened at all the firing. He came up and lay down in the bunk next to me, and bothered me several times during the night by asking unimportant questions, just to be reassured by my voice. I spoke comfortingly to him the first few times, then answered impatiently until he desisted. The poor fellow is greatly beset by fears. There are several others in the Battery who are terrified by the bombing and shelling. When the air raid alarm is given, they plunge into the shelters and remain there wide-eyed with fright until it is over. Nearly every raid produces some men who have suffered bruises in diving into the shelters in a panic; and Reick has had two front teeth knocked out thus. I hardly blame them, for it is a disconcerting experience to have 500-pound bombs exploding about one.

September 7, 1942 Monday
No. coast of Guadalcanal, B.S.I.P. Coords: 58.6-116.65,
near Lunga River bridge D-2 map #101, 18Aug42
      Rainy and cloudy all day. There was no bombing or shelling of our position, which is a great relief, as it would be most uncomfortable to have to get up in the middle of the night and run through the rain to a shelter. The chaplain has arranged for the "Flying Fortresses" which visit us to bring some gifts of toilet articles, clothes, and tobacco for the Battery. We are almost out of these articles, and can procure no replacements. We have not seen candy since landing on this island a month ago; and we are very short of tooth paste, shaving cream, razor blades, writing paper, etc. We have made several efforts to purchase these articles from the post exchanges of ships which bring supplies; but their stocks are depleted, and other organizations have been able to get there ahead of us. The various sections of the Battery are busy sending men to the new position which has been selected, and preparing for our moving there; which will take place about Thursday. I have not seen the place yet, but it is back in the hills to the south, and offers positive protection against shellfire and is much harder to bomb. It is also much higher than our present position, so that the rainy season will not affect us so adversely. It looks as though they plan to have us stay awhile.

September 8, 1942 Tuesday
No. coast of Guadalcanal, B.S.I.P. Coords: 58.6-116.65,
near Lunga River bridge D-2 map #101, 18Aug42
      It rained most of the day. The rain and cloudy weather prevented visits by enemy bombers or war ships. The various sections of the Battery

were busy working on the new position. At 0850, I with the Chaplain to the beach and we boarded the K-18, the former *Bellatrix*; and after much persuasion were able to get about $400 worth of cigarettes, tobacco, cigars, and some other minor articles. We could get no toilet articles, writing paper or candy, the last of which the boys crave so much that they were willing to pay a dollar for a nickel candy bar. On board this ship there arrived LtCol Stack, and Major Maas of the Paymaster Dept. They are to be billeted with our Battery. Major Maas brought applications for "family allowances" for the men in the last 4 pay grades (sergeant to private) to secure support for their dependents by contributing part of their salary. About 20 men in this Battery applied for these allowances. In the afternoon, Pvt Hodge of the 5th Batt. reported in and was assigned to duty as orderly to Col. del Valle. Hodge replaces PFC Routon, of whose antics the Col. finally tired. The new man looks like a neat and capable orderly. I spoke to Hodge on the responsibility he has in looking after the comfort and well-being of the senior officer in the Regiment. In the evening I held a "grab bag" with the odd items of post exchange articles that had been contributed by the soldiers on New Caledonia. (I have been told that there are 65,000 of them on that island who are still waiting for their first taste of action.) I had the men draw out of a helmet for the prizes. There remained some five articles that had not been drawn, and the men urged me to "raffle" these off. I did so, and received prices likes $2 for a can of talcum powder; $1.50 for four small tubes of tooth paste; etc. Money here has little value, as the men cannot get what they desire with it. The money I received on the auction was turned over to the Chaplain, who will use it to buy other items for free distribution.

September 9, 1942 Wednesday
No. coast of Guadalcanal, B.S.I.P. Coords: 58.6-116.65.
near Lunga River bridge D-2 map #101, 18Aug42
Most of the day was spent in preparing the new position for occupancy. The Battery will move tomorrow. At 0900 the Battery was paid, each man receiving $15. Those who did not wish to draw any money were not required to do so. I didn't draw any, for I have no place to spend it. There is talk of a post exchange of sorts being set up in the near future, but they handle mostly tobacco—cigarettes, cigars, pipe and chewing tobacco— so there would be very little I could use. It is a shame to see so much money wasted on tobacco that could be used in buying food, candy, toilet articles, etc. But the men crave their smokes (or at least they make a big fuss about it), so I guess it is just as well. If they had been permitted

to have liquor, they would have made just as big a fuss over their desire for that as they do over tobacco; but they seem to manage excellently without the spirits. Air raid alarm at 0945, and we to our shelters. There was much aerial activity by our planes, and there were some heavy thuds as though bombs had been dropped, probably on the beaches. (The beaches were guarded by Marines stationed there to protect shipping and guard against invasion.)

September 10, 1942 Thursday
No. coast of Guadalcanal, B.S.I.P. Coords: 58.6-116.65,
near Lunga River bridge D-2 map #101, 18Aug42
Word has been received that this Battery is to serve 3 meals per day, beginning today. I guess the supply system has been improved sufficiently so that we can be assured of plenty of rations. Breakfast was served at 0700; and immediately thereafter, the Battery began moving to its new position. The moving continued all day. At noontime I drove out to the new position, which is some 2.5 miles from the old location, and looked the place over. We are on the southern and western sides of a declivity, and on the edge of a drop of about 100 feet. There is a stagnant pool at the bottom of this drop, in which it is reported that alligators have been seen. The galley has been established, and the various sections of the Battery have their sites more or less completed. I have a spot selected for me near the galley. I was starting back to the old position when the air raid alarm was given. The bombers came over in quite a large formation and dropped a big load of bombs. The airfield was not hit, nor was the new airfield hit. The new airfield is just a short distance from the old one. One of our men visited the 3rd Battalion and reported that there were 9 casualties at "I" Battery and 5 in "H" Battery, from the bombing. The new position is much closer to the airfield and the bombs seemed to be a whole lot louder and nearer as I hugged the ground. After the air raid, I back to the old position and sent all the men to the new position. About 20 came back to sleep in the old position tonight. We have quite a bit of gear left in the old position, and I remained with it. At 1900, the Battery Commander of the adjacent Special Weapons Battery called me over and told me that an alert had been received, and gave me the following facts. There were some 2,000 Japs several miles to the east, and an attack was expected; Marine infantry and artillery were standing by, and all the men were to be awakened at 0130 in the morning to "stand to." I notified all my men, and went to bed cursing. I had expected a good night's rest tonight.

September 11, 1942 Friday
No. coast of Guadalcanal, B.S.I.P. Coords: 60.2-114.5,
Hill position D-2 map #101, 18Aug42

　　Kept cat-napping only all night, afraid that I would not be awake at the time to warn the men. I was also very uncomfortable with my sprained back. At 0130 1 woke all the men, told them to be on the alert, and then I back to my bunk and to sleep as well as my aching back would let me. Arose at 0600 and roused the Battery. I had them gather their stuff, and then I called for a truck to come and take them to the new position for breakfast. I read a book for a while, and then I wrote a long letter to Bess in reply to the several letters I had received from her. At noontime I had some more canned rations. There was an air raid about that time, which passed over me with very little effect; but when the other men from the Battery came over for our gear, they told me that the bombs had fallen in and around our new position, and that several men from the Pioneer outfit (who were building a road directly back of our position) had been hit, some very seriously. At 1500 I to the river, where I washed some clothes, shaved and bathed. Back and loaded my effects aboard the last truck for the day, and to the new area. I passed several big bomb craters that had been made in today's raid. A start had been made in erecting a combined office and sleeping quarters for me. I pitched my bunk on this platform, and settled down for the night. Heard that Routon, the man who had been relieved as the Colonel's orderly, had broken down during the raid today; and had been taken, crying and shaking, to the hospital. He was sent back to us after a few hours.

September 12, 1942 Saturday
No. coast of Guadalcanal, B.S.I.P. Coords: 60.2-114.5,
Hill position D-2 map #101, 18Aug42

　　Up, and my back much better. Two men have been transferred to the Battery to act as messmen — Carver and Klein. Breakfast was served at 0730. After breakfast I took a ride with one of the trucks and obtained some kerosene and some ice that is being made by some reclaimed Jap ice-making machinery. There was a short air raid alarm about 0830, but I heard no bombing. At 1130 a real raid was made, and some 25 bombers came over and did some serious damage, setting the gasoline dump on fire and knocking out a couple of radio shacks. But they paid a heavy price. Last night, 24 new fighting planes and 7 bombers had arrived for us. Our bombers left early in the morning, probably to give the Japs a little of their own medicine. When the enemy bombers arrived, all the fighting planes went up to meet them, and sure gave them hell. For the first time the 90mm guns gave a good account of themselves, and blew some bombers out of the air. I have been told that the reason they have been unable to reach the bombers before was that they had only 30-second fuses on their shells, which burst at a comparatively low altitude. They now have 1-minute fuses, and can now reach the planes. One of the men came in with a wing-tip from a Jap plane that had exploded over the airfield. The official count today was 10 Jap bombers and 2 Zero fighters accounted for, with 2 others burning and probably finished. We lost 2 planes. Later, Division Intelligence increased these figures to 13 and 3. At 1900 I went to bed. At 2200, four Jap cruisers opened a heavy shelling against the island. We took to our air raid shelters, and listened to the racket. It kept up for over an hour. We would hear a distant thud, and this would be followed by a loud "boom" at the shell burst. The shells were not falling on our position. Shortly after 2300 the shelling ceased. Major Clark came down the path and told us to awaken everybody, and for us to arm ourselves and to come with him. We went to the RCP, where we were split up and posted as guards after having been told that Jap forces had been contacted by the Raider Battalion to our south. A considerable amount of small arms fire could be heard from that unit, with occasional 37mm fire. They could be heard challenging and then firing all night. We had been on post but a short while, when the shelling resumed. We were now out of our air raid shelters, and about 4 shells went over our heads and burst behind us. After the first flash and boom of the cannons, I dropped to the deck so hard that my elbows were sore for two days. The men scattered, taking cover in any shelter they could find. I dropped back down the far side of the hill from the shelling. We had to continue our watch, however, because the small arms firing on the south would break out with renewed violence every few minutes. In between volleys from the enemy cruisers, we went down to the Ordnance Section and brought up a .50 cal. machine gun and set it up. The artillery shot a few shells at the cruisers, which thought they were bombs from an air attack, and they turned on their powerful searchlights and swept the skies. They finally ceased shelling at about 0200 on Sunday morning, but we continued watching for possible Jap attack.

September 13, 1942 Sunday
No. coast of Guadalcanal, B.S.I.P. Coords: 60.2-114.5,
Hill position D-2 map #101, 18Aug42

The small arms firing continued at intervals all night, and kept us on the alert. Word was passed for us to break up into pairs, and one of us to keep watch while the other slept. I stayed awake until 0330, then lay down near a sentry post. A single plane had taken to the air immediately after the shelling, and it continued flying back and forth over the beach and back into the hills, droning around and keeping us all guessing. It dropped flares at one time; and once the 20mm guns opened a burst of fire that drove it off in a burst of speed. Our men kept challenging all night long without receiving any hostile replies. Their nerves were on edge. At 0505 the air raid alarm was sounded, and the officers all took off for their shelters. Our sentry positions on top of the hill were in a very exposed position. I told the men that I was going to my air raid shelter. I had no authority to order them to abandon their posts, but after I told them my intention, they didn't need any orders, but scrambled for their shelters. Airplanes began to fill the air; and soon the ground shook with the vibration of their motors. But they were the loud-sounding Grumman fighter planes of ours; and though I lay in my shelter with my heart pounding in terror, awaiting the dreaded whistling of falling bombs and the rending blasts that followed, I was most agreeably disappointed. No bombs fell. I learned later that the alarm had been given when 24 fighter planes arrived to join our air fleet. That makes about 50 fighter planes on this field. Had a late breakfast, and was not through with it very long before the air raid alarm went again. Many of our planes took to the air, and I heard some zooming as of planes in combat, but I heard no bombing. Immediately after the bombing I dug my shelter a foot deeper. It had been too shallow, and I had been getting very scared during the last few raids, feeling very exposed and unprotected. There was another air raid before noon, and my air raid shelter felt immensely safer. Things remained quiet the rest of the day. In the evening I started to set up my sentries; but Capt. Harris told me the situation around here was becoming more dangerous and we set up 3 posts instead of the former single one, with 2 men on watch on each post at all times. This was at 1800. As soon as the guards were posted I spread my blankets and went to sleep, anticipating a good night's rest. Some shelling from our 105 guns started, and they were firing over our heads. The noise kept me from falling asleep, so I took my blankets and spread them in the air raid shelter, and I lay down intending to sleep through any air raid or shelling that might occur. I needed sleep. But at 2000 the Battery Commander came down and told us that every man was to be posted all along the front of our position, as it was believed that a Jap patrol with a mortar had broken through the Raider Battalion lines and was trying to get to the airfield. If the opposition grew too strong for them, they might try to get around the flank by coming through our position. I woke all the men in the Battery Police Section and in the Mess Section, and strung them along the bottom of the hill on which the galley is set. This is a sort of valley, and our line extended until it joined that of the Quartermaster and the Transport.

There was a man every 5 or 10 yards. We had a machine gun, .50 cal., set up on our flank. The artillery started up, and was throwing an intense fire over our heads. They were cutting loose with everything they had — the 75s, the 105s, the 37mm, and all the other weapons. The din was terrific. The guns were so close we could hear the commands to shift them. I could hear in the distance in the direction of the beaches the thundering rumble of naval gun fire. The firing kept up, increasing in intensity. Our men lay along the valley, listening intently to all sounds, and expecting Jap snipers to fire upon us at any moment. At 2300 the Battery Commander came down and told us that the line of sentries should pair up, and one man should sleep while they stood watch. I said I would lay down for an hour, and left word to be awakened. I didn't get any sleep, as the constant explosions of the 105 fire didn't permit; but I got an hours rest. Then I arose and told the Police Sergeant he could get some sleep. I sat and listened to the battle going on. Shortly after midnight the Battery Commander came down and told me to get the Battery ready to evacuate if it became necessary. He said the Raider Battalion was under pressure, and was being forced back. I was much surprised and shocked at this news. I expressed surprise that with all the men we had on the island, we should be forced to evacuate. Capt. Harris then told me that there were some Jap destroyers in the harbor that were giving the 1st and 5th Marines trouble, so that they could not be called upon for support. That explained for me the firing I had heard in the direction of the beaches. Capt Harris said that when we evacuated, we would not take any of our gear; and that we would have to move fast. He said he would take the men on the other side of the hill out with him; and that I was to take out the men in the valley in which I was. We were to leave by the garage path; and the Capt. gave me directions for getting to H&S Battery, 2nd Battalion, to which we were to evacuate. The directions were not quite clear to me, but I told him I would be able to find the place. He then went back. I resumed my watch, greatly depressed. It was a sign that we were being defeated if we were going to evacuate; and we might even lose the airfield, toward which the Japs were pushing. I decided to sleep no more, but to stay awake to watch for any Japs that might break through and reach our position. I sat there miserably, realizing that if we lost the airfield, and the Japs brought in planes, we might be killed or chased off the island. I had some official papers with much information of military value, together with two books containing the record of events from the day we landed on this place. I gathered all such papers and debated for a time whether to destroy them immediately to keep them from falling into the hands of the Japs, or to try to save them for our essential records — the roster, muster roll, payroll. It would be a serious loss to dispose of these papers, so I decided that I would take the papers out with me — and I meant to get myself and the men out when the time came! About midnight or shortly thereafter there was heard much popping, as of fire crackers (from Jap .25 cal. rifles), and a wild yell from the Japs, indicating the start of a Jap bayonet charge. The small arms firing increased in volume, and the cannons were roaring and pounding away without intermission.

September 14, 1942 Monday
Hill position: Coords: 60.2-114.5; and Lunga River bridge pos.,
58.6-116.65, D-2 map #101.

The cannonading continued past midnight, and there was a ceaseless crackle and chatter of small arms fire. There could also be distinguished the "wham" of hand grenades and the hollow roar of mortar fire. As it got on toward morning, the high report of Jap .25 cal. bullets became more and more evident. The bullets began coming across our position. It is said that the Japs employ a bullet that explodes. Whether this is so, I do not know, but there was very distinct popping and cracking, exactly like the sound of a sharp explosion, in the trees over our heads where the Jap bullets were striking. The firing increased, and soon was joined by some .25 cal. Jap machine gun fire. Our men were forced to get down and take cover, as the bullets were coming dangerously close and the men were becoming scared of ricochets. Tracer bullets began to bounce off the trees and fall in our position. It looked as though the Japs were right in the field on the hill above our valley. I began to fear that they would reach the edge of the hill and pour machine gun and hand grenade fire down upon us. I figured it would be a good thing to go up to the edge of the hill and check to see if there was any friendly fire that we could support; or if there were only Japs in the flat field on top of the hill. I wanted to send a 2-man patrol up to investigate, but didn't know whom to send. My job was to take care of the official papers of the Regimental Headquarters and Service Battery entrusted to my care, and to see that they didn't get into the hands of the enemy; and to get the Battery out if necessary. But I didn't like to send anybody on a mission on which I would not go myself. So I selected a young fellow named Bryan, who had expressed a desire to "get a couple of Japs," and told him to come with me. We were armed only with a pistol apiece. We crept up the hill in the dark, with our pistols loaded. When we reached the crest, we looked over, trying to see where the .25 cal. firing was coming from. We could see nothing in the darkness. The firing seemed to come from a short distance away in the flat field before us. I was not positive that it was actually .25 cal. firing; so I told Bryan to move down from the edge of the hill for a short distance, and I yelled out: "Who's firing up there?" I called twice, and received no reply other than the snap and rattle of continued firing. About 50 yards along the crest of the hill, we had a .50 cal. machine gun set up. I decided to make my way to this spot to see if they could give me any "dope" on the situation. Bryan and I crept along the edge of the field; and when about 15 yards from the gun, came across the crew in a depression. They told us that the field in front of us was full of snipers, some with machine guns. Our machine gun had been set up to fire in the direction of the airfield, and their rear was exposed. The firing today was coming from that direction, and they had moved into the depression in which I found them to escape the snipers' bullets. They told me they were waiting for daylight so that they could pick off the snipers who were in the trees in the field in front of us. I asked them how many rifles they had, and they said two. I told them that that amount was not enough, and that I would send them another rifleman to take care of the snipers as soon as it grew light enough. I told Bryan to come down with me and exchange his pistol for a rifle, and then rejoin the machine gun crew. We went back and got the rifle. As Bryan and I were going back up the hill to the machine gun position, I saw a shape on top of the hill crouching and peering down into the valley where our men were, with what looked like a rifle in his hands. I pointed this out to Bryan, and asked him if he thought it was a Jap. He looked for a while, and then said he could not be sure. I was going to find out by taking a shot at it, because the actions were so suspicious. But I had only a pistol, whereas Bryan now had a rifle; so I told Bryan to pick him off with his rifle. Bryan loaded a shell into the chamber of his rifle and fired. I didn't see the shape fall, so I thought Bryan had missed, and I immediately fired a .45 slug at it before it got away. I knew I had not missed; so when the shape still didn't fall, I realized it was just a bush waving in the breeze. We then continued to the position held by the machine gun crew, where I left Bryan, and I returned to the valley. I got two Reising guns and set them up on the flank that was toward the battle. The .25 cal. firing increased in volume, and the tracer bullets were ricocheting all around in our position. It was getting on toward morning, and I hadn't heard from the Battery Commander for several hours. I didn't know how the situation was developing, or if our danger had increased or decreased. I began to think that the officers had all been forced to leave, and had been unable to get word to us in the valley on account of the snipers covering the route of their approach. It was then 0500, and in another half hour it would be light. I had a chance of getting the men out and to safety in the darkness; but we would be cut to pieces if we tried to get out under the heavy fire in the daylight where we could be seen. The chief of the machine gun crew came down, and I told him to work his way along our line of sentries to the Quartermaster Section, where there was a telephone, and to call the Battery Commander and ask for instructions. He came back in a few minutes and reported that he had been unable to get connections with the office. That practically clinched my impression that the officers had already left. I told the machine gun section chief that when he got back to his gun, he was to send a man along the edge of the field to the officers' quarters, and see if there any officers left; and to get his report back to me in a hurry, as it was getting very light. In a few minutes, to my great relief, the Battery Commander came down and told me that we were holding the Japs, that we were not going to evacuate, and that the .25 cal. firing that we were being subjected to was coming from about 300 yards away; and that it was the popping of these bullets that we were hearing and not that snipers were in the field in front of us. I went back to my position and passed down along the line of sentries, giving the news and cheering them up. The only danger in our position was from the ricocheting tracer bullets, or from some sniper that might possibly break through. It kept getting lighter, and our artillery fire slackened somewhat. There were a couple of Jap machine guns still firing away in our direction but soon 3 American planes came along and strafed them out of existence. As the morning wore on, the volume of firing decreased, and the remnants of the Japs fell back. We had won another engagement. During the night, the Special Weapons Battery across the road had been shot up, and forced to move out of their position. Their Battery Commander, Major Viall, had been nicked by a glancing shot across his shoulder. Several of the men from the Raider Battalion had fallen back to the Special Weapons position. A Special Weapons officer, Marine Gunner Paul R. Michael, told one of these men to get up on the firing line. The man refused. The Gunner insisted, and the man shot and killed him. As this happened, Sgt. Militano (the same man with whom I had that fight during the blackout in Wellington) pulled his pistol and shot the man from the Raider Battalion dead... The Special Weapons galley was under fire, so that Battery ate breakfast with us this morning; as did 80 men from "I" Battery who had been firing during the night, and who had fallen back to reinforce our lines in the morning should there be a breakthrough by the Japs. The "I" Battery men left after a while, but Special Weapons stayed with us in our position all day, and ate with us again at 1500. There was the sound of continued "mop up" operations on the hill where the battle had taken place. At 1600 we were given orders to move back to our last position near the bridge across the Lunga River. We left all our stuff; and taking only blankets, we drove back to the spot from which we had moved recently. We were to spend the night there, while an infantry outfit moved in where we were located and prepared to defend it against any Jap attacks that might occur. I was glad to get back to the old place, as it afforded me an opportunity to visit the river and take a much-needed bath. The night here was quiet, and we all felt more secure. Our purpose in moving from this position had been to get away from the low ground before the onset of the rainy season.

September 15, 1942 Tuesday
No. coast of Guadalcanal, B.S.I.P. Coords: 58.6-116.65,
near Lunga River bridge D-2 map #101, 18Aug42
    Up, and we sent the galley crew back to the hill position to start cooking our breakfast. The Battery packed up its gear, and trucks kept running back and forth until the men were all back at the hill position. We had breakfast, Special Weapons again eating with us (they had moved back to the old position with us). I deepened my air raid shelter, and submitted some reports. We fixed up the galley, and spent the day improving and strengthening our position. I tried to get permission to visit the battlefield, but the Battery Commander said it was still too dangerous. We had two meals again today, the second at 1500. We started to move at 1600 to our position near the Lunga River. We spent the night at that position again, without any untoward incident. Some artillery fire was heard in the northwest during the night, but it was nothing affecting us. I shaved and washed a shirt in the river before dark.

> (The purpose of our coming back to the Lunga River position last night and tonight was to clear the hill position of artillerymen, presumably less qualified for infantry combat, and permit an infantry unit to man the position in case of a counterattack by the Japs.)

September 16, 1942 Wednesday
Hill position, No. coast of Guadal., B.S.I.P. Coords: 60.2-114.5,
D-2 map #101, 18Aug42
    Up at 0600, and the Battery packed up and we moved back to the hill position. Two meals again today. I took a trip out to the battlefield today. We ran into the remnants of the Raider Battalion. The 5th Marines were up there supporting them. About a mile from our position they had dug a long pit, and they were throwing therein the bodies of the dead Japs. The day was hot, and the bodies had a horrible odor. They were swollen and bloated, and were twisted in all sorts of distorted positions. Jap gear and Marine gear was mingled all over the area, indicating where the tide of battle had swung back and forth. I saw the hill where the Japs had made

their bayonet charge the time I heard the yelling a couple of nights ago, and the hillside was strewn with their effects. It was only 300 yards from the RCP; and had they succeeded in taking this hill, we would have had to fall back, thereby placing the airfield in the greatest danger. I walked along looking at the positions which the Japs and the Marines had dug, and mentally reconstructing the battle. Those Japs fight desperately, and are not afraid to die. The Marines on the hill had all sorts of souvenirs of the battle, including some exquisite swords. They had a purse from one of the Japs containing money from many of the South Seas countries, including the Netherland East Indies, and even about .65 in U.S. money. I noted many automatic weapons among their gear. The men I was with picked up a heavy machine gun, a rifle with bayonet, clips of machine gun ammunition, and several other souvenirs. We didn't touch anything on the bodies of the Japs, as they were in too decomposed a condition. The Marine casualties had already been removed. Rumors state that only 60 Marines had been killed, but that many others had been wounded. Back to camp, and on the way we found the diary of a parachute trooper of the 1st Parachute Battalion who had been among those who took Tulagi Island, which contained entries dated from 7 August to 28 August... I have had the men fix me a combination office and bunk, with a roof over it. My air raid shelter is directly underneath. We were ordered to stay in our position on the hill tonight. I set watches along the valley west of our position, and settled down for a good night's rest. Special Weapons Battery is encamped in the field on top of the hill on which we are. They have been given the order not to shoot into us. They furnished a machine gun and crew for an exposed position on our line.

September 17, 1942 Thursday
No. coast of Guadalcanal, B.S.I.P. Coords: 58.6-116.65,
near Lunga River bridge D-2 map #101, 18Aug42
    The night had been without incident (for me). There had been some firing of small arms during the night, but it had probably been from nervousness only. The day was quiet, so I took another trip to the battlefield. The bodies of the Japs were in still further condition of deterioration, and the odor is overpowering. They have burying parties working, putting a rope around the bodies and dragging them into the foxholes the men had dug during the battle, and there burying them. Came across a Jap bayonet, a pistol holster, and some Jap pictures which had been ripped from an album. They had probably been taken by paratroops on Tulagi, and had been left by the paratroops when they were forced out of these positions. Marine gear was scattered everywhere. Mixed with this gear was that of

the Japs… Back, and word was given that the Battery was going to move
back to the Lunga River position, to stay for the time. After our afternoon
meal we began to move, taking only personal gear. Battery property will
be moved tomorrow. We got to the new place, and the 3rd Defense Battalion was moved out to make room for us. We bedded down, and it rained
during the night, making it uncomfortable for me, as I had to use my poncho to cover the papers and records I was carrying.

September 18, 1942 Friday
No. coast of Guadalcanal, B.S.I.P. Coords: 58.6-116.65,
near Lunga River bridge D-2 map #101, 18Aug42
      Up, and the Battery began getting trucks and hauling gear from the
hill position to our river position. I went up to the hill position and did
some paper work while watching the men dismantle the galley and other
structures we had erected. Back to the river position in the afternoon. In
the evening to the river and shaved and washed some clothes. The 7th
Marines, Reinforced, arrived today. There are several thousand Marines
with this organization, and they are a most welcome addition to our forces.
One of the reinforcing units is the 1st Battalion of the 11th Marine artillery. They will revert to our command now. Among the new arrivals is Lt.
Bove, who was the former 1stSgt of this Battery, and who left with the 1st
Battalion (and whom I relieved as 1stSgt, my present job). He visited us,
and he and I swapped experiences. He has been on duty in Apia and Samoa,
and has been transferred from the 11th Marines to infantry duty with the
7th Marines. We discussed all our old friends, and gave each other the news
of their disposition. We had much to talk about, as we have not seen each
other for about 6 months.

September 19, 1942 Saturday
      About 0015 we were all aroused by the firing of some heavy guns. The
sky lit up, and a plane was heard in the air. The plane dropped a series of
flares. The firing came from the direction of the beach. Word was passed
that two enemy cruisers and two destroyers were shelling the island. The
shelling lasted less than half an hour, and I heard that the shells landed on
the beach near Kukum, killing two there; and on the airfield, without any
casualties. It rained during the night. I was sleeping on a poncho on the
ground, and I was getting quite wet. Finally moved my poncho under the
canvas covering the officers' mess, and spent the rest of the night there.
The morning was spent hauling Battery property from the hill position. I
ordered the men to build me an office. They fixed me up an excellent one,
consisting of two sections—one for the office and one for sleeping. To the

battle area. The 7th Marines are taking over the positions there, and they are big-eyed over the signs of battle still visible. The departing Marines had put up a sign reading: "Battle road, scene of the battle, 50¢ admission." It rained in the afternoon, and two of our trucks got stuck in the mud and had to be pulled out by tractors. I fixed up my bunk and to bed early tonight.

September 20, 1942 Sunday
No. coast of Guadalcanal, B.S.I.P. Coords: 58.6-116.65,
near Lunga River Bridge D-2 map #101, 18Aug42
Up after having spent the most restful night in a long time. My new bunk is a honey. Work slackened off today on account of its being Sunday. I to the river in the morning and did a big wash, and shaved and bathed. An air raid took place during this time, but I ignored it; although I heard the thud of bombs being dropped in the distance. The bridge at which we bathe has not been bombed, as I guess the Japs consider it too minor a target. But it would greatly inconvenience traffic if this bridge were destroyed; and there are always several men in the vicinity. At 1650, Chaplain Dittmar held prayer services. I did a lot of writing, and caught up on the office copies of the Record of Events.

September 21, 1942 Monday
The police truck was prevented from hauling gear from the hill position today by the 7th Marines, who are occupying these positions, and who were firing today. I accompanied the truck on a trip to the beach for sand. We drove way out to the west, to the extreme west flank of our positions on the beach. There I talked to a sergeant who described the battle that had taken place there on the night of 13-14, when we had all the excitement at our position in the hill. The sergeant said that the Japs never stood a chance there, our positions being too well fortified. The Japs probably intended this for a diverting action, and they paid dearly for it. They were allowed to get between two machine gun emplacements, and cut to pieces. Among the Jap casualties had been an officer of the equivalent rank of LtCol., and on him had been found important maps and plans and other intelligence. The sergeant told of blasting a pit for burying the Japs; and of placing all the bodies in the pit, with the LtCol placed according to his rank on top of the heap. Back and spent the afternoon in the office. Wrote a letter to Bess. I wonder how things are at home, and how poor Bess is doing.

September 22, 1942 Tuesday

In the morning to our former hill position. Intended visiting the front lines, but was told that everything was quiet and that there was nothing new up there. Met Bove, who is stationed within 50 yards of our former position, and talked a couple of hours with him. He is now a 2ndLt, and he was telling me of his difficulties. He is assigned tasks which he is unable to perform, not having had training in them (he has had no college or military academy education, and has previously had only enlisted service). He is with an infantry organization now, but is greatly desirous of getting back to the 11th Regiment. He came down to my place later in the day and left some candy for me, and asked me to give some to Major Viall. He also distributed some gifts to other officers, and is "playing politics" trying to get back... After leaving Bove in the morning, I started back to my outfit. I had just passed one of the bombed hangars on the airfield, when I heard the steel beam framework collapse. There were men living under these beams, so I hurried over; but only one man had been injured. An ambulance which was passing was halted, and the corpsman gave the injured man some morphine and they took him off to the hospital. At the scene, I met a couple of friends from the Newark reserves, and we exchanged experiences; and I was invited to come over sometime and see their souvenirs. So back to camp.

September 23, 1942 Wednesday
No. coast of Guadalcanal, B.S.I.P. Coords: 58.6-116.65,
near Lunga River bridge D-2 map #101, 18Aug42

The Corpsman, Sampson, and Pvt Klein both came out of the hospital today after having been treated for malaria. They both have lost weight and look pale; they will require treatment the rest of their stay on this island. This Battery was allowed one Staff Sergeant promotion, and I swung it to Sgt Scalcione, as I think he rates it above Sgt Way; and I think I can get more advantage for the Battery from Scalcione. They both have taken an examination for Platoon Sergeant, and Way made a couple of points more than Scalcione. In the morning I to the river and shaved and bathed leisurely, and washed some clothes. Things are getting very quiet around here. No bombing or shelling today.

September 24, 1942 Thursday

Started filling out the Fitness Reports for all the enlisted men in the first 4 pay grades. Then I took a walk out to Division Headquarters, looking for Sideman, with a view to getting him to develop some of my film; but he was not there, being on the beach on watch at the Observation Post.

Met there instead a man who had been in the reserve outfit in Newark about 4 years ago, and who had left to join the regulars. From Division I went to "D" Battery and visited some of the former reservists from Newark. Back to my Battery in time for lunch. Stayed in the office all afternoon, working surreptitiously on this diary. A new request for recommendations for appointment to the ranks of Marine Gunner and 2nd Lieutenant was received. In view of my probation, I am not eligible for these promotions. In the evening there were strong rumors to the effect that 22 enemy ships were in the neighborhood, and that our planes were bombing and torpe-doing them. There was much aerial activity to support these stories. Also, it is said that Japan itself is being bombed. I was issued a cot today, and slept in a bed for the first time since landing. I was getting accustomed to sleeping on boards on the ground.

September 25, 1942 Friday

Awoke after a very restful night's sleep. It is great to be sleeping on a cot again, instead of on hard boards with only a blanket beneath one. The day was hot and sunny, and very peaceful. I spent the whole day working on this diary. Things are as quiet as back in camp at New River. There is only an occasional salvo from the artillery to remind one that there are enemies on this island. I am eating heartily, and getting very little exercise. I am putting on weight, and getting out of condition. I hope this war is over soon, and that I get back to my civilian pursuits. I am either terribly scared at imminent danger; or, most often, just greatly bored by the life here. It is very monotonous, deadening, and coarsening. I have had no sight of any woman, white or black, since leaving Wellington almost two months ago; there are no movies, libraries, or other social diversions. I guess I just need more exercise.

September 26, 1942 Saturday
No. coast of Guadalcanal, B.S.I.P. Coords: 58.6-116.65,
near Lunga River bridge D-2 map #101, 18Aug42

A cloudy day. I worked on this diary in the morning. In the afternoon to the river for a shave and a bath. The following notices have come out today: Individuals are throwing away clothes that have become soiled in preference to washing them, and steps should be taken to prevent a continuation; roads are deteriorating too fast, and excessive speed of vehicles is a contributing factor, so a speed limit of 20 MPH is set except in emergency; jeeps are not to carry more than 4 men; all enemy arms, ammunition, explosives, and equipment will be turned over to the Division QM Salvage Section to be forwarded by the Intelligence Section to higher authority for intelligence purposes; and that mail is not to be left with the Division Post Office — it is to be submitted to the Battery censor first; and a system was set up for reporting on personnel "killed in action" on the field where it is impractical to evacuate the body due to "battle conditions" or "enemy-held territory" and the body is never recovered. In the afternoon some units of the Marines on this island went out and contacted the Japs, and they (the Japs) were getting lots of artillery support. The cannons could be heard until late in the evening. It began to rain in the evening and kept it up until past my bed time.

September 27, 1942 Sunday
No. coast of Guadalcanal, B.S.I.P. Coords: 58.6-116.65,
near Lunga River bridge D-2 map #101, 18Aug42
   Up, and the rain had stopped. At 0600 our artillery started and kept firing sporadically all day. The sound kept moving further to the southwest. In the morning, nearby Batteries were supporting the fire; but as the action moved out of range, there could be heard only the sound of the 75mm units accompanying the action. I hear that units of the 7th Marines are reinforcing the Raider Battalion, and they are out and have met a considerable number of the Japs and are engaged in heavy fighting. The air raid alarm was sounded at 1400, the first time in several days. We went leisurely to our shelters, figuring that our planes would intercept them again. But something went wrong, and soon we heard the 90mm guns pounding away. Eighteen bombers, accompanied by 13 fighters, came over. They let loose with many bombs, and the bombs fell all around and in our position. They fell so close to my shelter that I was shook up and the air was filled with dust and powder fumes. I expected each succeeding bomb to fall directly on our shelter and wipe out the six of us in it. It sure was close. The Communication Section was not so lucky. They had a direct hit with one or two personnel bombs right on their position. It blew their jeep out onto the road, setting it afire and burning it completely. It wrapped the runner's (messenger's) bicycle around a tree, destroyed much equipment, pierced and exploded all the 5-gallon water cans, and resulted in the following casualties among the Communication personnel: Cpl Hirt, bomb fragment wounds in right arm and head; Sgt Harrington and PFC McCallon, ruptured tympanic membrane, right ear; Cpl Nichols and PFC Haryan, both shell-shocked. A runner named Loveland, from another Battery, was also wounded and taken to the hospital. Hirt, Nichols and Haryan were taken to the hospital. The others were not. Other casualties were suffered by two Motor Section men, PFCs Kuboff and St. Martin, both of whom received bomb fragment wounds in their left legs. They were not

sent to the hospital, as the wounds were superficial. Special Weapons Battery had a bomb hit in their garage, and one jeep was totally burned, a 1-ton truck was destroyed, and another was shot full of bomb fragments. One of their men was badly wounded. A bomb landed near the Col's quarters, and blew up the officers' head… When things had quieted down somewhat we had supper; and at 1715 Chaplain Dittmar held prayer services. At 1830 I saw the Corpsman running past our position, and I followed and found that one of the sentries on watch at the river back of our camp had shot himself through the foot with his .30 cal. rifle. It may have been accidental, but such wounds are always suspicious. In the evening the artillery increased its activity, and I went to bed with the 105s shooting over my head. I learned later that the Marines had found the Japs too strongly entrenched, and had withdrawn with the intention of making a stronger attack at a later date.

September 28, 1942 Monday
Guadalcanal
Spent the day working on the bringing up-to-date of my diary. It was a hot, sunny day. The air raid alarm was sounded at 1330, and I to my air raid shelter, looking forward to the bombing with great apprehension. I hoped they would not bomb twice in the same place. Heard some of our 90mm guns firing and waited with dread for the thudding concussions of the bombs. But nothing happened over our position. Later we were given the following "official" story: Twenty-seven Jap bombers had come over, but our fighters had intercepted them and made them drop their bombs on the west part of the island, possibly on their own troops in that region. Our planes were credited with downing 23 bombers and one Zero fighter; with only one of our planes damaged. Today they evacuated Corp Nichols, who is suffering from shellshock; and Pvt Paul A. Renfrow, Jr., who has possible internal injuries from concussion. There is no information available as to the ships on which they were evacuated, or to what place they were taken. (This information is generally required to be included in the Muster Roll Report.) The men are in a rather nervous state.

September 29, 1942 Tuesday
The air raid alarm was sounded at 0940, and secured at 1025. There were no enemy planes sighted, and I heard no bombs. I think this one was a false alarm. Another air raid alarm went at 1345, and was secured at 1430. Our planes were quite active, but I saw no enemy planes and heard no bombing. I hear rumors that only a few Jap Zero fighters came over, and that two of them got on the tail of one of our fighters and shot him down. They had not sent over any bombers this trip. The Japs lost no planes. Our

TechSgt (Mess) Fowler was told by the Colonel that he will be recommended for transfer to duty in the U.S., and the man is greatly relieved. He is a regular, 48 years of age, and the air raids have been having a bad effect on his nerves. He is rather dirty, and keeps coming to me with all his troubles, so it will be a relief to me also when he goes. He is in great disfavor with the Battery Commander, who is always "riding" him, often unjustly.

September 30, 1942 Wednesday
A cloudy day in the morning. I to the river and shaved and bathed. I came back at 1030, just as it started to rain. The rain kept up all day, making everything muddy and unpleasant. There was a sale of post exchange items after supper, and I was able to get a bar of candy, toothpaste, and a nail clipper. (These items were slipped in by plane from time to time, and divided up among the various units on the island. They were always in short supply.) I collected the NCO Fitness Reports today from the various sections of the Battery, and the Battery Commander has marked all the men in his section (including me) with markings lower on the average than those of any other section. I received the lowest markings that I have received since coming on active duty. The average of the markings for the other sections is 89, while that of our section is only 77.

October 1, 1942 Thursday
A bright, sunny day, which is a great relief after yesterday's rain. In the morning I took a trip out to visit Bove. Got a ride almost to the 7th Marines camp from John O'Connor, who was the former police sergeant of E Battery when I belonged to that outfit. He is now the 1stSgt of H&S Battery of the 3rd Battalion; which amused me, as he can barely sign his name. He has two clerks doing the work for him (the clerical work; he was a good field man). When I got to the 7th Regiment I was told that Bove had been transferred to a position on the beach, where he was in charge of two 75mm guns. While there, I took a walk over to where the 5th Battalion was situated, and visited Jasinski and Bill Murray. Then I walked about 3 miles back to my camp. Spent the rest of the day in the office. To bed about 1900. At 2040 four loud "whams" were heard, as of exploding bombs, and a plane could be heard roaring off. We all ran for our shelters. A big searchlight on the airfield illuminated the skies. It remained on for a few minutes, and then was turned off. Later I heard conflicting reports that the explosions had been bombs dropped near the air field; and also that it was shelling from naval vessels or from our guns.

October 2, 1942 Friday
Guadalcanal

At 0415 I was awakened by the drone of planes overhead. They didn't sound like our planes, and I listened to them with mounting apprehension. I sat up and put my shoes on, intending to go to my bomb shelter and stand by there and give the alarm as soon as the air raid siren was sounded. But the more I listened, the more it sounded like Jap planes, and I could not understand why the air raid siren was not being sounded. It was very dark, and I hesitated before waking everybody for a possible false alarm; but finally I became so firmly convinced that it was Jap planes that I could control myself no longer and involuntarily started yelling: "Air raid! Air raid!" Everybody got up and took to their shelters; and not a moment too soon, for immediately after could be heard the whistling of the bombs hurtling downward. I do not know how these planes could have slipped by the sentries and the air raid watch, for even I recognized the sound of the Jap engines. The planes loosed a few bombs, and then took off. The bombs started a fire to the southwest of our position that blazed for half an hour. I remained awake the rest of the night. After breakfast to the beach to look for Bove but was unsuccessful. There was another air raid at 1250, in which Zero fighters came over and tried to attack two ships in the harbor. Two of their planes were shot down, and we lost three. TechSgt (Mess) Fowler received orders today transferring him on the first leg of a trip back to the U.S. He is 48 years old, and has not been giving satisfaction around here. He has over 20 years of service, and the air raids have been getting the best of him. Many others are getting nervous from the bombings.

October 3, 1942 Saturday

At 0410 the air raid siren was sounded, awakening us from a sound sleep. To the bomb shelters until the raid was over. I stayed awake the rest of the morning. Took a walk of about 4 miles to I Battery in the matter of one of our men who formerly belonged to that Battery. This man had made out an allotment to some girl while drunk, and had tried to get it stopped in I Battery, but had not succeeded. His family had written to headquarters, and the Adjutant and Inspector sent an order for us to cancel the allotment and make out a new one in favor of his family. Got a ride back. To the river and shaved and bathed before lunch. After the air raid this morning I took Fowler to the airfield and saw him aboard a plane bound for "white poppy." Shortly after noon there was an air raid in which only Zero fighters participated. They lost 7 planes to our fighters, and 2 to our anti-aircraft batteries. We lost 1 plane, but the pilot was saved. In the evening word was passed that about 4 enemy ships were in the vicinity of our island, and an "alert" condition was ordered for all night. I arranged a series of watches in the police and mess sections, and all the other sections did likewise. Then I to bed. But at 2130 the air raid alarm was given. To the air raid shelters, where I remained until 2340, when the "all clear" was given. Enemy planes could be heard overhead during this period, but no bombing.

October 4, 1942 Sunday

The "alert" condition continued all night until 0600. There was an air raid about 0130 that lasted for over an hour. All the men were pretty sleepy by now. To bed, and there were no more raids before morning. Capt. Mossburg, the officer who had me court-martialed, was evacuated this morning. I do not know the cause, but I saw him in the sick bay being checked by the doctor. I suspect his nerves are gone. Mess Sgt Adolph Manasse was transferred to this Battery, and promoted to the rank of StaffSgt (Mess). PFC Semler was promoted to Corporal. Both of these promotions are by "spot warrant." There also joined this Battery a Capt. Smart, who will replace Capt. Mossburg. I took things easy today, and caught up on some of my work. The interrupted sleep at night, and the waiting around in earthen bomb shelters for the air raids to cease is making me groggy and irritable. To bed at 1900, and I was called out two times for plane alerts, so I finally went back to bed with my clothes on. It is hot in the early part of the night, and no blankets are required.

October 5, 1942 Monday
Guadalcanal

Up after having had a good night's sleep despite the interruptions. There was no air raid during the day. Our 105mm batteries continued intermittent fire against the Jap positions all day. They fire over our position, and the concussion is unpleasant. I was told to promote Manasse to TechSgt (Mess) today. A new and bigger map of the Guadalcanal area has been adopted by the Division — Map 104. In the evening Pvt McDonough, the same man who had trouble about the allotment he had made out to some girl while drunk, shot himself in the left foot, near the toes, while cleaning his Reising gun. They tell me that he took the air raids hard, and was very nervous. He doesn't look very intelligent. They took him to the hospital. To bed at 1900, but was awakened at 2130 by the men telling me that a strange plane was approaching. There was no air raid alarm, but their fright communicated itself to me. I lay and listened to the plane, and it finally turned out to be one of ours, but I was disturbed the rest of the night. Our planes were very active (I hear they hit and possibly sunk 2 cruisers), and every time they came in to land I would listen to them and try to catch the landing lights (indicating they were ours). All in all, it was a wretched night. Everybody is jumpy.

October 6, 1942 Tuesday

Our guns were quiet today, and did no shelling of the Jap positions to the west. This was a great relief, as the firing at unexpected moments was making everyone nervous. Things in camp are quiet and almost as serene as back in New River. One can hardly realize that a couple of miles to our west Marines and Japs were killing each other. I read in a book, did some paper work, and in the afternoon boiled some clothes and then took them to the river for washing. There was no air raid during the day. I to bed early for a good night's rest. There were no air raid alarms tonight.

October 7, 1942 Wednesday

Up and it was quite cool in the morning. I had had a very good night's sleep. Shortly after breakfast our guns let loose with a furious cannonade, combined with aerial attack, on the Jap positions to the west. They kept this up for about fifteen minutes to half an hour. All during the rest of the day they kept an intermittent cannon fire against the Jap positions. Several new Air Cobra planes arrived today (about 10 or 15). I heard that the man who shot himself in the foot two days ago had been evacuated yesterday. Today we sent Sgt. Austin G. White to the hospital with malaria. I to the river in the afternoon and spent a nice time, and shaved. Had my hair cut by one of the men. Bove visited me during the day, and he gave me the location of his position, where he is Section Leader of two 75mm guns. He is making efforts to return to the 11th Marines, and may yet be successful. There were no raids by enemy aircraft today. It became cloudy in the evening. There was a feeling of excitement in the air as word was passed around that tomorrow at 0600 the Marines were going to attack the Jap positions and clean them out. I went to bed with a strange feeling. In the hills to our west were several hundred Japs, alive tonight, that tomorrow would be rendered shattered and mangled corpses. It seemed queer to know what was going to happen to that group of human beings, and to do nothing about it. In the last couple of battles the enemy attacked us, and therefore merited our retaliation. But here, coldly we were planning to go out and kill a large number of living young men, persons with families and relatives and loved ones at home.

October 8, 1942 Thursday

Shortly after midnight our artillery began a harassing fire against the Jap positions. They were firing so close to us that I could hear the officers' fire commands; and the roar of the guns disturbed my sleep all night. It sprinkled a little rain during the night, and in the morning it began to rain in earnest. The rain fell all day. This was a great disappointment to me, as I had entertained hopes of going out to the battle front to take pictures and to pick up some souvenirs. The rain didn't prevent the attack. I heard that our men had not been able to get in position at the time expected, so that the attack didn't start promptly at 0600; but it did get started. There was much artillery fire all during the day. The Marines were finding the Japs strongly dug in. They were not making much headway. In the evening the rain stopped, and the Japs were subjected to a particularly heavy cannonade. Planes could also be distinctly heard "strafing" the Japs. The casualties began drifting in. Col del Valle has received a radio, and it was set up outside tonight and over it we heard the news broadcast from the U.S. stating that there was a "lull" in the Pacific fighting. Whoever figured that one out should have been up in the hills for a first-hand observation of the "lull." To bed at 1930. At 2055 the air raid alarm was sounded, and it remained in effect almost continuously until 0240. During this time a single plane could be heard flying back and forth across the island. The 75mm howitzer battery near us continued firing when necessary, but the rest of the nearby area was blacked out.

October 9, 1942 Friday
Guadalcanal

The air raid alarm was in force from 2045 until 0240 — almost 6 hours. We all stood by our bomb shelters and listened as the enemy plane droned slowly back and forth across the sky. We grew weary and sleepy, and were very glad when the "all clear" signal was finally given. Up at 0600. The results of PFC Conley's trial was published today. He was tried and convicted by a Summary Court Martial for "Sleeping on Watch;" and was sentenced to be reduced to the next inferior rank and to lose $25 per month for a period of 2 months. But the fine was remitted. So he only loses $4 per month until he is again promoted to PFC. Quartermaster Clerk Gibson was transferred today to Division Headquarters Battalion. About 1000 a Jeep was going out to repair a radio near the front lines, and I accompanied the other occupants. The radio was attached to the 5th Battalion, 11th Regiment, and was set up on a promontory overlooking the battlefield. I got a good, long-range view of the battle. As we left that position, the air raid alarm sounded, and we were halted for almost an hour. We then continued on to the actual battle-front itself. Saw many weary Marines coming in. Most of the battle is over. Some of the Marines had not had a drink for two days. Dead Japs were lying all about in foxholes. The stench was awful. Food and water was moving up for the Marines. Worn out Marines could be seen sitting in among the dead Japs (who were all around) eating hungrily of canned rations, while the shiny green blowflies buzzed and swarmed over the adjacent horribly-bloated corpses. The Military Police were busy collecting bodies with the assistance of the Korean prisoners. We stayed only a very short while because the men I was with could not stand the awful odor. So back to camp, delayed somewhat by a large truck loaded with dead Marines on the way to the cemetery, which took up most of the road. Saw several wounded Marines being taken in for treatment, some of whom had been hit yesterday, but who had not been able to get to medical attention. To bed at 1900 after having heard over the radio that a Russian column was endeavoring to relieve the beleaguered Stalingrad, and that our forces were having good results in the Aleutian Islands. At 2330 some large calibre cannons opened up. We could see the flash, followed soon by the heavy roar of the explosion. It came from the direction of the beach, and soon we could see flares. We all thought it was enemy naval gun fire, but I could not hear the "zinging" of the shell fragments through the trees, and I thought it was queer that no alarm was being given. I called our telephone control, but they could give me no information. Finally Capt. Harris called me and told me it was the 5-inch guns of our own Defense Battalion that were firing, and that they were shooting out to sea.

October 10, 1942 Saturday
The firing of the 5-inch guns started again at about 0100, and this time the men were even more scared. But nothing serious happened, and we finally went back to bed; but our rest had been broken up. At about 1000 I with another Private to the front, thumbing rides to get there. The place is practically cleaned up. There are only a few Japs left to bury, and the Marines have moved up to the hills on the heels of the few remaining Japs. Our planes came over to do some bombing of the Jap positions, but through some mess-up in the signals dropped the bombs close to our men, slightly wounding a few. I was able to get a Jap cartridge pouch, a Jap canteen, and a 10-yen note. Some private on duty there had come across a dead Jap officer, and had acquired a beautiful sword, a pair of field glasses, and a Colt .38 cal. revolver, besides quite a bit of Jap money. We stayed there until past noon, dining on a cocoanut, then made our way back to camp. I to the river and walked in fully dressed and washed every bit of my clothes, including my shoes, to rid myself of all traces of my contact with the battlefield debris. Back to the office and dug into the paperwork. There were no air raid alarms, the radio news was favorable, and I to my bunk early.

October 11, 1942 Sunday
Guadalcanal

Up after having spent a restful night undisturbed by air raid alarms or shelling. I to work and cleaned up my place a bit. Stayed in my office all day. It had rained during the night, and it was cloudy today. It rained lightly a couple of times during the day. At 1250 the air raid alarm was sounded and the condition lasted until 1500. We heard much activity by our planes, but I am unable to get any exact figures on what actually happened. It seems that about 15 Jap Zero planes came over, escorting between 20 and 30 bombers; and that due to the cloudy condition, the Japs could not find the airfield and dropped their bombs on the beach. I was unable to determine if there were losses on either side. Corp Siegler, who holds an organizational (?) warrant, was issued a temporary warrant in the same rank. Later in the evening I was told that the official score in the raid today was 8 bombers and 4 fighters lost by the Japs while we lost 2 planes, the pilot of one of these planes being rescued.

October 12, 1942 Monday

Had a good night's rest, during which 2 loud explosions were heard, but they didn't disturb me. In the morning heard that there had been a naval engagement, and that we had sunk 4 destroyers and one cruiser of the enemies and we had lost one destroyer and had another set afire. There were no air raids during the day, and I had a relatively pleasant time. Took a swim in the afternoon. Spent part of the day cutting up strips of metal from a Jap bomber that had been shot down. All the men in the Battery are doing this, and from the strips are fashioning bracelets and identification tags. The aluminum alloy takes a high polish. In the afternoon there were many rumors of big naval engagements in the nearby seas, and stories of whole task forces being involved. Also, some contingents of the Army are due in tomorrow.

October 13, 1942 Tuesday

Up after a restless night. The Army arrived this morning — a regiment of infantry and a battalion of artillery. I understand they are to take up positions to the east, near Beach Red, beside those of the 1st Marines. I tried to get to the beach to see them come in, but the Lunga River bridge was out, and the river itself was unusually high, so I didn't go. The air raid alarm was sounded at 1135, and the raid lasted until 1240. Bombers came through and dropped bombs on the airfield. The alarm went off again at 1320 and lasted until 1430. Again the bombers got through. Hits were made near the runway, and about 150 feet of runway damaged. The Flying

Japanese cruiser *Furutaka*, sunk 22 miles northwest of Savo Island on October 12, 1942, after taking 90 hits in the Battle of Cape Esperance. (Imperial War Museum, courtesy of William H. Bartsch.)

Fortresses that had been out on a mission were forced to circle about and wait for the runway to be repaired so that they could have a long enough runway to come in on. I to the river and took a quick shave and bath. Soon after supper I was getting set to make my reports and get to bed, when a large calibre gun was heard to fire, followed soon by the whistle of a flying shell. It came from the west, passed alongside our position, and landed in the vicinity of the airfield. This was at 1830. The gun kept up an intermittent fire until close to 1200. Our artillery opened up and may have silenced it. We received orders to establish listening posts all along the front of our Battery area. I arranged the watches for the men near me, and to bed. At 2305 the sentries aroused the Battery with the announcement that the gun in the hills was shelling the airfield again. It fired about 4 shells, and then stopped. I stayed in the shelter until 2330, and then back to bed with my clothes on. I anticipated further trouble, and I was not disappointed. This night proved to be one of the worst I have ever had.

October 14, 1942 Wednesday
     At 0100 we were all awakened by the air raid alarm. To our bomb shelters, and soon a single plane was heard. It went over to the airfield and dropped a flare. This was followed by regular explosions which seemed to

fall across the ridge to our south, near the airfield. At first I thought it was bombs; but when the single plane continued circling and dropping flares on the airfield for a long time, I realized that it was artillery fire. The plane was dropping the flares and directing the fire to guide the gunners. I finally deduced that it was naval gunfire. I could see a flash, which would be followed after quite an interval by the dumping of a large amount of explosives, which exploded near the airfield. Some of the shells fell short, and landed most dangerously near our shelter. The shells roared overhead like freight trains, and the ground shook and quivered, and large trees could be heard cracking from the blasts and concussions. It sure looked bad for us for a while. This relentless fire kept up from 0100 to 0300. It seemed to me that our artillery ceased firing, and none of our planes took off. None of the men in our immediate area had been hit, but I heard a hacking near Col. del Valle's tent; and going over, found that two or three shells had made direct hits on his position, completely destroying his sleeping quarters and upsetting and damaging the R-3 tent and its contents of important maps and papers. I didn't stay long, however. At 0330 a plane could be heard overhead. Got to my shelter just as the bombs started whistling down. The plane was bombing the airfield, and his target was lit up by two huge fires started by the previous shelling. After the plane had dropped its bombs, it took off. We came out of our shelters, but not for long. Another plane came over and dropped a brilliant parachute flare, by the prolonged light of which he dropped another load of bombs on the airfield. These bombs, in coming down, sound exactly as though they are being aimed at one's head. It is only after the explosion that one knows how close they actually are. After this plane went, we stayed close to our shelters; and shortly before 0500 still another plane came over and dropped five bombs on its trip across the airfield, and two more on its return trip. It began to get light, and we out of our shelters to check the damage. There were no deaths in our immediate area, and only 2 or 3 slight injuries from concussion and flying coral. The Command Post was a mess. The Communication Section had had a large missile land in front of its position. Everybody estimated that we had been fired upon with 8-inch guns, but soon pieces of shell and "duds" shells began to be brought in, and it was found that we had been fired upon by 14-inch shells. They are immense things, these shells, weighing almost a ton. They sounded like a freight train when they were coming in. At 0530 the galley was told to get the fires started, and to get hot coffee and breakfast for the men. But our troubles were not over. At 0540, just as the stove was lit, the big Jap gun on the island started firing again. We all dispersed, and the gun fired about six times. It sounded as though there might be two of these guns. It will be

The head of a Japanese 14-inch shell fired from a battleship on the night of October 13-14, 1942, against Marines in the area of Henderson Field, Guadalcanal. Photographed October 14, 1942.

very bad for us if these guns remain. We will never know when we are about to be shelled. Word was passed that the shelling during the past night had come from a ship almost 20 miles out to sea. There are rumors that a naval engagement took place after the enemy ships left; and other rumors that our PT boats accounted for 2 destroyers in the enemy fleet that was doing the shelling. Received word today that Col. Pedro A. del Valle has been promoted to the rank of Brigadier General on 9 October, to rank from 15 September. Also found that there had arrived last night StaffSgt Holden of the Quartermaster Dept. He had been left on board ship when we landed, and in the naval battles that followed, the ship had left without disembarking him. Two new messmen from the 1st Battalion have joined as of yesterday. Also, Chaplain Dittmar has gone to the Division Field Hospital with malaria. At 0930, and at intermittent intervals during the day, the Jap artillery to the west would send over a few shells. They were aimed at the airfield, but we could hear them whistling past our position, and could never be sure when he would decide to deviate a bit. So we would go to the edge of our shelters and listen to the whistling. During the day, Corporal Braddock and PFCs Maloyd and Tee were sent to the Division Field Hospital suffering from hysteria. Sgt. White was released from the hospital after treatment for malaria. The air raid alarm was given at 1830, and lasted until 1940. We were told that in the morning raid our planes and anti-aircraft fire had accounted for 8 bombers and 3 fighters. Set up all-night watches again tonight, and I lay down, but was awakened almost every hour by shelling from the enemy artillery; or by my sentries hearing noises in the bushes or some other cause. I slept with all my clothes on, including my shoes.

October 15, 1942 Thursday

At 0140 I was awakened by the sentries who told me that a plane was approaching. I didn't think that any of our planes were airborne, so I watched this plane until it got over the airfield and dropped a flare. I knew what to expect, so I sent all the men into the shelters. Soon thereafter an intensive shelling from enemy naval vessels started. It seemed to be of smaller calibre than yesterday's shells (which were 14-inch shells), but fired at a much faster rate. The shelling lasted until 0215. I sat around until 0300; and when the shelling was not resumed, I to my bunk. At 0545 the enemy artillery to our west sent over several shells that interrupted our breakfast preparations. It lasted for about 15 minutes, and then we back to getting breakfast. But before we were finished the air raid alarm was sounded at 0647, and was not secured until 0800. We fed the men in small groups at a time; and soon after breakfast, at 0950, the air raid alarm was again sounded. It lasted until 1025, but I heard no bombing. The men are busy repairing the damage done to the Command Post. All this bombing and shelling seems to indicate that a major attack on us is pending. The men are getting very nervous and their appetites are affected. At 1050 a Jap fighter plane sneaked in, but all our guns turned loose on him and brought him down. One of our planes was damaged. No air raid alarm had been given. (The sounding of the air raid alarm presented a problem. To sound the alarm unnecessarily, or for unwarranted lengths of time, tired and depressed the men; interfered with duty, meals and sleep; kept the men confined unduly long in hot, fetid, cramped earthen shelters. Not to sound the alarm soon enough or for a long enough period exposed the men to danger from the bombings which fell unpredictably in all areas, particularly the airfield and vicinity.) Word got around that about six enemy transports were in the harbor unloading troops. Our Flying Fortresses sent two or three to the bottom. The gun in the hills kept sending over shells at intervals all day long. There was an air raid alarm at 1240 that lasted until 1400. A number of bombs were dropped in the vicinity of the airfield, and I didn't hear any of our planes fighting them. It is said that an admiral arrived today. I sure hope that the fleet he commands is not far behind.

The next few days are going to be very tough ones. They may be my last. The enemy transports that landed the men today were all either sunk at sea or blown up on the beach and set afire. There were air raid alarms and bombings at 1525 to 1555; 1610 to 1705; and 1930 to 1945. And in between that enemy gun in the hills kept sending over a few shells at intervals. We were able to feed only two meals today, due to the constant interruptions from air raids; and these two meals were served with many interruptions. The men would just about get the food on their mess gear when the alarm would be sounded. They are getting nervous and sleepy, and their stomachs are all upset. They are spending several hours a day in the hot and stuffy shelters. The "alert" condition was in effect all night, and we had 3 sentries posted continuously, but we were all awake most of the night.

October 16, 1942 Friday
Guadalcanal
     At 0025 a plane came over and dropped flares, so we all took to our shelters. The flares were immediately followed by a heavy and continuous naval gunfire against this island that lasted for an hour. There were no casualties in this Battery, the fire seeming to be directed at the airfield. A very large fire was started in an ammunition drop to our east, and this blazed for a long time. It sounded as though gasoline was exploding, and ammunition could be heard going off. We were told that two supply ships of ours were in the harbor unloading gasoline for the planes (we were running short of this gasoline). I don't know how they fared when the enemy naval vessels started shelling. It seems to be the most accepted opinion that 7 transports were in the Jap fleet that landed men on this island. They pack them in on the Jap transports, and there may have been as much as 3,000 men aboard each transport. If so, that would give them about 20,000 men here, which makes them about as strong as we are in numbers. They have artillery; and strong naval support, as evidenced by the shellings for the last 3 nights. Our navy has not extended any support to us these last 3 days, and this leaves the situation in a serious state. The men were very depressed until this morning, when rumors got around that our Navy would soon be in a position to take care of the situation. Also, there were reports that the radio had announced that our Navy had sunk 18 ships in the last few days in this area, and that Jap troops had been landed on the west side of this Island. So it seems that our Navy hasn't been laying down altogether. This news had a very cheering effect upon the men, and there was a noticeable boost in the morale. The Jap cannons didn't fire into us all morning, and there were no air raids. It was very cloudy all morning, with occasional rain. Everybody got a good rest. I told the galley to make every effort

to serve 3 meals today, and to put out its most appetizing food and fruits. The purpose of this was to get the men to eat again and get something on their ribs should coming events decrease our rations; and for us to eat the best parts of our rations now, in case we had to abandon any to the Japs. The morning was so quiet that after lunch I to the river and bathed and shaved. Also washed some clothes. This is the first time that I have had my clothes or shoes off in 3 days. I even slept in them. There is much activity by the Marines and Army. Trucks and tanks are dashing back and forth. In the evening word was passed that one of our planes would be airborne from 1900 to 2300 in an effort to intercept that single Jap plane that keeps coming over every night. But our plane didn't meet the enemy tonight. We set up watches, posted our sentries, and then we all to bed to await what the night would bring.

October 17, 1942 Saturday

Spent a quiet night for a change, to everybody's great relief. The men all looked much more cheerful this morning as they ate a breakfast of pancakes. At 0745 the first air raid alarm was sounded. We sent up 8 planes to meet the fighters and bombers that the Japs sent over; and between our planes and the anti-aircraft fire, we accounted for 16 Jap planes. There were other air raid alarms at 0825 to 0840 and at 1010 to 1030. At 1220 the air raid alarm was again given. It lasted for quite a while, and seemed like just another harmless raid. Then the bombs started dropping. The bombs fell all over our position. I thought sure I was going to be hit this time. The ground shook and rocked, and the dirt thrown up by the explosions just showered down into our shelters. After it was over one of the men in there with me began to laugh so hard that he became hysterical. We out and looked around. The officers mess had been demolished by a direct hit. There were shrapnel holes in our water cans, among the canned foods, in the Lister bag (the drinking water container), through the quarter-inch steel frame of the water tank, and in all the canvas around us. My office had about 7 or 8 shrapnel holes, my mosquito net was all torn, and my table damaged. It was a good thing I was not in the office at the time. This sure impressed upon me the wisdom of seeking shelter during any air raid. Other bombs had hit in various sections of the Battery position. General del Valle's quarters were pretty well banged up again. We were told later that our planes had received word too late to intercept the bombers, but had followed them and shot down 15 out of 17 of them. This, together with the 16 this morning, makes 31 planes today. I was pretty well shaken up, but soon recovered. We received 33 cartons of cigarettes and some candy and peanuts which I distributed among the men. We are eating very well these days. I patched up my office and lay down early to get whatever sleep the night would permit. Word was received that Corp Braddock, PFC Maloyd and PFC Tee were evacuated on the 16th. They were suffering from hysteria. Sgt Dzizynski went to the hospital yesterday with malaria. At 2045 1 was awakened and told to caution my men to be on the alert for a possible visit by a Jap amphibian plane. I notified the sentries and gave them instructions, and then back to bed with all my clothes on. At 2235 the air raid alarm was sounded. We to our shelters until 2340, but heard no bombing.

October 18, 1942 Sunday
Guadalcanal

Right at one minute after midnight some enemy vessel or vessels opened shell-fire against this island. The shelling had not been preceded by any aerial observations, and seemed to be without any specific target. It lasted for five minutes. We sat in our shelters for another half hour, then I to bed. At 0040 heavy shelling could be heard out to sea. It lasted until 0050. I heard no thuds of shells landing, and it seemed to me that no hits were made on land. Perhaps there was some sort of naval engagement. Back to bed again, and this time was not disturbed until morning. Our Battery and Special Weapons Co. are supposed to move today further to the north. We fed Special Weapons in the morning, so that they could go right ahead and move their galley and they would feed our Battery in the afternoon. I down to the river after breakfast and found that it had risen during the night and washed away the wooden bridge. The steel replacement bridge is less than half finished. The rising river had also torn down many wires that had been attached to the bridge. We spent the day moving to the new position, which is in a cocoanut grove. There has been very little bombing or shelling of this position to date. It is close by the 3rd Defense Battalion, and there is a 90mm battery about 500 yards away. I moved my office over today, and we started digging air raid shelters. There was an air raid, but the bombs fell nowhere near us. Most of the Battery slept in the old area, but I stayed in the new position with about 15 men. We set up a system of sentries for the night. Chaplain Dittmar went back to the hospital with malaria.

October 19, 1942 Monday

Up after having spent one of the most restful nights in a long time. There was no enemy activity to disturb us. The Battery went to work moving our stuff to the new position. Police Sgt Sladovich took sick with what seems to be malaria, and has been ordered to bed. He had intended to dig an air raid shelter for us two and two others, but he was ordered not to work and one of the others was sent on a working detail. So the other man and I spent the day digging three foxholes which will be the beginning of the shelter. There were two air raid alarms during the day, but I heard no bombs dropping and didn't notice any enemy planes. The cocoanut trees, while offering excellent cover, shut off the view. Most of the Battery was moved by evening, and there is an adequate amount of shelters. At about 2100, PFC Routon began crying and screaming, and didn't respond to my orders, so Dr. Queen ordered him to the hospital. Supply Sgt Quilter was transferred to the 1st Battalion to replace casualties there.

October 20, 1942 Tuesday
The day was spent in moving the rest of our gear to the new position, in digging air raid shelters, and improving the position. There were a couple of air raids during the day, but our planes seemed to take care of the enemy, dispersing the bombers and making them drop their bombs out at sea. Had my "office" shack moved to the new location, and have started a new shelter that will be as secure as the old one. Learned today that Chaplain Dittmar had been evacuated on 18 October; and that PFC Routon was evacuated today. Sgt Sladovich was sent to the hospital with malaria. That makes 3 men we have in the hospital with that ailment. In the evening the Jap artillery in the hills sent over a few shells toward the air field. At 1930 some Jap planes sneaked in and dropped a few bombs and until 2130 Jap planes came over at intermittent intervals. Our searchlights tried to pick them up, and our 90mm guns fired at them, but without success, I believe. After that there was a couple of more alarms, but the planes were ours.

October 21, 1942 Wednesday
Guadalcanal
There was an air raid shortly before noon, but our Battery was not affected. The day was spent in improving the air raid shelters and our positions in general. Two men from the Communication Section went to the hospital with malaria, and one with an infected foot. The morale of the men is improving daily. It had been decidedly low.

October 22, 1942 Thursday
A cloudy, rainy day. The air raid shelters are in pretty good shape. The enemy artillery is getting busy, and he is shelling several points on the island. He is hitting on or very near the runway. Yesterday I visited the hospital to see Sladovich, and there observed shelling at first hand. It is a sad thing to see the sick patients trying to get to cover when the shells start

bursting. A man in the nearby 3rd Defense Battalion shot himself through the leg today. A load of mail came in today, and I received a letter from Bess, which cheered me up immensely. There are very strong rumors that Gen Holcomb is on the island. The newspapers the men received today in the mail are those of August, and they describe our landing on this Guadalcanal Island. I guess the people back home have not lost track of us entirely.

October 23, 1942 Friday
There was an air raid today at 1115 during which the bombs fell closer than usual, but still quite a distance off. Corp Semler broke down today and was taken to the hospital. Two men came back from the hospital yesterday, leaving 4 still in there with malaria. We are furnished anti-malaria pills at regular intervals. The Jap artillery was very active today. I took a trip to the old area for some stuff, but was forced back because of the flying shell fragments. After supper the shelling resumed and came very close to our position. One shell hit so close that I flopped to the ground with the greatest haste, breaking my glasses. This is a very serious loss, and an irreplaceable one while I am here. The shelling increased in volume, and soon our guns began replying with a heavy barrage. Word was passed to us to look to our weapons, ammunition, and water; and shortly we learned that the enemy was attacking on our western flank on the Matanikau River. It is estimated that there are from five to ten thousand Japs in the force on this island, and we got set for some serious business. Our guns were firing forcefully. I lay down with my clothes on for a while, but couldn't sleep for the din. I arose and to the Operations tent, where I listened to the fire of the entire Regiment being directed against the enemy. We gave them plenty of steel, and it began to have its effect. At 2045 it began to rain. I stayed in the tent in the Operations dug-out until past 2200, at which time it looked quite favorable for our side, we having knocked out several tanks, and the enemy beginning to withdraw.

October 24, 1942 Saturday
At about 0200 the tide of battle began to recede and some of the guns were rested. By morning things were pretty quiet. Rumors said that we had accounted for 10 enemy tanks, and possibly 14. The Japs had been forced to withdraw. In the morning I to the beach with Special Weapons Battery, where I test-fired my Reising gun and found that it worked very satisfactorily. In the afternoon I received four rolls of film from Bess, for which I blessed her. I would have been willing to pay $15 per roll for these films. I was greatly aggravated at all the opportunities for taking pictures that I had to miss by not having film. If I can get these pictures after the war,

they will have the greatest interest value of anything I could bring home. I tried to get transportation to the front but was unsuccessful until after 1500. Then I started with my camera (Kodak Monitor 616 folding camera) and new film, but the Jeep in which I was riding was loaded down with too much ammunition and water, so I went only as far as the old position. There I dropped off and dug up some of my souvenirs and brought them back to the new position. I had hoped to take a bath after supper, but the Jap artillery started heavy shelling in the vicinity, and soon it started to rain. The enemy artillery kept firing until almost 2000. I was in bed by then. There had been no enemy air raids today.

October 25, 1942 Sunday
Guadalcanal

During the early morning hours there could be heard heavy firing of small arms and mortars in the vicinity of the position this Battery once held for a short while in the hills. It continued until past daylight. The rain had stopped some time during the night. We learned later that there had been a fairly heavy Jap attack on the Marine and Army forces in the neighborhood of the place called popularly "Battle Hill" or "Raiders Ridge" (in honor of the excellent fight put up by the Raider Battalion at that point). Word was passed down that the Japs suffered losses of from 300 to 500 men. At about 0745 the first air raid alarm was given, and for nearly all of the rest of the day it was in effect. There was constant and heavy air activity all day. There was probably a strong force of enemy naval vessels in the vicinity, from which these planes took off. They were mostly fighter planes. Our fighters were landed on the fighter strip to the east of the improved runway, and this fighter strip was more than ankle deep in mud from the rains of the last two nights. The fighter planes could not take off from this strip. At first the Jap planes had things pretty much their way, but finally our fighter planes were towed over to the improved runway and were able to take off from there. The Japs kept sending over flight after flight of fighter planes, and one bombing attack. By evening there had been shot down, by means of anti-aircraft fire and our planes, 22 of their fighter planes and 6 of their bombers. We had spent most of the day in or near our air raid shelters, and the anti-aircraft had sent a lot of metal skyward. A Regimental Memo was published commending the 11th Regiment for its conduct during the enemy attack occurring the night of 23-24 October along the Matanikau River. It stated that the Commanding General of the 1st Marine Division had personally called and thanked the Commanding General of the 11th Regiment. It praised the 11th for its contribution to the repulse of the attack, and stated that 10 tanks used by the enemy had been destroyed. The Battery Commander came along and told me to pass the following information: There had been 2 hits with 1000-pound bombs on a Jap cruiser, and one near miss on it during the day. Also, that a friendly naval force was going to strike in this area tonight. This latter information, I learned from rumors, concerned a Jap force that had been landed from two transports on New Georgia Island that our naval forces were going to attack in a sort of "commando" raid. This news was very heartening, as it feels good to know that our side is doing some offensive fighting also. To bed at 1900, but at 1955 was awakened by a heavy shelling that seemed to come from some enemy naval vessels, and it continued until 2040. After that stopped, I to bed again.

October 26, 1942 Monday

Just at daybreak there was a sharp increase in the small arms and mortar firing that had been going on since shortly after midnight. We learned later that the Japs around the "Battle Hill" area had forced the Marines back and occupied the machine gun posts for a while, but that the Marines had counter-attacked, retaken the positions, and captured several Jap machine guns. Things quieted down during the day. An air raid was organized against the Jap cannon in the hills that keeps shelling the runway and other positions, but it was unsuccessful. One of the corpsmen named Notaro was put up for office hours today for insolence and for refusing to obey an order. He was awarded 5 days bread and water. I took him to the Military Police Company for confinement, but they refused to accept him. They said they only took General Court Martial prisoners. I brought Notaro back, and Gen. del Valle recommended him for General Court Martial. This time when I brought him to the MP Co., he was accepted.

October 27, 1942 Tuesday
Guadalcanal

At 0330 the air raid alarm was sounded. An unidentified plane came over and after cruising around over our position, went into the hills where the Japs are located, dropped a couple of bombs, and took off. Got my work straightened out in the morning, and at 0930 with another man to the 5th Battalion, where we picked up Jasinski. We three then took off for the front lines around the "Battle Hill" (Raiders Ridge) area. We did much walking through the jungle, getting a lift now and then. Finally arrived at a point about 3 miles from the original "Battle Hill," and found about a hundred dead Japs lying about. They had been hit with 37mm canister shells, and

1st Sgt. Felber's office and foxhole at the third position of H&S Battery, 11th Marines, in coconut grove, Guadalcanal, October 26, 1942.

were all torn apart. There were loose arms and legs lying about, and the bodies of the Japs were badly ripped. I took one picture, and then joined the others in the purpose of our trip — hunting souvenirs. I got some pictures from the Japs, a rifle and bayonet, a sword scabbard without the sword, and a pistol holster. Jasinski found a cheap camera. These Japs must have come from the Dutch East Indies, for they had "occupation money" from that country and papers printed in the Dutch language. They were seasoned veterans. On nearly every body was found condoms, and several carried pornographic pictures. The Army had participated with the Marines in the fighting in this sector, and being equipped with many automatic weapons plus Garrand rifles, had done a good job of blasting the Japs. We stayed on the field until about 1400, then snipers began firing all around us, so we three took off back through the jungle trail. The firing became quite active, and I was as afraid of getting shot up by enthusiastic Marines as I was of being picked off by a sniper. The snipers had accounted for several casualties that morning, and we had met Marines who said they had just shot some. But we got through to the back lines safely. Back to camp and was told that Major Viall had told the men that our Navy had intercepted 3 Jap task forces during the last few days and had beaten them decisively. He said the naval officer in charge had also promised us his fullest support. During the morning I saw 9 planes leaving to dive bomb the Japs near the Matanikau River; and again at 0400, 9 planes did the same.

Carl Jasinski with dead Japanese the day after the October 25–26, 1942, Battle of "Raiders Ridge," Guadalcanal.

As soon as I got back to camp I to the river and took off and washed all my clothing, including my shoes. After supper, there was about $20 worth of post exchange supplies to be sold. As the Chaplain has been evacuated, the sale was made by me. There had been no bombing raids after the morning one, and the Jap artillery in the hills appears to have been silenced, for it didn't fire at all today. To bed early. There was much firing going on soon after dark. It came from all sides of us.

October 28, 1942 Wednesday

As on yesterday morning, at 0330 there was an air raid alarm which lasted about an hour. I heard no planes or bombing. Got my work cleaned up in the morning. Arranged for a truck, and with two men rode out to the battlefield again. There had been brushes with the enemy all last night, but these clashes had not been in this sector. We poked around for a while. The Military Police Company was having our Korean prisoners bury the dead Japs, who were by now in an advanced and horrible state of decay. Back shortly after noon without having found the scene of last night's encounters. Spent the afternoon getting a truck and going out to the Division brig to get a statement from Notaro, the General Court Martial prisoner. In the evening had my hair cut, shaved, bathed and washed all my clothes again. There were no air raids by the enemy aside from the early morning one.

October 29, 1942 Thursday
Guadalcanal

For the third successive morning Jap planes came over between 3 and 4 o'clock in the morning. Today two were picked up by our searchlights. We fired some anti-aircraft, but without apparent success. The planes made one trip across only, and the "all clear" was sounded a half hour after the alarm. There had been quite a bit of small arms firing during the night. I tried to get information as to just where the fighting took place, but could not get anything exact. In the morning I stood by while I sent my clerk to get a signature from Notaro on the typed copy of his statement, and to get a set of finger prints taken at the hospital. In the afternoon I helped the clerk get out a corrected roster of the personnel of this Battery. In the evening I was seized with a painful attack of cramps that made me most uncomfortable, and disturbed my sleep all night. It must have come from bad food or dirty mess gear.

October 30, 1942 Friday

Our planes kept up a constant patrol all night long. In the morning 4 of our destroyers and one cruiser took off to the west of the island, and with our Major Nees and Capt. Appleton aboard to direct fire, they shelled the Jap bivouac areas and their equipment. At 1405 there was an air raid alarm that lasted until 1450. I saw no enemy planes. I took things easy all day, getting rested up after the bad night I spent. My stomach is in good shape again, and I ate 3 hearty meals. Wrote a letter to Bess, enclosing some Jap money for souvenirs. Also wrote letters to the Battery clerk, Murray; and to the Marine Corps Schools, telling the latter that I would continue my lessons when I caught up with my textbooks. Estimates of the shells fired by our vessels this morning varied from 3000 to 5000 rounds. Was visited by Jasinski in the evening, and he told me the artillery is scheduled to move up to positions on the Matanikau River front for a big push in a day or two. I wished him luck.

October 31, 1942 Saturday

At 0220 the air raid alarm sounded. We dressed and sat around until 0315, when some plane dropped a brilliant green flare in the direction of the airfield. Nothing happened, however, and the "all clear" signal was given at 0335. Wrote another letter to Bess today, and took a shave and a bath in the morning. After lunch started a letter to my brother Jack. Then out and took a couple of pictures. Visited Jasinski, who is moving up to the front lines near the Matanikau River in preparation for tomorrow's big push. I borrowed a radio from him, but when I finally got it to my tent, I

October 31, 1942. More "Japanese calling cards": naval shells fired against Marines in the Henderson Field area.

was told that a certain part was missing, and that I didn't have enough batteries to run it. In the evening it started to rain, as it has done for the past 3 days. The rain was slightly heavier tonight, but it didn't rain all night, and the roads are not too bad. But it must have been uncomfortable for the men on the front lines, who have no shelters. We have many men up there. A convoy of our men is rumored as arriving soon. To bed uneasy with the knowledge of what is impending tomorrow.

November 1, 1942 Sunday

Our planes were active from the first crack of dawn. I finished the work that I had to do as quickly as possible and turned the Battery over to the clerk. I couldn't arrange for transportation, so I started out on foot for the front lines. By dint of much walking and thumbing of rides I made my way out to a point near the Matanikau River. There I came across the official photographer of the Regiment, and with him up the banks of the Matanikau River to where the infantry had built some pontoon bridges over which we crossed. The Engineers were busy constructing a more substantial bridge over which trucks will be able to ride. We followed a trail through the jungle until we came upon a crew of men fighting their way through with a cart full of mortar ammunition. It was heavy going in the dense underbrush. We followed them, and they led us to where a mortar unit was stationed. We stayed for a short while to see the mortar fire several rounds at the Japs to the front, then continued on. The Japs had some artillery and were firing over the ridge on which we were and into the men on the other side of the river. Our artillery was replying, and the shells from both sides were whistling over our heads. We were told that there was the remains of a Jap machine gun nest on the top of the ridge, and we went up to see. We walked along the crest of the ridge until we were at the forward observers' post of the mortar unit, but all we could find was a place that had been covered over, and from which a white skull protruded. We walked further along this ridge, and soon shells began hitting in our vicinity. We sat down, and some of the shells went within a hundred yards of our position. I think these shells came from our own batteries, for we were on the northern slope of this ridge and facing toward our guns. Some Very pistol signal shells went up from the spot where the shells were hitting, and the fire lifted to well past Point Cruz in enemy territory. We met a man coming back from the front lines, and he told us that our front line was just two knolls ahead, and that our men were stopped by heavy Jap machine gun fire from positions which they could not locate. There were several wounded men there, with no corpsmen or means of getting them out. The photographer with me began urging that we start back, as it was 1400 and he was hungry and thirsty. So we started back. We passed a badly shot up Marine lying in the road in the blazing sun, and some exhausted Marines nearby were arguing as to whether he was dead or not. A corpsman had told them he was dead, but they said they could see the man's muscles seem to twitch from time to time. It was probably the effect of the hot sun on the body. We saw two small Jap field pieces (cannons) of about 30mm. They looked as though they were animal-drawn, for they had harness attached. Further along we saw a squad of men who had two seriously wounded men with them and no means of getting them out for treatment. There was no corpsman about. There were some Higgins boats in the distance toward Kukum, but too far away to be signaled. We went on and came to the mouth of the Matanikau River, where there were several of the Jap tanks that had been knocked out in the battle of 23 October. I took some pictures. We were ferried across the river by means of a rubber boat from some airplane, saving us the job of having to go up along the riverbank to the footbridge. On the other side we saw some officers and told them the situation about the lack of corpsmen and facilities for evacuating the wounded. They called up Division Hq. about the matter. We got a ride on a truck going out, and passed a group of Army trucks that were being sent in to bring out the wounded. The Division Hq.

had acted promptly and effectively. Continued back to camp, and took things easy the rest of the day. Heard that our advance was bogged down. To bed early.

November 2, 1942 Monday
Guadalcanal

The night was quiet. I heard no heavy artillery firing. Reports indicate that our men were making but slow headway. I decided not to go to the front lines again until a big engagement took place. Puttered around in the morning. Lt. Bove came over to visit me and we had a long talk and discussed some of our North Carolina friends. In the afternoon I washed some clothes and bathed and shaved. A large convoy of ships came in

Left: November 1, 1942. Men of the 5th Marines lug mortar shells through the jungle west of the Matanikau River. *Right:* November 1, 1942. 81mm mortar crew of the 5th Marines in action west of the Matanikau River against enemy on the other side of the hill.

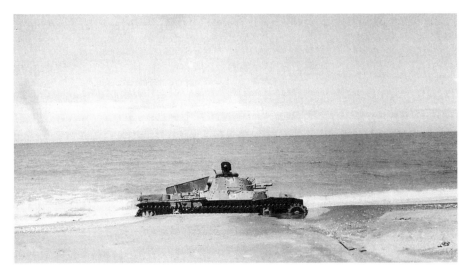

Top: Japanese Type 97 (1937) tank wrecked during an attempt on the night of October 23, 1942, to cross the mouth of the Matanikau River. Photographed November 1, 1942. *Bottom:* Japanese tanks knocked out in the assault of October 23 at the mouth of the Matanikau River, Guadalcanal. Photographed November 1, 1942.

today — 2 transports, 1 cargo ship, and several destroyers, according to one report. The 5th Defense Battalion landed, as did some Army units. They brought with them seven 155mm cannons — not howitzers. These cannons have a much longer range than our howitzers. They were set up in the afternoon, and fired some rounds, putting an enemy anti-aircraft emplacement out of commission. Some of our ships came in and unloaded today without trouble.

November 3, 1942 Tuesday

In the morning there was the sound of heavy gunfire at quite a distance out to sea, but I could not get any information as to what took place. One reliable source said that our planes patrolled an 80-mile radius of this Island without encountering signs of any naval battle. It started to rain in the early morning hours, and cleared up about 0730. It was cloudy and drizzly the rest of the day. The 155s did some firing in the morning. I could get no word as to our progress on the Matanikau. In the afternoon I to one of the huge 155mm guns located nearby and took a picture of it. Saw many of our troops moving eastward from the Matanikau in the direction of Beach Red. Later there were strong rumors that a Jap force of about 3,500 men had landed around Beach Red. The neighboring Special Weapons Battery got their machine guns together and with their crews took off for somewhere. Our planes droned overhead insistently, and they could be heard dropping bombs to the eastward. Heavy artillery fire could be heard in that direction also. The 155s kept up a slow rate of fire all night, disturbing our sleep.

November 4, 1942 Wednesday
Guadalcanal

At about 0400 was awakened by a shot and calls for help. A sergeant in the adjacent Special Weapons Battery had been having a nightmare, and had shot himself through the left palm with his rifle. The bullet, in going through, had made only a small hole in the palm, but had left about a 1.5" hole in the back of the hand. He will probably lose his left hand. Heard reports that a regiment of Japs, about 3,500, had landed past Beach Red early Tuesday morning. That was why all our troops and guns had been headed in that direction. At 0830 I decided to go to our eastward front to see the action. Found some amphibious tractors headed that way and hopped aboard with my camera. The tractors went down the east branch of the Lunga River out to the ocean. They then headed eastward, keeping a short distance off shore, snorting and wallowing in the waves. The harbor near the fighting contained 14 of our ships—3 transports and the rest destroyers and cruisers. The transports were unloading rapidly, and there were groups of natives on shore helping with the unloading. Our planes were on constant patrol. The tractors took me as far as the mouth of the Ilu River. There I sat for 45 minutes and watched 4 of our war vessels shell the Jap positions on shore. They did a most thorough job, even using "Time

Top: November 4, 1942. Amphibious tractors moving down the Lunga River to the ocean. *Bottom:* November 4, 1942. Amphibious tractors in a jungle river, Guadalcanal.

fire" and having the shells burst in the air. I crossed the Ilu River and found our neighbors, the Special Weapons Battery, had moved to this position and had spent the night there. Saw some light tanks, and I counted 32 of them. After passing this group there was a stretch of about 2 miles where I saw no one. Passed a deserted native village and spent some time examining

A 155mm "Long Tom" cannon of the 5th Defense Battalion landed on November 2, 1942. Lt. Eaton on track. Photographed November 4, 1942.

the architecture and handicrafts lying about. Took pictures of a rude native bridge and of some of the huts. They had lime and mango trees growing about, and a short distance away was a pineapple patch. Saw some of their cooking utensils, and visited their school house. I continued on and came across a unit of the Special Weapons Battalion and the 7th Marines. Finally arrived at the mouth of the Malembui River. This represented our furthest eastern flank. Our troops hold a rectangular position extending 400 yards up the west bank of the river and about 600 yards westward. The Japs are on the east bank of this river. They had landed 2 nights ago to the east of our present position. The 7th Marines had been on that side of the river, but the Jap force that landed was so superior numerically, and had such fire superiority with the presence of the 2 destroyers that were landing the troops, that the 7th had not engaged them, but had withdrawn back across to the west bank of the Malembui River. They had no field phone lines connected at the time, and their radio was not functioning properly, so they had been unable to notify Division of the landings, thus permitting the Japs to land unhampered, and to get away with their ships without contact. At 1430 I started back. Plowed through a sandy road for about 3 miles until I reached the Special Weapons Battery position. Got a lift there from an officer attached to the 8th Marines (2nd Marine Division), and he told me that there were 4,900 men from the 8th Marines landing today, and that Col. Carlson's Raider Battalion was also landing. This latter group is the one to which Major James Roosevelt, the President's son, is attached. Got rides pretty nearly to my camp, and arrived in time to join the rear of the chow line. After eating, to the river, where I washed all my sweaty clothes and took a bath.

November 5, 1942 Thursday
Guadalcanal

Our artillery had been firing casual shots all night. At lunch time the air raid alarm was sounded for the first time in several days. About 26 enemy planes came over, but our anti-aircraft batteries got only 6; and the planes we sent up failed to make contact. Spent the morning in the office, and in the afternoon to the beach where I took some pictures of the natives unloading ships. To bed early. At 2245 the air raid alarm was again sounded. The alarm was in effect for 2 hours. A single plane was heard during that time. The searchlights were turned on, but didn't seem able to locate the plane. The plane dropped a flare to the west of our position, and after a while another in the vicinity of the airfield. I didn't hear any bombs. Our 90mm guns didn't fire. The plane left at 0045 of Friday morning, and we all back to our interrupted slumbers.

November 6, 1942 Friday

We had not been in bed long when the air raid alarm was again sounded at 0230. I stayed awake until about 0300, when the "all clear" was

November 5, 1942. Melanesian natives unloading a ship, Guadalcanal.

given, and then back to sleep until morning, this time with my clothes on. In the morning I heard reports that our PT boats had sighted 2 cruisers or destroyers, but had lost contact with them. There had been the sound of heavy firing out to sea, but nobody knew what had caused it. Spent the morning checking the men for their blood type, for the information of the "sick bay." Did some work in the afternoon. Heard that there were 2 cargo ships on the beach, but somehow I didn't get around to going to the beach. The battles on our east and west flanks are continuing, and we are progressing slowly.

November 7, 1942 Saturday

Was able to secure a truck at 1000, and to the 5th Battalion area, where I picked up another part for my borrowed radio. Drove to Bove's position, which is now in the hills, and with him traveled eastward along the beach to the Malembui River. Two days ago this had been the furthest east flank of our position; but today found that the 7th Marines had crossed the river and were advancing eastward, without meeting opposition. A unit of the 164th (Army) was across the river and south of the Jap positions. We have a unit of the Marines on the east of the Jap positions. The Japs are surrounded — if they remained in that area and didn't take off to the south and the hills. Bove would not go across the river, so we rested. Saw a small cargo ship near the Tenaru River that had been hit by a Jap submarine which had come in and fired a torpedo at it. The destroyers standing by had released many depth charges, which had rocked the Island. It was reported that one submarine had been sunk, and possibly a second one also. The Jap torpedo had struck the cargo ship in the center, which was fortunate; for the ship was loaded with 500-pound bombs forward and aft to steady it. Had it been hit on the bow or stern, it would have blown the bombs. Back to my office and found Jasinski waiting for me. We all to the beach and arranged to get enough batteries from the amphibious tanks to run the radio set which Jasinski had loaned me. There were a great many planes in the air in the evening — torpedo planes and bombers and several other types. There are rumors that a large Jap naval force is headed this way.

November 8, 1942 Sunday

Up and there were reports that our planes had come across 1 Jap cruiser and 10 destroyers. The torpedo planes had released their torpedoes, 2 hitting the cruiser, and a third hitting a destroyer. The cruiser had also been hit with a 1000-pound bomb, and had been struck a glancing blow from another bomb. It was reported as sunk. Some of the destroyers were also sunk. None of the ships attacked the Island. It rained all day. I visited the Division Photo Section in the morning, and was drenched. There are many rumors of Army units due in tomorrow and the next few days, and our possible early relief from this Island. It is even rumored that we will go back to the U.S., but that doesn't sound reasonable to me. To bed early, but at 2145 there were two tremendous explosions at a great distance. They sounded like salvos from a battleship, and I got set for a shelling of the Island. But nothing happened. There was the sound of artillery fire and mortars to the west near the Matanikau River.

November 9, 1942 Monday
Guadalcanal

Up and it was a sunny, hot day. In the morning shaved and finished a long letter which I had started Nov. 1st. It was to my brother Jack, and gave a description of the Island. In the afternoon I had a truck for a couple of hours. To the beach and tried to find the torpedoes that had been fired at and had missed the cargo ships about to unload. These torpedoes had been removed because they constituted a menace, so was unable to get a picture of them. The torpedoed ship was still in the harbor; and I was told that it was beached on a coral shelf. To an aviation unit and

The 8th Marines move to the front at the Matanikau River on November 9, 1942, for the next day's attack on the Kokumbona area.

November 9, 1942. Japanese Type 3 (1914) 76.2mm naval dual-purpose gun in emplacement at Kukum. (The gun was widely believed to be British, captured by Japanese.)

arranged to have my pictures developed in a couple of days. Then out to the beach again and got a ride almost to the Matanikau River. Found that we are moving up 11,000 rounds of ammunition for the guns, and there were major-unit troop movements toward the west. There is a big push due very soon. I hope they clean out the Japs and we get relieved soon. Took 6 pictures during the day. In the evening to the river, which was quite high, and did a big batch of laundry and bathed. To bed at 1900, my usual retiring hour. It rained during the night. The rainy season must be approaching.

November 10, 1942 Tuesday

At 0900 left for the west front. Got a ride, but an air raid came up and the truck I was in went back and stayed near the air raid shelter until the raid was over. Then the truck took me to the bridge across the Matanikau. From there I walked to the front. Saw (and smelt) occasional dead Japs, and saw evidence of their former occupation of these positions. Saw wrecked Jap field piece. The 8th Marines held reserve positions. They had marched up with much equipment, including full packs and horseshoe rolls. They were losing or throwing away quite a bit of this stuff, especially gas masks. As they neared the front they placed their rolls and gear in piles and went up with combat equipment only. I saw one of the positions from which a big Jap gun (captured from the British) had been

shelling the airfield. I greatly ad-
mired the Jap foxholes and dugouts, at which they are very in-
genious and proficient. At 1300 I
started back to Point Cruz to meet
a Marine who was going to be there
with a truck to take us right up to
the front. Had gone but a short distance when a Jap patrol cut loose
with rifle fire at the road on which
I was traveling. The Marines all
scattered and took to cover. I got
behind a truck and drew my pistol.
Though looked carefully and intently, I could see no enemy, and so
didn't fire my pistol. But the men
all about me were blazing away into
the woods from which the Jap firing
was coming. They didn't seem to
be getting results, so I decided to
continue to my appointment. The
Jap bullets were snapping all about,
but by stooping low and running
across open stretches, I got past the
sniper-infested area. Saw a provision truck, and borrowed some
canned rations. Then walked about

November 10, 1942. A Japanese dugout
west of the Matanikau River.

another two miles to Point Cruz. The man I was supposed to meet was
not there, so I chose a spot where the odor of rotting Japs was not too
strong, and I opened and ate the contents of the canned rations. Then I
up and walked about 3 miles westward until I was told by a "forward
observer" officer, shielded behind a tree, that I had reached the furthest
edge of the front lines—that there was nothing but Japs ahead. There wasn't
much exciting happening at the moment, so I to the beach and lay in the
sand, watching the crystal-clear water breaking on the white coral beach
sand, and keeping a wary eye open for Jap snipers, as I was right up the
front. At 1500 I arose. The 164th Army troops were falling back to where
I was, in order to establish a defense line for the night. They were setting
up machine guns, and occupying foxholes that the Japs had dug. I started
back, and walked about 4 miles to the Matanikau River bridge before I got
rides back to camp.

November 11, 1942 Wednesday

Heard of an aviation unit that was doing photo developing work, so with Pvt. Lawrence Ashman of the R-2 Section (a combat photographer) to their office and obtained permission to use their dark rooms. Ashman developed 8 rolls of film for me, some of which were exposed 3 months ago. He did a poor job, and I had to wait a very long time for the film to dry in the muggy weather. While waiting, I saw an air raid by 26 Jap bombers. It was a beautiful sight to see them coming over in formation, and the pattern of the 90mm guns. I was in an open space and had an excellent view of the whole affair. I was very disappointed at not having my camera with me at the time. Back to the Battery, and much mail has come in. Sorted and distributed it to the various units. I received several letters from different people back home. After supper a report got about that a Jap task force, the largest in Jap history, composed of about 80 ships, was headed this way. Everybody felt very depressed. The Marines in the east flank have cleared up the Japs they had surrounded, and they were being drawn back. It was supposed that some of the Japs got away. In the west, our forces were drawn back about 4 miles to the Matanikau River again, and they were digging in all over the island should the Jap task force arrive. The amphibian tractor men had their machine guns packed away in preparation for a quick getaway from this island should they be relieved; but today they broke them out again and set them up for action in what looms as a possible last ditch struggle if the Japs arrive.

November 12, 1942 Thursday

In the morning learned that there were 2 troop transports, 4 cargo ships, and 16 fighting ships of ours in the harbor. More mail came in. There was a report in the morning that 4 waves of bombers had been headed this way, but had been intercepted by some of our carriers. At about 1300 there was an air raid by 16 Jap planes, 15 of which were shot down. Distributed a lot more mail today. Several new planes were added to our force today, including eight P-38s. Early in the morning there had been some heavy shelling somewhere at a great distance. About 1100 a big Jap gun fired a shot at one of the ships in the harbor; and our destroyers and cruisers opened up on the Jap positions and shelled them for several hours.

November 13, 1942 Friday

At 0120 the air raid alarm was sounded. I dressed and sat around. The sky was lit with flashes, as though a great naval battle was in progress, but I could hear no bombing. The ground shuddered several times, as though depth charges were being exploded. A plane came over and dropped an orange flare in the west. At about 0245 the "all clear" was sounded, and I back to bed. In the morning our planes were very active, taking off with bombs and torpedoes, and returning empty. Finally got a report on what was occurring. There had been a big naval battle a short distance away. However, a later report stated that 2 Jap aircraft carriers had been hit with no report as to what resulted from the hits; one battleship had been hit and was now burning a short distance off Savo Island; our torpedo planes had put a torpedo into another Jap battleship and had crippled it so that it was making only 15 knots an hour, escorted by 3 Jap destroyers; 1 cruiser had been sunk; and one other ship had been sunk so rapidly that its class had not been determined. One of our destroyers was reported burning. Our planes kept up a ceaseless activity all day long. The ground shook a couple of times, as though from explosions out at sea. I spent most of the day sorting out the mail that has been delivered in the last couple of days. I received 12 letters and a package of film from Bess. Learned that her brother Bill, the physician, had been recalled to the service with the rank of Major. Also, that an elderly aunt of mine had remarried. It began to rain in the evening, as it has done for the past several days. The rainy season will soon be here.

November 14, 1942 Saturday
Guadalcanal

At about 0130 I was awakened by a burst of shellfire. I gave the alarm; and we all dressed and to our shelters. The rain had stopped. The shelling continued steadily until about 0200. The shells didn't fall in our immediate vicinity but I could hear the fragments screaming through the air. In the morning learned that about 3 cruisers had attacked us. A notice on the bulletin board said that 2 torpedoes, and possibly a third, had hit on the Jap cruisers; and that two 1,000-pound bombs had hit another cruiser; and that both were sinking. In the afternoon an emergency gas mask inspection was ordered. Word passed around that a Jap task force, which included 12 troop transports, was headed this way, and due to arrive at 2000. Extra ammunition was passed out. Spirits dropped low, and there was a marked loss of appetite at supper. The officers seemed fairly cheerful. I passed Gen del Valle's tent, and he called to me and gave me a can of beer which he had managed to make cold somehow. Though I am not a drinking man, that beer was the most delicious thing I have had for a long time. A detail from our Battery was sent to reinforce the Special Weapons Battery defense lines for the night. Adjacent units also set up defensive measures for whatever might happen tonight. All the normally non-combat troops (cooks, clerks, vehicle operators, etc.) were ordered out and assigned defensive responsibilities and placed in the perimeter defense in anticipation of a big Jap offensive tonight by the troops of the approaching Jap task force. Our planes were kept busy all day shuttling back and forth. Several planes from the carrier *Enterprise* landed on our field after dropping their bombs on enemy vessels. At 1900 Capt. Harris passed on to me the following information, which he said Gen. del Valle had secured from Division: Of the 12 transports that had started with the Jap forces, 1 had been hit; 1 had been sunk; 2 had been hit so badly that they were unable to move; 3 were burning and stopped; 5 were smoking from hits; and 1 was unaccounted for. I to our lines and passed this news on to our men, upon whom it had a very cheering effect. It was a bright moonlight night, the first in several nights. This is in our favor, as our planes can get on and off the Island unhampered by mud. I took most of my clothes off and lay down to get some rest before what promised to be a very hectic night. At 2325 I was awakened by very heavy firing out to sea. There was a naval engagement in progress. I heard reports that our ships were pursuing Jap vessels. To the Operations dugout, where I found Gen. del Valle, and he confirmed these reports. In the darkness I made my way to our lines and passed on this information to the men, who had been wondering what the shooting was about. The news that we were the aggressors, and that our navy and air force were doing so much to intercept the enemy and keep them from activities against our lines, made them very happy. Left them on watch, and I back to bed.

November 15, 1942 Sunday
    Slept the rest of the night through without incident. In the morning heard that 5 Jap light cruisers had been sunk by planes from the Enterprise, and that we had lost no planes in this operation. It was also reported that the Jap fighting ships accompanying the task force that had been on its way to this Island, had left the transports behind and had gone off. It was also reported that 4 Jap transports had landed this morning on the western end of the Island. Our planes worked hard all day, bombing the Jap transports that landed, and the troops from them. Our artillery did some shelling of the Japs on the Island also, and the 155s hit several shells into the transports. I wrote a long letter to Bess. Stayed around the office all day. I have several magazines, that arrived on the last mail shipment, that I am reading. Also, there were several old newspapers that were available. To bed early tonight.

November 16, 1942 Monday
Guadalcanal
    A comparatively quiet day. Yesterday there had been 2 air raid alarms, but today there were none. During last night our artillery had kept up a

Top: Japanese battleship *Hiei*, abandoned and scuttled on November 15, 1942, after sustaining severe damage in the Naval Battle of Guadalcanal, November 13–15, 1942. (Imperial War Museum, courtesy of William H. Bartsch.) *Bottom:* Japanese troopship *Yamazuki Maru*, beached in Doma Cove, Guadalcanal, after having been bombed and strafed during the Naval Battle of Guadalcanal, November 13–15, 1942. (National Archives 127-N-53412.)

constant harassing fire against the Japs to the west. This was continued during the day. It was a cloudy day, and it rained a couple of times. The roads are getting very muddy. Wrote a letter to Glen (?). Spent most of the day reading.

November 17, 1942 Tuesday

Received several letters addressed to Bove, so in the morning up to his quarters. We had a long talk about our correspondents. We have received news from Newark that the Postmaster has not been re-nominated, for which I am glad, as I never liked him or his autocratic ways. While there, I visited Jasinski, who has come back from his position near the Matanikau River. He has reclaimed his radio set. He gave me a Reising gun, and I let him keep the storage batteries. In the afternoon I tried to get my movie camera exposure meter exchanged for a still camera exposure meter, but without success. Did a lot of reading during the day. Not much of a military nature going on. We shell the Jap positions sporadically day and night for harassing effect. The two sides are counting losses in the recent naval battle, and the Japs are making extravagant claims as to the damage they have inflicted on our navy.

November 18, 1942 Wednesday

In the morning cleaned up the Reising gun which I had obtained from Jasinski. In the afternoon did some laundry. There is a different paymaster on the post, so I polled my Battery as to how much money they want to draw — up to $25. To the pay office and got some sheets to use as SMR (Special Money Request) forms. The day was without significant military incident. In the morning a large concentration of heavy planes left this Island on some mission about which I could get no details, except that we lost 1 Flying Fortress during the operations. The local news bulletin carried a dispatch from Washington on the action during the night of 13-14 November, and the day of the 14th. It listed the following Jap losses: 1 Jap battleship sunk; also sunk were 3 heavy cruisers, 2 light cruisers, 5 destroyers, 8 transports loaded with Jap troops, and 4 cargo transports. Besides this, they damaged 1 Jap battleship and 6 destroyers. Losses on our side were 2 light cruisers and 6 destroyers. Enemy casualties were estimated as over 10,000 men.

November 19, 1942 Thursday

Today's news bulletin estimated the number of Jap troops downed in the naval engagements of the past few days as 24,000. That is quite a big job of fighting that we have been saved. Spent the day making up the Special

Money Request and getting it signed. The days pass very quickly here. Our troops in the west are again advancing past the Matanikau River and pushing the Japs westward along the beach. I guess the Japs cling to the north coast so as to have a place of entry for supplies and reinforcements. Otherwise, it would seem that the hills inland offered the greatest security for their numerically inferior forces. It rained again tonight.

November 20, 1942 Friday
Guadalcanal
     In the morning I took the Special Money Requisition to the Division Paymaster and arranged for the money to be picked up Sunday. While out, I tested the Reising gun that Jasinski had given me, and it fires well enough, but when I manipulated the cocking device it sometimes jammed. So back to my office and "detail-stripped" the gun and fixed a certain piece on it, and now the gun does not malfunction. There are some very strong indications that we may move out of here soon. The Police Section (maintenance unit) was told to submit a list of property boxes by size and weight; certain units in the vicinity are packing their gear; rumor has it that the Quartermaster is preparing to move; etc. I sure hope that the signs are correct this time. A commendation from the Commander, South Pacific Force and Area, Admiral Halsey, was published to the men who were engaged in the operations of the last few days. In my opinion, the Navy is especially to be commended for its fine, brave and excellent work. They engaged a tough and numerically superior enemy with courage and vigor, and won a notable victory. They have the honor, respect and gratitude of all of us here.

November 21, 1942 Saturday
     At daybreak the Japs west of the Matanikau were subjected to a fierce bombing and shelling by planes and artillery. Soon after breakfast I out for the front lines. Did much walking to get there. We are pushing forward (westward) strongly, with the Army units in front and the Marines holding the secondary positions. I crossed the Matanikau about 300 yards up from the mouth. Had a tough time in the jungles back from the beach. The Japs are inland about a mile, among the foothills. I did some steep climbing. In passing along one ridge, the Japs shelled a passing Jeep truck, and the shell landed about 50 yards away. While there, three more shells landed uncomfortably close. They were all small calibre — about 37mm, I think. There didn't seem to be any definite front line. I was quite tired and all alone. It was well past noon, and I had been traveling continuously in the heat of the sun without food or drink since morning. So I turned back and made my way back to camp. It rained in the evening. To bed early.

November 22, 1942 Sunday

A hot, sunny day. Washed some clothes in the morning and got cleaned up. The Battery Commander went to the Division Pay Office for our payroll, and at 1030 we paid the Battery. I spent most of the day reading some of Joseph Conrad's works. In the west the Army troops were still pushing the Japs back slowly. Signs are increasing everywhere that we will be relieved from this Island soon. I hope so.

November 23, 1942 Monday

Shortly after 0600 all the available artillery opened up a heavy bombardment of the Jap positions in the west. Spent the day just puttering about. After supper sat in a card game in a blacked-out tent, and was not very lucky. To bed at the very late (for me) hour of 0930.

November 24, 1942 Tuesday

A hot, sunny day. Did a lot of paper work. It is now definite that we are soon to be relieved. The forward echelon is already being selected. I expect to be out of here inside of two weeks. There are all sorts of rumors as to our destination and future activities. The fighting in the west is progressing slowly. I am starting to get my things together in preparation for departure. In the evening I played cards again for a couple of hours, quitting when I was even.

November 25, 1942 Wednesday
Guadalcanal

Another hot, sunny day. The weather has been exceptionally nice the last few days. Our sleep was disturbed during the early morning hours for the first time in quite a while. At 0230 a verbal alarm was given, and an unknown number of enemy aircraft came over and dropped some bombs in the vicinity of the airfield. Our Battery was not affected, and we soon back to bed. But at 0400 we were again awakened by (4 or 5 illegible words). A single plane flew overhead, but I observed no bombing. (4 or 5 illegible words) my stuff and puttering about the office. Only slight activity in the west.

November 26, 1942 Thursday

Thanksgiving Day. Again we had early morning callers. At 0305 the air raid alarm was sounded. Some planes came over, but no bombs were dropped in our area. At 0435 the "all clear" was sounded, and I back to bed until 0700. This broken sleep is bad. It gets quite chilly in the morning hours, and the men get out of their warm bunks in a hurry. There are several colds in the Battery despite the fact that it gets so warm during the day that one sweats profusely even when most lightly clad. It is getting hotter here all the time, it seems. But I am not complaining. I am very glad that I am not one of the infantry, who have to sleep in foxholes with the ever present danger of the Japs to disturb my slumbers. The men in the west are sure having it tough, especially in rainy weather. But tougher than their lot is that of the Japs, who are doomed. They are being surrounded by our troops, and I expect a big push to drive them out any day. I spent most of the day playing poker, with only slight loss.

November 27, 1942 Friday

The third successive morning Jap bombing craft got us up. Today they came at 0340, and they dropped their bombs closer to my present position than ever before, but still a good distance away. The "all clear" was sounded at 0415. Borrowed a typewriter and worked all day with my clerk getting out rosters and warrants for the promotion of 12 communication men. In the evening played black jack for a short time and won $6. The forward echelon has not yet left, and it looks as though my Battery will not be relieved until late next month.

November 28, 1942 Saturday

Again the air raid alarm awoke us in the early morning hours, this time at 0225. There was much activity by our aircraft, but I was not aware of any Jap planes. The alert lasted until 0415, after which I went back to bed again. The situation in the west remains the same; we are slowly whittling away at the Jap forces, and making slight gains of ground. The Japs must be pretty well dug in. Today's news bulletin carried items about the slowing down of the United Nations drives at Buna in New Guinea, and in Northern Africa. The Russians are still developing their offensive on the Stalingrad front, and opening up a new one in the Moscow sector. The news also said that it was a single plane that bombed this Island on the 25th, and that there were some personnel casualties. A small item that may have large consequences stated that Spain is calling up 4 classes of men for military duty. A previous report had stated that Spain would join forces with the enemies of any country that attacked her. I spent a quiet day. I am slowly getting things ready to leave this Island.

November 29, 1942 Sunday

Again awakened at 0330 by Jap bombers. I heard 8 explosions, and they sounded like 500-pound bombs at quite a distance. "All clear" at 0355.

Japanese Model 92 (1932) 105-mm cannon used by "Pistol Pete" to shell Henderson Field, seized in November 1942 during drive on Kokumbona. (National Archives 127-N-53489.)

At breakfast the ground shook and rocked, as though several depth charges had been exploded in the harbor. The rest of the day was uneventful. Spent most of the day reading magazines.

November 30, 1942 Monday
Guadalcanal
　　For the first time in almost a week there was no early morning air raid by the Japs. After breakfast I set out to get some pictures. As I passed the bomb dump I was horrified to see a 1,000-pound bomb roll off a truck and fall on the ground about 25 yards from me. I expected a tremendous blast to blow me into eternity, but nothing happened. The fuse had not been set into the bomb. I took several pictures of the bomb dump, and then proceeded to the beach. The supply ship *Alciba* has been afire for the last 3 days. Some reports say that it was struck by a torpedo, and others say it was spontaneous combustion. The fire was confined to one hold, and most of the cargo had been unloaded. They were still unloading her today. I got

a ride on a large ramp boat, and took some pictures of the burning ship. It began to get dark and cloudy, and by the time I got back to my office it had started to rain. It rained all afternoon and evening. Right after supper word got around that a large convoy of Jap ships was headed this way. There were supposed to be 8 troop transports and numerous destroyers. Everybody's spirits dropped, and anxiety and disappointment took hold. This may delay considerably (permanently for some) the date of our leaving this Island. I got into a black jack game to take my mind off the matter and won $15 by 2030, when I retired. At 2330 I was awakened and told to get the Battery up and on the alert, as Jap ships were approaching. The air raid alarm was sounded soon after. I got the Battery up and had them check their weapons, helmets and gas masks, and fill their canteens. From way out at sea to the north could be seen almost continuous flashes as our Navy engaged the oncoming Jap fleet. They were so far off that no sound of the battle reached us—only the flashes. We "stood to" until 0110 of the following morning, Tuesday.

December 1, 1942 Tuesday

The "all clear" signal for the air raid alarm (which had started at 2330 last night) was sounded at 0110. During this period I had observed no bombing or noticed any hostile aircraft. The Battery Commander came down and told me I could secure the Battery, as our Navy was engaging the enemy. Back to bed; but at 0415 the air raid alarm was again sounded. I could hear what sounded like a single plane passing overhead to the east, and then returning. It made another trip at about 0500. During both trips the 90mm guns sent up about 15 shells, but I doubt if they made any hits. It was getting light by this time, so I stayed up. The galley fires for breakfast were not started until 0545, at which time our planes were taking off from the airfield and it was quite light. I felt very proud and fond of our Navy. Again they had saved us from a nasty mess. Tradition may hold that there exists animosity between Marines and the Navy, but all the Leathernecks on this Island have respect and admiration for them. They sure have been in there punching, taking some hard blows and saving us from much trouble. Admiral Halsey is my candidate for Secretary of the Navy. He sure is a (3 or 4 illegible words). He is one of the heroes of the men here. The men have little (1 or 2 illegible words) Gen McArthur. The latter is the butt of sarcastic remarks. The men seem to think that he protects himself too much, and his nickname is "Dugout Doug." I got into a card game and played all day, at one time being a loser of $18; but I recouped it all and finished $5 to the good.

December 2, 1942 Wednesday

Had a most restful and undisturbed night's sleep. Cleaned up some paper work in the morning. Bove came over for a visit. He is trying to get transferred to a Naval mail job. The Post Office Department is commissioning several officers for mail duty in the various branches of the service. I sure would like to see him get the position — I might try to get in there and get a commission that way. In the afternoon was visited by Jasinski. He had been stationed near the Matanikau River for a while, but was now back at his camp area. The Army is taking over the battle west of the Matanikau, and they are progressing very slowly. Jasinski thinks that our artillery may be called upon for some assistance. Played poker all afternoon and evening (it takes the players' minds off the desperateness of our situation), winning about $2. It rained all afternoon. Rumors are beginning to drift in about the results of the naval battle about 2 days ago. Again the Jap navy suffered a severe blow. Figures on the losses varied considerably; but whatever the figures are, the Jap losses are heavy. The figures will soon be published in the local press news.

December 3, 1942 Thursday
Guadalcanal

Spent the morning cleaning up my paper work. In the afternoon played cards until supper, making some money. After supper back to the poker game, and was losing slightly by 2230. At that time a sentry came in and told us to douse our lights and prepare for an "alert." The Battery Commander called me on the phone and told me to get the police section up and armed; and that he would send the R-3 Section to join them, and they were all to report to Special Weapons Battery to help reinforce the secondary defense lines. (Normally police, cooks, clerks, etc., were not used for combat; only under extreme conditions were they placed in the firing lines.) It seemed that reports had been received that several Jap warships were heading this way. I got the men together, checked their weapons and helmets, and sent them over to Special Weapons. The air raid alarm sounded. Our planes were active. I undressed and went to bed. (I wanted to be as well rested as possible for what promised to be an arduous night.) The air raid alarm was soon secured. The men on the defensive lines were shown their positions, and then dismissed and told to go to bed, but to be ready to take up their positions at a moments' notice. Word was received that our Navy was engaging the enemy, and that our planes had made contact with them.

December 4, 1942 Friday

Busy in the office in the morning. After lunch, Jasinski came around in a Jeep and invited me to go up to the front lines with him. I went up,

Mitsubishi G4M1 "Betty" bombers heading to Guadalcanal from Rabaul on an attack mission in late 1942. (Courtesy of William H. Bartsch.)

and the Army is in position about a mile past Point Cruz. They are not making much headway, and there is only patrol and artillery activity. The Japs are sending over some fairly heavy mortar fire. It started to rain while we were up there. We started back, stopping off at a 155mm gun emplacement manned by the Army. Got back to the Battery in time for supper. Bove called me and told me he was stationed on the beach again, and invited me to visit him. I played poker again until midnight, winning about $30. I have recouped all my losses and I am about $60 ahead of the game. The rain continued during the evening, and I had forgotten to take in my blankets. When I quit the game, they were wet and I had to go to bed without them. The Army 155s shelled the Japs during the night.

December 5, 1942 Saturday

A sunny day, and my blankets dried out quickly. In the morning did some paper work and took a nap. In the afternoon played poker and won $27 more. This is far and away the most I have ever won at cards. I have put away $150 to send to Bess as soon as I get to Wellington, N.Z. In a military sense, the day was quiet. The Japs to the west were shelled again, the Marines and Army sent out patrols, rumors were strong that a Marine Raider Battalion had finally surrounded and destroyed the big Jap gun that had been giving us so much trouble, and which had accounted for a number of casualties. There were several ships in the harbor. Word filtered through that Gen. del Valle stated that there were 5 battleships and 4 aircraft carriers in the vicinity of ours. This would indicate either that a large convoy of our troops was coming in, or that trouble with Jap naval units was expected. The forward echelon is still on the Island.

December 6, 1942 Sunday
Guadalcanal
Was busy in the morning with paper work. Had intended visiting Bove, but somehow just didn't get around to it. We received more free cigarettes, which I distributed. Much of our post exchange supplies while on this Island have been issued free to the men. In the afternoon, and up until 2230, I played poker, winning almost $50. In the last few days I have won about $200. This is too much for me to have about, and I am going to send some home to Bess before I lose it back at cards.

December 7, 1942 Monday
Spent the morning trying to get a Postal Money Order to send some of my money home to Bess, but was unsuccessful. Finally was able to get a Government check for $150. In the afternoon I washed clothes and paid a visit to Bove. This is the first afternoon in several days that I have not played cards. Found Bove well, and we talked for quite a while. Then I back to the Battery and had supper. After supper I played cards until 2200, winning $40 more. All day today, which is the anniversary of the attack on Pearl Harbor that started us in the war, our artillery pounded the Japs in the west. The 70mm howitzers in this regiment were pretty well worn; and today they expended so many rounds that they completed the wearing-out of their tubes (barrels). Besides this, the 105s and the 155s sent many a round to the Japs. The Japs were active, too. A submarine came to the surface in the harbor and sent another torpedo into the already damaged *Alciba*, making it necessary to beach her. The Island was rocked with depth charges; and when I visited Bove, I saw seven of our warships patrolling about the harbor.

December 8, 1942 Tuesday
Up and heard rumors that a Jap naval force had been engaged by our forces last night. Also, that the planes I heard taking off about 0500 this morning were going out to try to contact this enemy force. Other rumors are that Gen. del Valle is leaving us to go to Honolulu. If this is true, it might mean that we also might follow him there, and then on back to the U.S. I sure hope this comes to pass, for I would like very much to see my

wife again; and also my father, who is not very well, and is on in years. Did office work in the morning, played cards in the afternoon and won $6. In the evening I played again until 2230, having miserable luck and losing about $40. I wrote a letter to Bess, and enclosed the check for $150 of my winnings with it, as a Christmas gift for her. That is a sum I will not lose back to the poker game. I still have money to bankroll my playing.

December 9, 1942 Wednesday

Up, and after getting out my morning reports I took my camera and to "P" Battery, 5th Marines. There, after much delay, I took some pictures of the guns of the Battery. Had a light lunch there also. Back to my Battery in the afternoon and found a letter from Bess. The forward echelon finally left today. It is now said that they are going to Brisbane, Australia. There were 2 air raid alarms in the afternoon, but no bombing was observed (by me). I have stopped eating at the mess-hall for the last two days, and am living on the fruit cake sent to me by Glen (?). In the evening played cards again, with my normal good fortune, and won about $40 — almost as much as I had lost yesterday. It began to rain at nightfall, and it poured rain. At 2100 I was called on the phone and told to see that all lights were out in the Battery area. That broke up the card game. I got drenched inspecting the Battery in the rain.

December 10, 1942 Thursday

At 0240 the air raid alarm sounded. It had stopped raining, but it was quite dark. I dressed and could hear a plane coming overhead to the east, and after a while, returning. It made another trip across our position. I lay dressed in my bunk for about an hour, then undressed and back to sleep. In the morning learned that it had been our plane. Was kept busy in the office all morning. Received word that I am to prepare 25 rosters by tomorrow noon, indicating that we are to embark soon. All sorts of rumors are floating about. Visited the cemetery today and took some pictures. Played poker in the evening and lost $25. It began raining at 2100, and it rained all night.

December 11, 1942 Friday

Lt. (j.g.) James J. Fitzgerald joined us as Regimental Chaplain. He is a Catholic. He is a much younger man than Chaplain Dittmar (Protestant) was, and does not have the latter's suavity and charm. The new Chaplain fought with (accompanied) the paratroopers when they landed on Tulagi Island, and for his bravery under fire was made an honorary paratrooper. Worked on my embarkation rosters all morning (no photocopying equipment available, rosters had to be typed in batches). In the afternoon took some very good shots of various types of planes on the airfield. Visited Jasinski and took a picture of a heavily bearded member of his Battery. In the evening played poker and won $30. The 3rd Defense Battalion received several thousand cases of beer, and as they are leaving soon, they are trying to get rid of it. They adjoin us, and all day the road was jammed with trucks carting the stuff away at $3.60 per case.

December 12, 1942 Saturday
There had been much puking during the night from the over-enthusiastic beer drinkers. I had been too busy to indulge. I had been offered several bottles, but I had refused them. In the morning visited Bove. There are several ships in the harbor, among them the *American Legion*. The ship that is to take us off was not here yet. There are reports that about 12 destroyers of the enemy were in the vicinity, and that our PT boats had sunk 3 of them, with a loss of 2 of our boats. Began packing my stuff in preparation for leaving. Some of our boxes were moved down to the beach. There was no card game tonight, as the Army is moving in and taking over our area. At 2220 the air raid alarm sounded. The searchlights picked out a single enemy bomber. Though probably blinded, the plane dropped several bombs, none of them near our position. The "all clear" signal was given at 2255, and we all wearily back to bed.

December 13, 1942 Sunday
The new Chaplain (Fitzgerald) held an elaborate Mass at 0630 that lasted for more than a half hour. The Army took over the rest of the facilities here, and are now in charge of communications, operations, messing, etc. More Army units moved in. The Marines continued packing and moving their gear down to the beach. Some first class mail came in and was distributed. I received 2 very nice letters from Bess, and 1 from Max Gelfond. In the latter, Max told me that Bill Kuntze, my boss in civilian life, is now a lieutenant (I guess it is in the Army). Played cards in the evening, and won $10. Just as I was about to go to bed the air raid alarm was sounded at 2140. A single plane came over, and after a while the lights picked him up. The 90 mm guns opened fire and it was quite a sight to see the plane like a silver moth in the lights, with the bursting shells all about it. The plane was not hit, but the lights and firing drove it off. It returned again in a short while, and this time the lights could not find it and it dropped several bombs, none of them near my position. "All clear" at 2340.

December 14, 1942 Monday
The Army is feeding us today, as we have secured our mess facilities. In the morning took a trip to the beach, and there are many of our ships in the harbor, including the *Hunter Liggett*. The beach is swarming with men arriving and unloading ships; and with others loading ships in preparation for departure. In the afternoon we sent most of the rest of our gear to the beach, made up our packs, and policed the area. In the evening the Army units stationed here set up their band and gave a much-appreciated concert. Most of the men were on the beach loading the ship, and they stayed there for tonight. The rest of us slept wherever we could find unoccupied space that the Army units were not using.

December 15, 1942 Tuesday
Abd USS Hunter Ligget *at sea — bound for Brisbane*
At 0800 the Battery and the rest of our gear started moving to the beach. I took several pictures of the beach and the *Hunter Liggett*. The

A Marine Grumman F4F-4 Wildcat landing on Guadalcanal in December 1942. (National Archives 111-SC-50898.)

morning was spent in getting the guns, trucks, and gear aboard. I ate on the beach —canned rations. Shortly after noon we were all loaded, and the troops embarked. We moved right out, traveling at a good rate of speed. Got my men bedded down. The ship is overloaded by more than 300 extra men; and over 40 men from my Battery do not have bunks. These men sleep on the deck in any space they can find. I got life jackets for all the men. Just at nightfall the ship was shaken by depth charges. Soon after, "general quarters" was sounded, and we all donned life jackets and stood by, while the convoying destroyers released several more depth charges. After about 20 minutes the "general quarters" was secured, and I to bed. The compartment to which I am assigned is reserved for the first 2 pay grades only. It is very hot and the bunk is a very uncomfortable one. I spent a wretched night, but was thankful that I did not have to sleep where the lower pay grades slept, or on the hard deck.

CHAPTER 3

Australia and Cape Gloucester
December 16, 1942–February 7, 1944

December 16, 1942 Wednesday
Abd USS Hunter Ligget *at sea — bound for Brisbane*

Glad when dawn came and I was able to get out of my bunk. Had a good breakfast. Mustered the Battery and issued them 10 quinine pills each. This will be a daily ration for several days. In the morning there was an alert when a plane was observed, but it was secured when the plane was identified as friendly. We passed a convoy of several ships headed in the opposite direction to ours. We are traveling in a southwesterly direction. The quinine pills we are taking are making everybody dizzy. My head is ringing and my hearing is impaired. The meals are good. I played cards in the afternoon and evening, losing $37. To bed at 2200 and slept well.

December 17, 1942 Thursday
Abd USS Hunter Ligget *at sea — bound for Brisbane*

It had rained heavily during the night. We drew 10 more quinine pills today. (This regimen was intended to rid the Marines of any latent malaria.) There is a constant bitter taste of these pills in my mouth. The weather seems to be getting cooler. I played cards again, and lost all the rest of the money I had on hand. Before retiring, I took a shower. Fresh water is available at all hours on this trip.

December 18, 1942 Friday
Abd USS Hunter Ligget *at sea — bound for Brisbane*

The weather had been pretty rough during the night, and the seas had pounded the hull all night long. There was a stiff breeze blowing in the morning that sent the spray away up to the upper decks. We drew 10 more quinine pills today. These pills contain 3 grains of quinine each. The combination of pills and rolling seas is making everybody feel bad. I took a look about in the morning. Besides our ship, there was the *American Legion*, sister ship of the *Hunter Liggett*, and 2 destroyers for escort. Our Battery furnished the working parties for today. There were 36 privates and PFCs; and 4 corporals. They cleaned the heads (toilets) and decks, and painted boats. I took things easy today. We had ice cream for supper dessert tonight. The meals are excellent. There are strong rumors that we will dock tomorrow at Sidney, Australia.

December 19, 1942 Saturday
at sea — Brisbane

About 0930 we came in sight of land. It was Brisbane, Australia. The harbor is a bit shallow for the *Hunter Liggett*, and we had to wait for a high tide. We moved around the Barrier Reef at the mouth of the harbor and up to where it narrowed to what seemed a river. A tugboat helped swing us around facing down river, and warped us into a dock beside some warehouses. It was growing dusk. The men aboard ship had a great time, and were singing and whistling and shouting ribald remarks. They cheered lustily when they saw a billboard advertising beer. They shouted and halooed and waved handkerchiefs to all the girls they could barely see in the distance. These were the first girls seen since leaving New Zealand last July — 5 months ago. Brisbane is very flat near the harbor. There are mountains in the distance. We saw some queerly shaped hills just before entering the harbor. As we tied up at the wharf a group of Army Military Police stationed themselves along the pier so that no Marines could go over the side for unauthorized liberty. As the ship is due to leave immediately after unloading, the crew was given liberty. I played cards until 2400, winning $5. Shaved and cleaned up, got my gear together, and to bed.

December 20, 1942 Sunday
Camp Cable, Brisbane, Australia

Had breakfast and collected all my gear. The units began debarking. I formed the Battery on the pier, and we marched off. We were watched like criminals. We had to march between two lines of MPs (military police) to waiting trucks. We were set aboard these trucks and they started off at

a fast pace. The town of Brisbane is a sprawling place. I didn't notice any
high buildings. We soon cleared the town and passed through some farms
and ranches. Then we began hitting into land covered with scrub trees.
Finally, 40 miles from our starting point, we reached our camp. It is very
crude, with few facilities. It is in a sandy, scrub forest, and just buzzing
with mosquitoes. Much of the bark on the trees has been burnt, and the
place is full of soot, as in Verona at the New River, North Carolina camp.
We have showers, water for which is supplied from a tank that is filled daily
by a tank truck. The messing facilities are already installed. We live in
tents. This used to be an Army camp.

December 21, 1942 Monday
Camp Cable, Brisbane, Australia
   Spent the day securing the camp. I set up my office in an isolated
tent. All the boxes containing my office gear came in. I found my seabag,
which I had given up as lost. It contained much pressed khaki clothes. I
was very glad to see this bag again. All my desks and stationery boxes came
in also. There is an appalling amount of work for me to catch up with. The
food is good and plentiful so far, and I am reveling in fresh fruit and delicious cold milk. This is the first fresh milk since leaving New Zealand last
July. The mosquitoes are awful here. They bite right through our heavy
utility clothes. Several of the men have seen kangaroos in the vicinity.

December 30, 1942 Wednesday
Brisbane, Australia
   It rained all morning. There seems to be more rain than in Wellington. Reports came back that some of the roads were washed out. There was
difficulty getting a truck to haul us to town. Finally, after 1000 I obtained
a big covered truck, and we off on the 40-odd miles to Brisbane. Tried to
get accommodations at several hotels, but everything is absolutely snapped
up. The hotels are all filled, as are the boarding houses. The agencies in
town who have that responsibility are trying to place the overflow in private homes. The hotels have beds set up in corridors and on porches. I to
the Red Cross and arranged to get sleeping space on their ballroom floor.
Checked my bag and out to get something to eat. I could find no "fish and
chips" places in this town. The restaurants are definitely second class; and
in fact the whole town is like some hick city in the hinterland of the United
States, although this is the third largest city in Australia. By comparison,
Wellington is much more urban. I found that at none of the restaurants
and cafes that I visited do they serve napkins. All the store fronts on the
main street have hanging canopies that reach to the street and cover the

sidewalks. When I first saw these as I came into town when we arrived it puzzled me. But now I know. It is to shelter the people from the almost continuous rain. The natives seem not to mind the rain very much. The town is full of uniformed people, both male and female. Even most of the people in civilian dress carry some badge or insignia denoting service of some kind. I to the Kodak agency to try to get some film, but was unsuccessful; nor could I get two other articles that I inquired about. Photographic material is in short supply. This Kodak store does a large volume of business, however, despite the film rationing. To a barber shop and had my hair trimmed. Visited a newsreel theatre to see some pictures of Guadalcanal, and caught up with other events. The news at this theatre seemed much older than that which I had been accustomed to see in the U.S.A. These theatres do not provide such up-to-the-minute features. In the evening there was a dance at the Red Cross building. I watched for a while, then went out to a public dance hall called the Trocadero. The dancing here was more modern, and a good many of the younger set go in for this "jitterbug" stuff. They had quite a novel cooling system by means of huge fans that I thought very practical. Stayed there a while looking on, then back to the Red Cross to learn that the Army had failed to provide them with cots, and so there were no accommodations for us. We were offered bunks at a camp about four miles from town, but I was reluctant to leave town and go out in the suburbs again. I had been too long removed from normal human (civilian) company. So I stretched out on a chair in the game room and spent the night with all my clothes on, happy in the knowledge that all about me was a big city full of all sorts of civilian people, and no hostile Japs.

December 31, 1942 Thursday
Brisbane, Australia
Up in the morning and took a shower at one of the numerous servicemen's organizations. After breakfast to meet a fellow I had run into yesterday, who had to return to camp today. I arranged to take over his bed tonight. It is on the porch of the Grosvenor Hotel, and looks fairly clean. After some slight shopping chores, had lunch. Took my G.I. issue shirts and trousers to a tailor and left them to be cut down to fit me. Out, and while walking about town fell in with a drunken Marine and his two Australian friends. We had a few more beers together, I paying for most of them. The Aussies are good "chiselers." They are a big, robust race; and at first it was startling to see them going about in shorts—big six-footers and broad in the beam. But inside those shorts there are no "boy scout" sissies. I saw one of the men who had been at Tobruk, and he had a terribly

wounded arm. The Americans are making it tough for the natives. The Americans have accumulated so much money, and they are so free with it that many of the shopkeepers are taking advantage of their ignorance of the local money system and overcharging them. Many shopkeepers are refusing to sell to the Aussies, and sell the scarce goods only to the Marines for much higher prices than they can get from the natives. One man complained to me that at a certain place he could not get any whiskey because the proprietor was saving his limited supply to sell to Americans at exorbitant prices. Normally, however, prices are about two-thirds of what they are in the United States. At none of the restaurants that I visited did they serve napkins. All the main streets have big air raid shelters built on them, and all the walls are plastered with signs directing to air raid shelters. A number of the buildings are sandbagged against air attack. At night there is a partial blackout, which here is called a "brown-out" or "dim-out." Auto lights are hooded; and traffic lights are covered with only a slit left open. I dropped into a movie to pass a couple of hours in resting, having not had much sleep last night. Then out and to a dance hall called the Coconut Grove. There were many people there, this being New Years Eve. I left early and walked about town, observing the people, the architecture, and the customs. There was none of the hysteria that is prevalent in New York on New Year's Eve. The people were a trifle more animated than usual, and the Americans were running around trying to find where the New Year's celebrations were most hectic, but they were not finding much. It stopped raining, and the park on Adelaide Street was full of service men with their girls waiting for the advent of the New Year. I stopped off at a roadside wagon and had a bite to eat. Then to the Red Cross where I picked up my bag and to my bed dog-tired.

January 8, 1943 Friday
Abd USS West Point, *anchored off Brisbane*
    Shortly after midnight a ship came alongside the dock. Marines climbed aboard it until there was hardly room to stand. This ship started out, and I sat down on my pack on the deck and dozed. At 0300 we approached a ship which loomed up very large in the darkness. There were some lights showing on it, which surprised me, as I figured we were pretty far offshore and therefore in submarine territory. We went aboard this big ship, and in the night it seemed an enormous vessel. It is the *West Point*, the former *American*, now converted into a troopship operated by the Navy. We were assigned to bunks in a large compartment on C deck. I to sleep for about five hours, rising at 0830. My throat was very bad, and I was quite hoarse. The orders for reports and rosters began coming in. I

got the stuff out to them, despite the crowding and lack of facilities. Had breakfast. There will be only two meals per day aboard ship. The rumors are that between eight and nine thousand Marines will be embarked. Troops kept coming aboard all during the day. Loading of cargo also went on. I took a nap in the afternoon. At 2200 I to bed. The ship still had not left. It is rather warm aboard in the holds.

January 10, 1943 Sunday
Abd USS West Point, *bound for Melbourne, Aust.*

The Battery was again awakened shortly before midnight and sent up on a working party to unload personal gear from a ship alongside. They worked until about 0600 this morning. At about 0900 the ship moved out. We were accompanied by a destroyer on each side. Our ship has a cruising speed of 22 knots, and a top speed of 30 knots. We are cutting the water at quite a rate. This is the fastest troop ship I have been on. My headache continued to bother me. I spent the day between resting on my bunk and playing poker. I played until 2300, making about twenty pounds, or about fifty-five dollars. There is considerable sickness aboard ship, mostly malaria. Yesterday, a Marine died with malarial meningitis. Also, a Marine carrying a side of beef from the hold to the galley slipped and fell, and the side of beef landed on top of him. He suffered a fractured skull and internal injuries, and is not expected to live. He was bleeding profusely when carried off. I hope my headache leaves soon.

January 22, 1943 Friday
Ballarat, Victoria, Aust.

Learned that my clerk, when refused liberty yesterday, had gone to the Sergeant Major and requested permission to see the Adjutant to see if he could override me. I have stood for his laziness and his lack of knowledge (after all these months in the office he is still unable to make out the Ration Statement, Change Sheet, or Morning Report without help), but at this evidence of disloyalty I was thoroughly disgusted. As soon as I had an opportunity I cleared the office and told him to remove his belongings from the office — that he was no longer employed there. I told him to report to the police sergeant for duty. I will not miss him. It took me longer to explain how to do something than it would have taken if I did it myself. He never did anything unless I asked him to do it. I will try to get the battery clerk of Special Weapons Battery, which is about to be disbanded, transferred to my office. He appears to be a bright Italian lad with the rank of PFC, and he made a good record for himself with the rear echelon. Spent the rest of the day working at the office routine. The paper work is piling up. My desks have not yet arrived.

January 26, 1943 Tuesday
Melbourne, Victoria, Aust.

Up and took my camera to be repaired. Left a shirt to be altered. While walking down the street I was amazed and delighted to meet Fred Bove. He just came in about two weeks ago, and is stationed at St. Martha (Mt. Martha?), about 40 miles from Melbourne. I told him I had a luncheon engagement with the friend I had met last night. I said I would get rid of my friend as soon as I could, and meet Bove again. To meet this Australian friend, and after having lunch, bade goodbye, saying that I had other engagements. Met Bove in front of the Hotel Australia, and we spent the afternoon shopping and catching up on news. I learned that my former boss, Bill Kuntze, Supt of Vehicle Service, Newark, N.J. Post Office, had gotten married before leaving for the Army as a lieutenant in the motor transport. Also learned that John Hallo had resigned his position with the Panama (Canal Zone) Post Office Department, and was now working in the Newark Post Office in a temporary position; also that he was subject to draft into the Army. This Hallo has had a hitch in the regular Marine Corps and served in Nicaragua. He also has several years of (Marine) reserve service. He, Bove and I used to be very close friends, and we traveled all over together (twice by car to the West Coast and Mexico)... With Bove to the cocktail lounge of the Hotel Australia (which seems to be the social center of the town), and we were seated at a table with two Australian women. We had several drinks, and the ladies invited us to their homes in the suburbs. Bove had an appointment with a friend and I met another one. So we all to dine in a very nice place. From there we went to a cabaret, where we danced and drank until midnight. We ate again. There are "austerity" regulations here which prescribe the amount that may be expended on each meal, and that amount may not be legally exceeded. Bove had a very nice and gentle girl with him — a member of the Australian Women's Army Service (AWAS) and she promised to introduce me to her sister. It is very nice to be able to talk to the opposite sex after so long away from their presence.

> The gap in time between the last date above (January 27) and the following date (February 22) was caused by the pressure of work and by a period of depression. Work has been piling up, and I seem unable to clear it up. I am doing very little to catch up with the mass of paperwork (payrolls, muster rolls, all sorts of reports) that accumulated while I was on the island of Guadalcanal. I do not have a competent clerk, and I am trying to do too much myself. But my outlook has improved, and I am slowly making progress. There still remains a vast amount of work that I just can't seem to get started on. For a while I was so depressed that I

was entertaining some pretty bad thoughts, but I decided not to worry about things and I went out and attended the movies and some dances, and it took my mind off my troubles. I spend about fourteen hours a day in the office, but do not seem to accomplish very much in the way of bringing the work current.

March 8, 1943 Monday
Ballarat, Victoria, Aust.

Did some small tasks in the morning. The entire afternoon was wasted by my having to stand by as a possible witness in the General Court Martial trial of Private Mattus (?), the man who shot (Sgt.) Casey on the night of August 14 (on Guadalcanal) when he (Mattus) mistook him (Casey) for a Jap. I was not called, and the case was adjourned until tomorrow afternoon, when I will again have to stand by... There is much talk in camp about the Ninth Australian Division having come home from Tobruk and the eastern fighting and having found all their girls taken by the Marines in Melbourne. The story has it that the Australians (servicemen) ordered the Marines to leave town before midnight Saturday, and that several fights have developed over the weekend. One of the men returning today from weekend leave in Melbourne reported that the military police are rounding up the Marines and sending them back to camp. I will know more about this tomorrow.

March 9, 1943 Tuesday
Ballarat, Victoria, Aust.

Received conflicting reports about the hostile situation in Melbourne. Some reported seeing and engaging in fights, and others reported the situation normally peaceful. However, I note in today's paper that there will be a "get-together" held this coming Sunday at which 4,000 Australians and 3,000 Americans are expected. There will be free beer and sandwiches; and as a gift from the American forces, each Australian serviceman present will be presented with a metal souvenir — clasped hands with American and Australian flags to symbolize friendship. There are also planned radio shows and band concerts and dances for each other. So it looks as though there might be some grounds for all the stories, and that the authorities are taking energetic measures to cope with the situation... I cleared a lot of work through my office today. The place is beginning to look much better, and I have only the four months of Marine Corps muster rolls to worry about — but that is plenty. The new man, Goodheart, that they gave me is a good typist, and accustomed to office work. He keeps plugging at the work. I was supposed to be a witness at the manslaughter trial in the case against Mattus, but it (the case) was again adjourned. It looks as though the whole case may be dropped, which is the sensible thing to do. The incident occurred more than six months ago, and was most certainly an accident... Last night I wrote a long letter to Bess, and tonight I wrote to Bill Kuntze, my boss in the Post Office, who is stationed in Hawaii (with the U. S. Army).

March 11, 1943 Thursday
Ballarat, Victoria, Aust.
     Felt unusually well today, considering the small amount of sleep I had been able to get. Kept things going. Received permission to take the weekend off. I will go back to Melbourne. Mattus, the man being tried for killing (Sgt) Casey on the island of Guadalcanal, had his case dismissed today.

March 13, 1943 Saturday
Melbourne, Victoria, Aust.
     Awakened about 0900 by a chambermaid who was impatient to get my room made up. Russell had not slept in the room last night. I guess he made other arrangements at St. Kilda. (Because of limited space and great demand, hotels would not rent rooms to singles— so Marines doubled up on leave.) I did some shopping in the morning after breakfast. At 1530 Bonne called for me, and when I told her I had not seen much of Melbourne, she took me to the zoo and showed me all the Australian animals, including the emu. Stayed there until 1800, then back and I changed into my greens and we to the Wentworth Restaurant to have a very nice meal. From there we booked a table at the Coconut Grove cabaret. We drove out there rather early, and while waiting for the place to open we stood on the bridge over the Yarra River. This river is a narrow, dirty stream, but tonight, with the moonlight reflected in it, it was quite romantic. A river ferry came down the stream, and there were lights on it, and a machine was playing music, and the people aboard were all singing. It was a beautiful scene, and my thoughts drifted back to Bess, so far away, and I longed mightily for her. I tried to imagine what she was doing and thinking tonight... The (Coconut) Grove opened finally, and we in to our table. We drank only lemonade tonight. I danced nearly all the dances to 2330, then with Bonne to her home, which is quite a ways out of town. Back to my hotel and got to bed after taking a shower.

March 23, 1943 Tuesday
Ballarat, Victoria, Aust.
     Checked with the clerk who inquired about transfer to my Battery, but was disappointed to learn that he had been offered inducements to

March 17, 1943. Brig. Gen. Pedro A. del Valle presents medals for service on Guadal-canal at Ballarat, Victoria, Australia.

remain in his present position. Worked hard and accomplished little during the morning. The trial of Mattus for the shooting of (Sgt.) Casey was reopened today. The court has been directed to either acquit him or find him guilty, and thus to make final disposition of his case. I was called as a witness, and had to stand by from 1300 to 1600, and wasted the entire afternoon. While waiting, I sat in at a poker game going on in the mess hall where I was waiting, and I won seven pounds— more than $20; so the afternoon was not a total loss. Back and worked until 2200. I deeply regret not having been able to get that experienced clerk.

March 25, 1943 Thursday
Ballarat, Victoria, Aust.

Up after a poor night's sleep. Worked hard all day and accomplished quite a bit. I stood by as a witness for Mattus, but I was not called. At 1000 the case was completed, and Mattus was acquitted. He drew $80, and was granted the weekend off. This is the first liberty he has had since the slaying (accidental shooting of Sgt. Casey) last August. In the evening I to town and called Bonne, and she told me that she had been unable to engage a room for me. I arranged to meet her Friday evening, and told my Battery Commander that I had official business in Melbourne (to pay members of the Battery in the hospital there) and asked permission to take the weekend off. I intend to return Sunday.

April 17, 1943 Saturday
Ballarat

Inspection in the morning by the new Regimental Commander, Col. (Robert H.) Pepper. Gen. Del Valle has been detached, and is in the hospital with piles (hemorrhoids). The new colonel is very tough — hard to please and cranky. He gave us a thorough inspection and said he was satisfied, though he didn't give details. After inspection I asked

Right: 1st Sgt. Felber by his office, Ballarat, Victoria, Australia, in August 1943. *Below:* August 1943. Col. Robert H. Pepper (CO, 11th Marines) at left, Maj. Gen. William A. Rupertus (Commanding General, 1st Marine Division) center, and Lt. Col. Thomas B. Hughes (Executive Officer, 11th Marines) at right, Ballarat, Victoria, Australia.

the Battery Commander about recommending me for Marine Gunner, a warrant officer (rank), and he agreed. I will keep pushing this matter, but there will be many difficulties before I attain this promotion.

May 17, 1943 Monday
Ballarat
　　Felt very sleepy today. Got out quite a bit of work, but it keeps coming in so heavily all the time that I am constantly left with a sense of drowning in a sea of paperwork, of helplessness. Wrote a long letter to Bess, the first in several weeks. My conscience bothers me about the infrequency with which I write to Bess. I feel I am mentally ill. To bed early.

June 8, 1943 Tuesday
Ballarat
　　Still rather tired. Kept working all day. It is cold and wet around camp. There are all sorts of rumors concerning the time of our leaving Ballarat for combat — everything from within a month to four months. Wrote a letter to Bess. Received a letter from her. She is a darling about writing to me, especially when I reply so infrequently. Received a letter from Bove, and he has been transferred to a mail job. He states that the uniform where he is stationed at present is khaki, so he must be in some warm place. He offered to try to get me transferred to his unit, and I am giving it some consideration.

December 26, 1943 Sunday
Cape Gloucester, New Britain
　　Arose at 0530 and down below decks. Straightened my gear and lay down for another hour. It was not quite so hot. Had breakfast. I was disappointed that we were still at sea, and not at our destination, as I would have liked to see our ships pour in the scheduled 7,000 rounds of naval gunfire; and to see the bombing attacks. I got all my gear together, ready to disembark, then up to the top deck and played cards for about an hour. At about 1230 the crew was ordered to "beaching stations," I got the Battery to collecting their equipment and had them go to the bottom deck and wait besides the ramp doors. As soon as the ship beached, we were to go ashore. The vehicles would follow us. At 1325 our ship stopped off Beach Yellow # , Cape Gloucester. The shore showed evidence of the terrific shelling that must have taken place. Great gaps were cut out of the trees that lined the shore, and a hill to our left looked pulverized. The greater part of this hill had been denuded of all growth, leaving only churned-up brown earth. We received word that the landing had been successful, and that the Marines were pushing ahead and were close to the airfield, our

objective. At about 1400 our ship beached and we went ashore. There were several false starts before we could find our bivouac area. At each stop we made, the men began digging fox-holes immediately. At 1145 there was an air raid. From reports, only one Jap Zero came in. Several of our planes happened by at the time, on a bombing mission. All the anti-aircraft guns opened up — on the Jap and on our planes. Our planes were hit, and three were brought down. The others had to dump their bombs, and two officers and several of our men were killed by these bombs. Firing could be heard in the distance, and casualties were being brought in. Was told that the units making the landing had suffered very slight losses. We could see big squadrons of bombers come over to bomb the Jap positions, and we could see the bombs drop from the planes. We had complete air mastery. As we moved to our area, I took a look around. The whole beach road contained evidence of Jap occupation. There were all sorts of dugouts and installations, and a large quantity of supplies. There were several destroyed Jap field pieces. There was the stink of dead Japs, though I saw no bodies. There was a large quantity of Jap propaganda, intended for the Australians, with the purpose of creating hostile feelings between them and the Americans. Some of the leaflets were obscene. We reached our area, which was a patch of dense jungle, and we began to set up camp. It rained slightly several times during the day. There was a former Jap dugout along the road that I had passed several times. A Marine went into his dugout, and came out very fast — there were Japs still in it. Gasoline was procured and dropped into the hole and set afire. Two grenades were also tossed into the dugout. After all this, one dazed and shocked Jap came forth. He was dressed only in a loin cloth. The MPs took him away. We set up a guard for the night. The Battery Commander kept me so busy running around on silly little errands that I had no time to set up my bunk or to dig a foxhole. I spent the night sitting on a log against a tree. Japs kept sniping all through the night.

December 27, 1943 Sunday
Cape Gloucester, New Britain
It rained all day. I took a couple of trips out onto the road to look at the Jap positions and equipment. Found more of their propaganda

Opposite top: Aug. 17, 1943. Confidential USMC photograph (Neg. No. 3130) showing 1st Sgt. Felber demonstrating a camouflage suit, Camp Victoria Park, Ballarat, Victoria, Australia. *Bottom:* Aug. 17, 1943. Official USMC photograph (Hdqtrs. No. 60338), distributed by the Division of Public Relations in Washington, D.C., captioned, "JAP'S EYE VIEW — ADVANCING TOWARD YOU is Marine First Sergeant Abraham Felber, of 295 Avon Avenue, Newark, New Jersey, wearing a camouflage suit designed to blend with natural surroundings. You wouldn't have seen him a moment ago. But he would have seen you."

October 25, 1943. Natives constructing mess hall for the 11th Regiment, Goodenough Island, D'Entrecasteaux Group, off New Guinea.

leaflets. Jap snipers were busy all day. They come quite close to our area and snipe at the amphibious tractors on the road alongside our camp. They are rather ineffective. All day long trees crash to the ground, and leaves are falling constantly. This is from the effects of the terrific shelling, and the tremendous concussion of the aerial bombs dropped here. A falling tree killed one of the men in the 5th Battalion yesterday. The 12th Defense Battalion came in today. All day long finds LSTs landing Marines and supplies and departing hurriedly. Theirs is a much better organized affair than the landing at Guadalcanal. Set up our guard again for the night. I had

1st Sgt. Felber with Melanesian native chief "Charley," Goodenough Island, D'Enrecasteaux Group, off New Guinea, in late 1943.

been able to put up my hammock during the day. There had been no chance to dry out all day, and I didn't want to break out any dry clothes because they would be soaked quickly and I have few clothes with me. So I removed my muddy, soggy leggings, undressed, dried myself with a towel, and to bed. My feet look like those of a swimmer who has been in the water too long. During the night there was the sounds of a heavy action to the left.

December 28, 1943 Tuesday
Cape Gloucester, New Britain
Learned that the firing last night was a Jap attack on the hill to the southeast of our position. This attack had been repulsed with an estimated loss to the Japs of 200 men, while we had only one Marine killed. It rained all day today again. When I arose I just put on my wet and muddy clothes. It was no use putting on dry clothes, for they would become wet and muddy in a very short time. The roads are in terrible shape. The mud is knee deep. There is a constant, heavy traffic on these roads that keep digging them deeper. The only way traffic keeps moving is by being hauled by caterpillar tractors and by amphibian tractors. Even these vehicles bog down, and two or three of them have to chain up to pull the stuck vehicle out of the mud. There was a very heavy concentrated bombing attack on the airfield today... I saw Jasinski today. His outfit had been up on the front. He had strained his back, and he was in pain. They have done nothing about it yet. We got the word to move out after lunch. We packed quickly in the

December 28, 1943. A tractor stuck on a muddy road, Cape Gloucester, New Britain.

December 28, 1943. 75mm pack howitzers of D Battery, 11th Marines, in action against the Japanese, Cape Gloucester, New Britain. (Official USMC photograph, Neg. No. 12203.)

rain and sent our equipment out by amphibious tractor. The men loaded their packs and hammocks on their backs, and we started for the beach road. The trail out was very bad. The mud was knee deep, and at one section it was waist deep. When I came to this place, I stepped in and the mud was so clinging and I was so burdened with gear that I fell in the mud up to my neck. My gear got all wet and I had mud in all my pockets. The beach road was in fair shape, so our gear was loaded aboard trucks and sent to the new area. We walked about two miles to the place. The Battery Commander, Captain Fairclough (?), is a very trying individual. He is about twenty-one years of age, and almost childish. He gives very silly orders, and runs me around like an errand boy. He shoves everything onto me, no matter whose job it actually is. He doesn't give me a chance to set up my hammock or dig a fox-hole. In our position we have "D" Battery on our flank. They have a machine gun defense set up for local security. There is nobody in front of us but the front line about 8,000 yards away. We set up a couple of listening posts. An order came through to make up a 60-man outfit that was to stand by in case the Japs broke through our lines.

We would then go up to the front to assist our men. I had the deuce of a time getting the men's names and running around to all the sections. It was all the more irritating because it seemed so silly to me. The situation on the front was well in hand. The lines were 8,000 yards from our position. It would take at least two hours to get to the front in the darkness through the jungle and swamps; and if we didn't get shot by our own men upon arrival, we would have only the one unit of fire for each man. Even if it should become necessary to call out our Battery, all they would have to do is have the whole Battery fall out and take 60 men. But that would be too easy. So I had to make up two platoons, assign platoon leaders, divide the platoons into three squads, and assign men as squad leaders and designate which men were in which squad. It was dark when this task was complete. I took off my clothes which were stiff with mud, and took a towel and wiped off some of the mud from me, and to bed. Didn't have a very restful night, for "D" Battery besides us kept up an intermittent harassing fire all night long. There was a Jap bombing attack during the night, but they dropped the bombs on their own lines.

December 29, 1943 Wednesday
Cape Gloucester, New Britain

It didn't rain so heavily today. It only sprinkled lightly several times during the day. I worked on my Change Sheets and Morning Reports, bringing them current. The Jap airfield received a terrific pounding by air bombing and by ground artillery. There is a big final push to be made on the airfield. Stories are coming back of hundreds of Japs being killed and presenting a burial problem. There is also a small but steady stream of our men coming back as casualties. Our losses are unusually light. We have complete mastery of the air. Our bombers and artillery are doing a very good job and saving lots of our infantrymen. TechSgt Black, the combat correspondent, reported back for duty with this Battery... In the evening "D" Battery moved forward leaving us alone in our position. We set up all our six machine guns, and put watches on them that were to sleep by the guns all night. Took a bath tonight and changed clothes for the first time in three days. There was a misunderstanding, and the men on the machine guns who came off watch went to sleep in their hammocks instead of staying with the guns. Major Ennis roused the Battery Commander and gave him a good talking to for disregarding his orders. He made him round up all the men in the dark and get them on the guns again. The Battery Commander acts like a kid, and he is being treated like one. This doesn't help me.

December 30, 1943 Thursday
Cape Gloucester, New Britain

Didn't sleep very well last night. Up, and held reveille at 0600. It was still dark. Breakfast went at 0700. We were moving out today, so immediately after breakfast, we rolled our hammocks and broke camp. We loaded our trucks and were ready to roll by 0830. This looked like one time we would be getting to our new location in plenty of time to set up our camp and our hammocks. Just as we were about to move out we were ordered to stop the movement and stand by. We were told that we would not move until after lunch. We all sat about just waiting. Our galley was secured, so we sent a truck out and drew "K" rations for the men for lunch. After lunch the order came to move, and we all started off in a northwest direction along the beach road for about three miles. We keep moving toward the airfield as our troops advance. Our new location is in a patch of jungle right at the edge of the ocean. We set up the camp and put up our galley so that we could have hot chow tonight. Some mail came in and was distributed. Major Ennis ordered a machine gun watch set up, and put out five guns, with six men on each gun. These men were to stay with the guns all night. It took every available man to supply the guns. These men have to work all day, and then sleep by the guns all night. I was told that a Jap reconnaissance plane flew over our positions this evening, and that a bombing raid might be expected. It was dark by this time, but I dug myself an adequate foxhole before going to bed. This is the first foxhole I have dug on this island.

December 31, 1943 Friday
Cape Gloucester, New Britain

Reveille at 0700. It rained all morning. About breakfast time, one of the men on the machine guns heard a noise in the bushes. He challenged, and he said that somebody ran off into the bushes. He swung his machine gun around and let loose one shot before his gun jammed. As soon as he heard this, Major Ennis ordered all available men, and all those not actually standing gun watch, to form a patrol to see if they could find any Japs. The patrol went out, got separated, spent a couple of hours in the jungle, and came back empty-handed. There probably had been no Japs there, and the noise in the bushes must have been a bird or animal... The machine gun watches were maintained all day. The men are protesting at all this work. They do not have any time to themselves, and they are having difficulty finding time to bathe or shave or wash clothes between the time they are on duty or on gun watch. The rain let up for a while in the afternoon, and I shaved. I have some wet clothes that I have no facilities for washing or drying, and I do not know what to do with them ... shortly after noontime there was a definitely perceptible tremor of the earth. I guess this island must be subject to earthquakes, just as Guadalcanal is. Today, which is New Years' Eve, the American flag was hoisted over the Cape Gloucester airfield. I didn't get a chance to see the ceremony, nor have I had an opportunity to visit the front. I hear that there are a number of dead Japs at several places that we have not yet had a chance to bury... Received a letter today from my cousin, Morris Abend, who is a Master Sergeant in the Army and stationed at Fort Hamilton, New York. He is doing well, and is now married. To bed at 2000 on this quiet New Year's Eve.

January 1, 1944 Saturday
Cape Gloucester, New Britain
    It was clear in the morning. I did some paper work. After lunch I started out with Ashman, the photographer, and Black, the combat correspondent, for some pictures. As soon as we got away from camp, it started to rain. There was no place to seek shelter, so we continued on, getting thoroughly drenched. Reached the 5th Battalion area and stopped off there until the rain ceased. There were several dead Japs in nearby dugouts. They were in a very advanced stage of decay, and an overpowering odor hung about. I took a couple of pictures. Black suggested that we go to the airfield, about three miles further on. We started. The roads were jammed with all sorts of heavy equipment going forward — guns, ammunition, tractors, food trucks, water trailers, immense road building machinery, etc. The roads were being churned into a sea of mud. Even walking was difficult. We plowed through ankle-deep mud for a couple of miles, and then the mud became almost knee-deep. We turned back without reaching the airfield. Our front lines are now about three miles beyond the airfield. Reached camp just in time for supper. Mail was distributed after chow, and the men were issued a free ration of cigarettes and candy. Took a swim in the ocean and washed some clothes. To bed at 2000; but before I could fall asleep, the Battery Commander called me and told me that Division was moving out and that I would have to establish another machine gun post. He sent me digging up men in the dark. Finally got him his men, and then I back to my hammock.

January 2, 1944 Sunday
Cape Gloucester, New Britain
    It was a clear, sunny day for a change, and the men took advantage of it. There was much washing of clothes and tidying-up. I boiled some of my clothes and hung them to dry. They were dry by noon. I changed

into these dry clothes. I took a swim and did some sunbathing, which was a great help to the sores I have on my legs. These sores started with scratched mosquito bites, chigger bites, etc. and they do not heal. My clothes are wet continually, often with salt water, and the sores are irritated and grow steadily larger... In the afternoon did quite a bit of paperwork. It looked like a quiet night as I went to bed at 2000, but at 2030 Jap aircraft came over. They flew about in the dark, up and down the beach. Our guns opened up on them, and the sky was lit up with 20mm tracers and with 90mm bursts. They dropped bombs at several points. Some of these fell quite close to our position, and I could hear the whistle as they descended and was rocked by the blasts. None of them fell in our immediate area, and we had no casualties; but I hear that the 4th Battalion was hit and that several of the men were wounded.

January 3, 1944 Monday
Cape Gloucester, New Britain
      Another clear day. This makes two in a row, and the men appreciate it. Their appearance is greatly improved. Heard today that there were about 15 planes in last night's air raid. Eleven men from the 4th Battalion were wounded, one seriously. Orders were passed for all men to cover their foxholes with logging and sand bags. Much urging was not needed, and the men turned to with a will. The reason for the covering of the foxholes is that personnel bombs have a very sensitive detonator; and if they hit in among the trees, they explode in the air and strike into the foxholes... I worked all by myself, deepening my foxhole and covering it with twigs. I put one layer crosswise, and the next lengthwise; and I placed sandbags on top... Did some washing, and took a nice, long swim in the afternoon. I played some poker in the evening, losing seven pounds (Aust.). After dark to bed, just about the time the Jap planes came over. There was quite a bit of anti-aircraft fire, but I observed no hits. The planes made several runs over the area and dropped bombs, but none fell in our area. Between attacks I fell asleep in my hammock, and I was awakened by our anti-aircraft fire. When I awoke, the planes were right overhead; and in my sleepy condition I nearly fell out of the hammock and had a difficult time trying to get the thing unfastened. Ripped my hammock in the attempt. This is bad — mosquitoes and insects can get in while I sleep. My foxhole is plenty deep. No problem there.

January 4, 1944 Tuesday
Cape Gloucester, New Britain
      Another nice day. Heard today that one of the men wounded in the air raid a couple of nights ago has died. Several of the others are to be evacuated.

It was another clear day today, and I sure enjoyed it. Things are quieting down somewhat. Spent the morning cleaning my gear and doing a bit of paper work. In the afternoon took a swim in the ocean. Played poker after supper, and lost eight pounds. I sure am in a losing streak. The game ended at darkness. I out and sat on the beach for about an hour, waiting for the nightly Jap bombing, and for our anti-aircraft defense. No planes appeared tonight; and after it started raining, I back to my hammock for the night.

January 5, 1944 Wednesday
Cape Gloucester, New Britain
It had rained very hard all night. At times it seemed as though a solid sheet of water was descending. Many of the men had their hammocks soaked or flooded, and a couple of the men fell out of the hammocks while bailing them out. Mine stayed comparatively dry. I hated to get out into the rain to call reveille. The galley fly (canvas shielding the outdoor kitchen) had blown down in the night, and breakfast was a half hour late. Had to get up a big working party to secure the galley. It rained all day. Played some poker in the evening, and lost another seven pounds. To bed at dark. When it rains, there are no air attacks. I prefer the air attacks.

January 6, 1944 Thursday
Cape Gloucester, New Britain
It poured rain during last night. Everything was damp that was not sopping wet. Did some paper work during the morning. Played poker all afternoon and evening, losing another eight pounds. It rained off and on during the whole day. There are several sores on my legs, and they are having a difficult time healing, as they are wet for as much as three days at a time. They become irritated, and I scratch and enlarge them. It was raining when I went to bed at 2030.

January 7, 1944 Friday
Cape Gloucester, New Britain
It rained hard all night. The rain came down in a pounding solid fury that seemed about to drown out the whole island. It stopped toward morning, and it was not raining at breakfast. There had been some very loud thunder during the night, and the crack and explosion of the thunder seemed like naval gunfire and caused me to flinch and shrink every time it was heard. I never used to flinch at thunder before I underwent the naval shelling at Guadalcanal. When awake, thunder does not bother me; but when half asleep, I flinch instinctively... Got together ten men in the morning, who were to go forward to our new position on the other side of the

airfield and prepare it for us to move into. But when they started, they found that three bridges were washed out between them and their objective, so they could not go today. I did some paper work in the morning. In the afternoon I took a swim, and the ocean very rough and full of dirt that had been washed in by the rain. But the rinsing did my sores good. I played cards for about an hour in the afternoon, losing five pounds. I sure am having tough luck. I continue playing, feeling that my luck is bound to turn soon; but it will not take much more to convince me that maybe it won't... Took a trip to Hq and Service motor transport to try and check on that ammunition box I lost on Goodenough Island; and learned that it had been turned in to some gunnery sergeant who said he was acquainted with me and would return it to my battery. They gave me names to check with, and said that the unit which drove the trucks that I left my box on was still at Goodenough Island and was not coming out here. I will have to write to my rear echelon and get them to check for me... Did some paperwork in the evening after chow. Made a bet that there would be no air raid tonight, and I won.

January 8, 1944 Saturday
Cape Gloucester, New Britain
        The ten men who were to go forward to prepare our new area finally got away today. The roads were in fairly good shape, even though it had rained pretty hard last night. Spent my time rounding up working parties, and doing some paper work. Went in for a short swim, but the water was so rough and dirty that I didn't stay long. To bed early after supper but was soon awakened by an air raid alert shortly after 2000. There were planes in the air until as late as 2245. They dropped some bombs, but none fell near our Battery position. There was only slight anti-aircraft activity in reply.

January 9, 1944 Sunday
Cape Gloucester, New Britain
        It had rained again during the night, but it was dry during the day, though cloudy. The condition of the roads improved somewhat, and there was an increase in traffic. Our position is fairly quiet, but on both our flanks along the beach there is continuous activity. To the east, past the hill used for an observation post, there is continual contact with the enemy, and occasional enemy raids. To the west, past the airfield, our men are steadily pushing forward and extending our holdings. If the roads were not in such terrible shape, I would make some trips to the front, but they are impassable... Took a shower during the afternoon, and the salt water

bathing is helping my sores. I am working on a long letter full of information for the rear echelon… To bed in 2000, just as the air raid was sounded. It began to rain very soon after that, and that prevented any bombing. The "All Clear" was sounded soon thereafter.

January 10, 1944 Monday
Cape Gloucester, New Britain
    It had rained very hard during the night. There was still a slight rain falling when I gave reveille at 0700, but it stopped before long. Had some difficulty with the galley section this morning about discipline, and I had to run one man up before the Battery Commander. A Lt. Boland joined the Battery. He will not be attached to us for very long. Seven men more, plus two truck drivers and a corpsman, were sent forward to the new area to help prepare it for our occupancy. It was cloudy all day. Did some paper work, and got some candles and read a magazine before retiring at 2200.

January 11, 1944 Tuesday
Cape Gloucester, New Britain
    It didn't rain during the day, but it was cloudy and overcast. There was about a half hour of sunshine all day. It was quite cool. The sun is seen very seldom here. Some natives of this island have been obtained and they are working at piling commissary stores. They are very black, and some of them are quite primitive-looking. The natives on this island were formerly headhunters. I took a couple of pictures of them… In to take a swim, but I no sooner got wet than the Battery Commander called me out to make a thorough police of the area. I quickly dressed, only to be told that the policing would not start until after supper, as there were no men available. After supper I got all available men and we gathered together all the loose branches, twigs and brush, and piled them up. We could not remove the piles, as it was quite late and we would require a larger working party than available… A strong wind blew up after supper, followed by a violent downpour. After the rain subsided somewhat, I to my hammock. There was an air raid alert, but I paid no attention to it. The weather was quite bad, so I figured there would be no bombing. The "All Clear" came soon after.

January 12, 1944 Wednesday
Cape Gloucester, New Britain
    It had rained several times during the night, as usual. Toward morning there had been two air raid alerts, but I heard no bombing. I am afraid all this non-bombing activity is air reconnaissance, and a prelude to some

major enemy operation… This campaign has been very dull for my Battery. We are about to move forward for quite a distance, to the other side of the airfield. I hear we will be about 1,000 yards from the field itself. This puts us within bombing and shelling range of attacks on the airfield. We are due to move up there very soon. I hope I get close enough to the front lines to be able to visit them occasionally… There is much discussion here about a reported new law that has been passed in the United States requiring that those members of the armed forces who have served 18 months or more overseas be returned to the United States. I have served for about 19 months. I sure would like to get appointed a Marine Gunner before being sent back to the States. I have a much better chance out here of getting such a promotion… Things were quiet in the Battery today. I took a good swim in the afternoon. Jasinski visited me, and he has been used as an Acting First Sergeant. It didn't rain during the day today. There are several jobs to be done about the Battery area, but there is no personnel to do them. I to bed at 2000, after having read some magazines.

January 13, 1944 Thursday
Cape Gloucester, New Britain
    There had been very little rain during the night. Towards morning, there had been an air raid alert, but I heard no bombing. The morning was sunshiny for a change. A notice has appeared on the bulletin board that this Battery is to move to our new position right after breakfast tomorrow… I boiled some clothes in the morning. In the afternoon took a swim. Got together as much of my gear as possible, and to bed early to rest for tomorrow.

January 14, 1944 Friday
Cape Gloucester, New Britain
    Up, and it was pouring rain. We had breakfast, and despite the weather we were told to get our hammocks rolled and our packs made up. The first few trucks began leaving for the new area. The police (clean-up) of the area began, and as usual the area was in a very untidy condition. We went over the place several times, and there was still much property strewn about. Major Ennis complained about the condition of the area. It was pretty good by noontime. We ate canned rations for lunch. About noontime all the men and gear had left and the Battery Commander and myself got aboard the last truck and we turned the area over to some colored Army troops who were moving in. We rode for about five miles, passing the airfield, on which was standing an abandoned Jap plane. The roads were awful, and we passed many stalled vehicles. Tractors were busy pulling

out trucks that were stuck. The Engineers are busy constructing bridges across the many streams emptying into the ocean. It took us a couple of hours to make the trip. The actual camp area was comparatively dry, but the roads and area surrounding us is just a swamp... The rain let up somewhat in the afternoon, and I started putting up my hammock, in between calls for working parties. After I had a place all cleared away and was about to set up the hammock, the Battery Commander came and told me that I was not located centrally enough, and told me to move to a new position. I got set up there, and it was chow time. The men just finished putting a canvas over the mess hall, which had been constructed by the advance working parties. There is a big Operations dugout being constructed in the area. I missed not being able to get my swim in the ocean. To bed dirty and sweated up. The clothes I had washed yesterday were still wet, and had become quite dirty during moving. I have no others.

January 15, 1944 Saturday
Cape Gloucester, New Britain
Up, and it was raining. Every available man was called out on working parties. They were detailed to the construction of the Operations dugout, to erecting an Officers' Mess, to digging ditches to drain the area and to other details. There was much bickering among the officers as to whether they should be required to furnish men for the working parties. They all thought there was more important work to be done in their own section... In the afternoon our Property Sergeant came back with a couple of pyramidal tents which he had managed to steal, and I had one put up to be used as my office. Got my papers in from the rain for the first time since arriving on this dank and dripping island... Some humorist cut the ropes of my hammock, and soon after I got into it the hammock rope gave and I landed on the ground. I fixed it up and went back to sleep; but during the night the other rope gave and again I found myself on the ground... It rained several times during the night. In a couple of days I will move into the tent that I am using for an office. I would have done so immediately, but I am afraid the Battery Commander would want to move in also. Though he is a captain, he is only about 22 years old; and at times he acts like about twelve years old. He is childishly selfish, and has very immature ideas. His pettiness and lack of sense become exasperating many times.

January 16, 1944 Sunday
Cape Gloucester, New Britain
Again everybody available was called out on working parties. As usual, it rained most of the day. Church services were held in the afternoon. I

got quite a bit of work done, now that I have a place to work in that is not exposed to the rain. Our area was previously used by the Japs, and there are many of their dugouts around. The trucks are having a very difficult time getting through the roads about our area, and we are having difficulty getting water. To bed early today.

January 17, 1944 Monday
Cape Gloucester, New Britain
It didn't rain during the night, but it made up for it by just pouring most of the day… Private First Class Ernest, a truck driver, was picked up today and taken to Division Headquarters. He is accused of stealing a Speed Graphic camera from the Marine Corps and selling it in Melbourne. He will probably be given a General Court Martial… I did quite a bit of paper work during the day. Work is still continuing on the Regimental Operations dugout, and on a mess hall for the officers. There are occasional air raid alerts during the night, but no bombing in our area so far. Last night a Jap plane glided in and dropped some bombs among a group of C.B.s (Construction Battalion servicemen), killing four and wounding about 17. These men were at work during the night on the air field, and they had lights on. The plane coasted in with its motor cut… I finally got my first bath today. It was while it was raining so very hard. I just took my clothes off and stood out in the rain. It was as good as any shower. If I could get a dry set of clothes, everything would be O.K.

January 18, 1944 Tuesday
Cape Gloucester, New Britain
There was only slight sprinkling a couple of times during the night, and it didn't rain during the day. Received word that the Regimental Commanding Officer, Col. Pepper, is to be relieved at the end of this month. There is much speculation as to who our next Commanding Office is to be… Kept working around the Battery all day. If tomorrow is a nice day, I will try to get out and take some pictures. It began to rain toward evening, and it rained hard all night.

January 19, 1944 Wednesday
Cape Gloucester, New Britain
It was teeming rain in the morning. Everything is damp and rotten. Even the big trees here are soft and decaying. There are worms and bugs and grubs and insects and termites everywhere. And over everything there is the ugly stink of decay and death. Everything is blooming and gross with luxurious fertility; but it is a diseased growth, and everywhere bugs and

crawling things are eating away at the damp, rotting heart of it all. Mold forms on everything. I opened my pack today, and a new pair of leggings of stiff canvas were covered with green mold; and some film I had in the pack had the outer box eaten away by termites. This film is tropical-packed, and is enclosed in a hermetically-sealed metal tube, for which I was very grateful, as the termites could not penetrate this. I took all my exposed film and placed them in a tin box and sealed the box with adhesive tape to keep out termites and dampness. I had some chocolate bar "D" ration, in paraffin-sealed boxes, but even this was eaten through by rats; and flies, ants and termites were helping to dispose of it. It is all a wonderful experience, but I sure would hate to have to live in this place permanently... There were several air raid alerts in the evening, and some anti-aircraft firing, but I to bed and didn't let the noise and excitement disturb me.

January 20, 1944 Thursday
Cape Gloucester, New Britain

There were a couple of air raid alerts about 0400 this morning. It rained slightly during the night, but the roads appeared fairly firm. Took a truck and out to visit our outlying sections. Took a couple of pictures of wrecked Jap Zero planes. Visited our Ordnance Section. Had lunch at some mess that was feeding along the road. In the afternoon visited the Quartermaster and tried unsuccessfully to get some tents. We started to trace the location of a village where we heard there were several native women, but got side-tracked at a former Jap position and quartermaster dump. We spent about an hour investigating their dugouts, ammunition piles, cases of food, etc. While there, it began to rain hard, so we started back without getting to the village. Had a bit of trouble getting through the mud, but made it in plenty of time for chow. It rained all evening. There were no air raid alerts.

January 21, 1944 Friday
Cape Gloucester, New Britain

A beautiful, sunny day, and a very welcome relief from that ever-present rain and dampness. Things dried out a bit today. I got a 3-man working party to put up strongbacks for my tent. I worked around the office during the morning, and in the afternoon I to the Quartermaster by truck. Also visited the Ordnance. It was so nice and sunny that when we came to our former position, I in and had a refreshing swim in the ocean. I envy the Quartermaster their position, right on the bank of a stream flowing into the ocean. They are able to wash, launder clothes, and enjoy a daily swim. Got back to camp in time for chow, and the men had finished strongbacking the tent.

January 22, 1944 Saturday
Cape Gloucester, New Britain
　　Another sunny day today. The roads are getting nice and hard. The Colonel wanted the Fitness Reports today, so he could start marking and grading the officers. I worked on these reports all morning. There is only one typewriter available, and that is in the Sergeant Major's office. I have to wait until his clerks are not using it, then get in some of my work. I finished the reports in the afternoon, and turned them over to the Sergeant Major. I got the necessary data from the officers present, together with their signatures. But the officers who are on the rear echelon, and those detached had to have blank Fitness Reports made out for them. Col. Pepper is expected to be relieved on 1 February. The Battery Commander, Capt. Fairclough, is also being detached and transferred to the 1st Marine Amphibious Corps. I will be glad to see him go, as he is very incompetent. It is possible that he will get an unsatisfactory Fitness Report. Capt. Griffin, of the Plans and Training Section, will be the next Battery Commander... It has been dry for so long that this diary has lost its dampness, and the ink does not spread as it did during the rainy weather. However, I am taking a chance in writing with ink, because if this book becomes wet, the ink will spread and possibly become illegible. Pen writing is much neater, more exact, and more easily read. There were no air raid alerts today.

January 23, 1944 Sunday
Cape Gloucester, New Britain
　　The impossible has happened — there was another sunny day today. Did some work about the office during the early morning. Got a ride out to the airfield and took a couple of shots of the Piper Cub aircraft attached to the 11th Marines as aerial observers for the artillery. Back in time for lunch. Lou Pescatore, who used to be in the Newark, N.J., Marine Reserve Battalion, was there to visit me. We talked over old times. He is now a Gunnery Sergeant... After lunch took him with me and we to a camp nearby, where there were a number of natives living, including their womenfolk. We walked around a bit, watching them at lunch. They were eating rice topped off with corned beef. I took several pictures of the natives, and had hard luck with one of the rolls of film. The damp air had swelled the film, and it became stuck, making it necessary to open the camera and spoil at least half the roll of film... We stayed at the village but a short time, then left and stopped at the beach for a swim. Back to camp, and I set up a cot in the office tent and brought my hammock indoors and laid it on the cot. I will sleep under cover from now on... The switchboard has rigged up

some sort of hook-up whereby several phones can be connected to the radio to receive broadcasts. Last night I got on the line. I took my phone off the pole and brought it to my cot. I lay there in my cot with the phone alongside me and listened to some pretty good programs and the news. Some comfort!… Our Battery Commander, Capt. Fairclough, left today. He will probably wind up at Guadalcanal, the headquarters of the 1st Amphibious Corps.

January 24, 1944 Monday
Cape Gloucester, New Britain
     I am almost ready to believe anything now — today was another nice day. I did some work in the office and on the tent in the morning. Did very little in the afternoon. To bed early, so that I could listen to the radio broadcast over the phone… I have made arrangements to go to the front lines near Hill 660 tomorrow, if it does not rain.

January 25, 1944 Tuesday
Cape Gloucester, New Britain
     There were slight showers early in the morning, but the rest of the day was clear and sunny. After breakfast I assigned the men to the working parties. When all was cleared up, I in a truck with another Marine, and we rode about eleven miles southwest along the beach, past the air field and, to a hill called 660, because that is its approximate height. There had been much action here recently, and the perimeter of our defenses was along the base of the hill. We got out of the truck, and the vehicle left us. We decided to climb the hill. It was very steep, and we had to pull ourselves up hand over hand part of the way. The sides of the hill were pocked with dugouts, machine gun positions, and shell and aerial bomb craters. The fight for this hill had been furious, and had lasted for several days. It must have been a heartbreaking task for the 7th Marines to climb this steep and slippery incline with full battle gear and their weapons and ammunition. Even with the extremely light gear we were equipped with, we had to stop every few feet, to regain our breath and still our pounding hearts… The 7th Marines have been relieved, and the 5th Marines are setting up the defenses on this hill… When we attained the summit of the hill, we had an excellent view of the beach along Borgen Bay and Natamo Point to the east. Looking north we could see Hill 450, or Target Hill as it is known. The sides of this latter hill show great bare brown scars where artillery fire blasted its slopes. There are several observation posts set up on the top of Hill 660, and we had a very good view of the surrounding territory through the powerful glasses these posts are equipped with. We

January 25, 1944. Japanese trophies at the 1st Marine Division observation post on Hill 660, Cape Gloucester, New Britain.

wandered about the top of the hill for a while, looking at the Jap defense positions. Most of the corpses had been buried, but there were one or two still in inaccessible places that were emitting their horrible odor. Nearly all of the souvenirs had been picked up... We decided to descend the south-eastern slope of the hill and work our way back north and toward camp. Though our front lines were at the base of this hill, we had a patrol past Natamo Point, about 3,000 yards from Hill 660. They had gone to that point by boat, as the intervening terrain was too rugged, and there were two rivers to cross. We had intended working our way from the base of Hill 660 to the position of the patrol; but we were told that the jungle was too dense, there were no trails, and that the rivers were pretty wide. This area is also infested with Jap snipers. We made our way down the hill past all the evidences of the recent struggle, and began working our way toward the beach. It got a bit swampy near the shore, but we finally made it. Began walking and thumbing rides back toward camp. Passed a place where there were more than 25 Jap landing barges along the shore, blasted by our bombing. At the docks there were four LSTs unloading. Much mail came in today... We got back in time for supper. The man we had sick at Cape Cretin, and the two men who had been sick at Oro Point, came in today on the LSTs, and reported back to duty. One of the post office clerks, Tur-rentine, who had been left at Cape Cretin to guard the safe, came in also. He was censured for having left the safe, and was dismissed from his postal duties. He will report to the garage to work as a truck driver... I to the well we have dug and drew water for a bath before retiring for the night.

January 26, 1944 Wednesday
Cape Gloucester, New Britain
   Another nice day. Received two packages— one from my brother-in-law, Bob Panitch, containing toilet articles, a good sewing kit, and a box of excellent cigars. The other Christmas parcel was from Bess, and she sure made up a swell gift box. It contained the vitamin pills and cigarette lighter that I had asked for; and besides, it contained soap, tooth paste, candy, gum, razor blades, tooth brush refills, and several other very useful items. Also received a letter from her. In the mail came much literature and magazines for the enlisted men's library, and I had an orgy of reading papers and magazines.

January 27, 1944 Thursday
Cape Gloucester, New Britain
   It was nice during the day. It is beginning to rain a bit in sudden, short-lived showers. It rained at night. I worked on office work when I was not engaged in reading Life Magazines. Received another letter from Bess today; also from her nephew Sheldon, and from the Chinese AWAS I knew in Ballarat. Everybody has been receiving delayed Christmas parcels, and the camp is full of candy and fruit cake. I to bed early tonight so that I could lie there listening to the radio broadcast over the telephone hook-up.

January 28, 1944 Friday
Cape Gloucester, New Britain
   Spent most of the day reading. It was quite hot and sunny most of the day, but there was a light shower or two. Things are very dull here. Col. Pepper is making preparations for leaving, and we are expecting the new Regimental Commander very soon. There was a farewell party today for all the officers in Col. Pepper's honor. He is in a pleasant mood... Listened to the radio over the phone.

January 29, 1944 Saturday
Cape Gloucester, New Britain
   The Sergeant Major told me today that he had been told to get up a recommendation for himself for Warrant Officer, and that Col. Pepper would sign it. I sure wish I could get another recommendation for myself, but I do not know how to arrange it. Read most of the day. Washed some clothes. It was hot, with occasional quick showers. The air raid warning

system here is very poor. Jap planes sneak in on us every so often, and there are many occasions when the alarm is given at the approach of our own planes. There was an air raid alert after dark tonight, and our entire aircraft defenses put up a sizeable barrage, but nothing happened. The plane left the area, and we all to bed.

January 30, 1944 Sunday
Cape Gloucester, New Britain
A quiet day today. Major Ennis desired that all available men continue working today, just as on a weekday. We are putting up another tent for the new Regimental Commanding Officer... I finally wrote a letter to Bess today. The Battery Commander, Capt. Griffin, came back today. He is the Assistant Plans and Training Officer, and he was out surveying the recently captured Hill 660. We got along very well today. I hope he is more aggressive and active than Capt. Fairclough was... About 1695 a Jap plane sneaked in and dropped a bomb near one of our destroyers. The air raid alert was sounded after he had gone... The amount of rain falling daily is increasing, and it rains during the night.

January 31, 1944 Monday
Cape Gloucester, New Britain
Col. Pepper has left the Battery, and the new Regimental Commanding Officer has moved in. Col. Harrison is a tall, thin man, who arrived with an electric refrigerator and washing machine. He has a special trailer to carry his gear. The Battery Commander kept me busy getting up a chart of the area for the allocation of fifteen tents that we are going to draw. With this issue of gear, we will have tents for all our men. I wrote another short letter to Bess today.

February 1, 1944 Tuesday
Cape Gloucester, New Britain
Quiet day today. I fiddled around the office, reading most of the day. I am terribly bored with this campaign. I am going to try to get another recommendation for Warrant Officer put in for me, then I will see about getting home. There is very little actual work for me here, and even that little I have no ambition to do. The only actual desire I have at present is to be made Warrant Officer.

February 2, 1944 Wednesday
Cape Gloucester, New Britain
The Battery Commander finally broke down and let me have a clerk for my office. He is a private named Burnett, and I have had my eye on

him for a long time. I believe I can train him to be a first class clerk. I did more work today than for the past three days put together, with the help of this new man. I am getting quite ambitious, and I am irritated that I cannot work after dark... I sat around for quite some time after dark before going to bed tonight. It was quite cool.

February 3, 1944 Thursday
Cape Gloucester, New Britain
 It was a nice day today, and it didn't rain once. I did quite a bit of work with the new clerk. We received a "safe hands" delivery of mail from the rear echelon today, and it contained a letter from Ramsey, the clerk at Goodenough Island. He gave me a lot of news about events back there, and included lots of regulations concerning administrative procedure that will be of great assistance to me. He does not state definitely that he has that ammunition box in which I kept my stationery and records, but he says he is sending me the stuff I asked for, to me in two packages. I hope especially that he sends me some of those Record of Events books.

February 4, 1944 Friday
Cape Gloucester, New Britain
 It rained in the morning. In the afternoon, working parties cleared out the area, removing brush and twigs. There are rumors that we may move from this position. I sent back a 5-page letter of information to the rear echelon. Got out a roster of men on this island. Gosh, things are dull here for me.

February 5, 1944 Saturday
Cape Gloucester, New Britain
 Up, and a 50-man working party started clearing up the area. They worked hard all morning, and made much progress clearing the jungle. It rained slightly during the morning. In the afternoon, we started clearing the area again, but the Battery Commander came out and told us to knock off— that the Colonel had decided to move from this location. A universal groan went up from the men, who had spent much time and great effort to clearing the site and to putting up tents, strongbacks, and other fixtures. We will probably have to build a new Operations Dugout, which is a big job. We have not been told the location of the new camp site... Distributed a cigarette ration of one carton per man today. In the evening sat in on a poker game, and the long lay-off seems to have been lucky for me, for I won 17 pounds (more than $50).

February 6, 1944 Sunday
Cape Gloucester, New Britain

No work done in the morning, this being Sunday. At first the men just hung around, not wishing to do any more work on an area that we are going to abandon. Then word was passed that there had been a change in the plans, and that we were going to remain at this location. The news was received with delight by the men and officers. The orders were that the men were to clean up around their own tents, and that tomorrow there would be a big working party to clear up the rest of the area. It was a hot, sunny day, so I with two other men to the native village to the west. As we neared it, we heard the beat of drums and the chant of native singing. When we arrived at the scene, we found all the natives in the center of their village doing some tribal dances. The drumming was coming from a 55-gallon steel gasoline drum which had been set up on edge and on which several of the natives were pounding with stones. That was all the music. The natives were all dressed up, with new grass on the women's skirts; all the heads shaved, except for a round patch on top; and what little hair was left was tinted deep red and black. The drum was located in the center of the clearing; and the dancers, both male and female of all ages, were in a large circle. When the drummers began pounding on the gasoline drum and chanting, the dancers picked up the chant, and linked arms in groups of four or five, with the end dancers carrying a 6-foot long bamboo staff. They closed in on the drums, both drummers and dancers singing. When they reached a tight circle about the drum, they continued singing and dancing. The dance seemed to consist of one simple step. They kicked forward with the left foot, brought it back and placed their weight on it, then kicked back with the right foot. That was all the dancing that was done. From a loose circle with gaps in it they moved up on the drummers into a tight circle, and then kicked back and forth until the end of the dance. The dances lasted a short period of time — about three or four minutes. There was a short pause between the dances, then they were resumed. The singing sounded all alike to me, but perhaps they sang different songs for each dance. The Division Intelligence Officer was there with a party as guests of some Australian officers who controlled the natives. Col. Buckley, the Intelligence Officer, had some cameramen with him, and they were busy photographing the dances with still and movie cameras. We sat quite a while watching the dances... At about 1600 the dance broke up, and the natives went to their shacks and began preparing their supper of boiled rice surmounted with canned corned beef. I back to camp. After supper I played poker, winning three pounds. An unusual hand occurred during the game. I held a pair of fours, and drew

Natives and Marines on a truck, Cape Gloucester, New Britain, in March 1944.

two more fours, so that I had four of a kind. I kept raising and being raised until all players dropped out except another man who had drawn three cards. We kept raising each other until I began to suspect that he also had four of a kind. As mine were very low, I finally called; and sure enough, he had four aces. There was at least eight pounds (about $25) in that pot. The game ended shortly after 2100, when the air raid alert went. I to bed, but got little sleep, as there were about three other air raids during the night. I didn't get out of the cot, but the banging of nearby guns kept me awake.

February 7, 1944 Monday
Cape Gloucester, New Britain

The new Battery Commander had given me my orders last night, and I had transmitted them to the Section Chiefs. At reveille, the Chiefs got their men up promptly, instead of letting them stay in their sacks as long as they wanted to. The line at breakfast was the longest since we hit the island, and most of the men preferred to stay in bed and miss breakfast; but as they had been aroused, they decided to eat. It was 0800 before breakfast was finished, and we could not get the men out for the working party at 0800 as planned. It was 0815 when the call was given for the working parties. They broke out rapidly, and were put to work. They were quite tired, as there had been about three air raids during last night, and the raids had lasted for some time. I hadn't arisen for the air raids, but they had kept me awake. There were about forty men on the working party, and they did a lot of work in cleaning the place. Pay Clerk Eggers and Paymaster Sergeant Skupien arrived today to make arrangements for paying the men. I played poker in the evening, with poor luck, winning ten shillings.

CHAPTER 4

Return and Rebuilding
June 2, 1944–December 31, 1945

2Jun44

Embarked aboard USS *General Robert L. Howze* at Pavuvu Island, Russell Island, British Solomon Islands and sailed there from same date. Arrived at Lunga Point, Guadalcanal, British Solomon Islands 2Jun44 and sailed therefrom 4Jun44. Arrived and disembarked at San Francisco, California June 19, 1944.

July 25, 1944 Tuesday
Station Hospital, AAB, NAAF

(No entries) (This was an Army Air Force (?) hospital located in Weequahic Park, Newark, N.J.)

Was being treated for malaria.

August 17, 1944 Thursday
295 Avon Avenue, Newark, N.J.

Today is my fourth wedding anniversary. Bess and I puttered about the house during the day. In the afternoon Bess and I downtown, and she had the beneficiary on her life insurance policy changed from her mother to me. To the War Manpower Commission to arrange for a release for Bess, so that she could get a job in California if she wished, but it was too late in the day. We ate at a Chinese place, and then to a local movie. Stopped off at a cafe called the Hour Glass, and had a couple of drinks before going home.

September 3, 1944 Sunday
San Diego, Calif.
       Up and packed Bess's stuff. We had a late breakfast, and took a walk
to the beach afterward. Back to the house and told the landlady that Bess
was leaving today. She took it very nicely, and we parted on good terms.
We to San Diego, and to the house of our new landlady, Mrs. Meyers. Left
our bags there, and back downtown. Had a light snack, and then by taxi
to the border. Went across into Mexico, and had just time to purchase our
tickets and get seated before the bullfights started. The two matadors today
were Armillita and Perez. They had 3 bulls each, and these bulls were very
fierce — much fiercer than the bulls I saw about 2 months ago. One of the
horses was severely gored; and one of the men handling the capes was
knocked down; but the bull was drawn off before he could be hurt. Perez
was very poor today; but the other matador was magnificent, even to one
as little versed in that cruel and stupid game as I am. Bess liked it fairly
well, but was horrified by the cruelty and brutality of the sport... All the
places were crowded in Tia Juana, so we back to San Diego to eat. Then
to our new place on Texas Street in San Diego, where I spent the night.

September 6, 1944 Wednesday
Camp Pendleton, Oceanside, Calif.
       A very slow day today. In the afternoon we were called into the office
of the Colonel commanding this regiment, and he told us that we were all
going to move to a new area, and have the new area to ourselves. The area
is No. 17, and is nearer to the road to Oceanside by about a mile. I asked
when we might expect to move, and we were told "tomorrow or the next
day." We are to get the recruits we are to train in the very near future. I
am assigned to a Headquarters Company; so I will not do any troop training. My work will be paper work in the administrative end of the job. At
1630 Holt called for me, and I home. Sat around reading for a while, and
then early to bed, as I felt tired.

September 7, 1944 Thursday
Camp Pendleton, Oceanside, Calif.
       Suffered an attack of malaria today. I had been feeling the symptoms
increasing each day; and this morning, riding to the barracks, my stomach felt queer and I thought I was going to vomit. My bones ached, I felt
a chill, and I had a severe headache. I took 2 of the quinine pills that my
brother-in-law, Bill Panitch, had given me. I repeated this dose at 4-hour
intervals during the day, and my headache cleared up and I was able to
keep going all day. When I arrived at the barracks, I found everybody in

the process of moving. I got my stuff together, and despite my poor condition, I managed to get moved to the new Area 17. Everything was in a state of much confusion. We were paid at 1400, and I received all the money I had saved overseas. I had asked for a check, but received the money in cash. Things got very busy in the afternoon, and I had just about decided to stay in the barracks tonight and continue on my work, when Holt arrived with his car and urged me to go home with him. I went. Found that our two suitcases had been delivered by the express company. Wrote a letter to my brother Jack, and spent a couple of hours unpacking before going to bed.

September 12, 1944 Tuesday
Camp Pendleton, Oceanside, Calif.
Worked pretty hard today. Things are straightening out in the office. In the afternoon Holt called me and said he had to go somewhere tonight, and couldn't take me home; but he had arranged a ride for me. At 1730 a fellow called and took me within a short trolley ride of the house. We have received several letters— including some that have been readdressed from our Newark address; so I guess our letter carrier has our change of address. I wrote a letter to Bill, Bess's brother, thanking him for the quinine pills he gave me that prevent a serious malaria attack. Bess has not been feeling well lately, and has vomited a couple of mornings.

September 14, 1944 Thursday
San Diego, Calif.
Up, and to work in Holt's car. It was a cold, raw day. Kept busy all day. Home in the evening, and was greeted by Bess with the news that she had been to the doctor's, and he had told her that she was pregnant. This news made me very, very happy. I took her out and we to an ice cream parlor to celebrate.

September 16, 1944 Saturday
San Diego, Calif.
Slept late today. Up and wrote letters to Bove and to Bill Kuntze. In the evening downtown and to a movie with Bess. Ate after the show, and then walked about town window shopping. Home fairly early. Bess is feeling better since the doctor gave her some medicine to prevent her early morning sickness.

September 19, 1944, through November 17, 1944
(No entries)

November 18, 1944 Saturday
Camp Pendleton — San Diego, Calif.
    (No entry)

November 19–20, 1944
San Diego, Calif.
    (No entries)

> (During the above periods, Bess was informed that her illness was due
> not to pregnancy, but to a malignancy. Her condition rapidly worsened
> to such an extent that I requested emergency leave for myself. Arranged
> for a registered nurse, who attended Bess on our trip by train back to New-
> ark, where she could be looked after by her brother, Dr. William Panitch.)

November 25, 1944 Saturday
arrived in New York, N. Y.
    (No entry)

> An ambulance met our train in New York. Through the efforts of her
> brother, Dr. Bill Panitch, Bess was admitted to Sloan Kettering Memor-
> ial Hospital in New York. (York Avenue at 68th St.)
>   On November 27, 1944, Bess passed away.
>   Buried November 30, 1944, in Hebrew Cemetery, Newark, N.J.
>   (No further entries in 1944)
>   (Since the last entry, September 18, 1944, I had been assigned as First
> Sergeant of Headquarters and Service Company, 4th Infantry Training
> Regiment. The death of Bess had been a desolating loss, and I was feel-
> ing lonely and rootless. The diary resumes with the following entry.)

January 2, 1945 Tuesday
H&S Co., 4th Infantry Training Regiment
Area 17-B-I, Camp Pendleton, Oceanside, Cal.
    Received a letter from my lawyer, Louis K. Press, telling me he was
proceeding with the closing of Bess's estate. Also received a letter from the
Abends, expressing sympathy at the news of the death of Bess last Novem-
ber 27th. I have a lot of correspondence that should be taken care of, but
I find great difficulty in getting myself to write.

January 5, 1945 Friday
    Paid the men today at 1300. I didn't draw any money, letting my pay
accumulate on my pay account... I had a headache, and felt poor all day.
Took an atabrine pill in the morning, and a couple of quinine pills at
night. It feels like an attack of malaria. This is being written after taking

the two quinine pills, on an empty stomach. My hands are trembling, and I am having difficulty controlling them.

January 6, 1945 Saturday

The barracks were inspected this morning by the Company Commander, Warrant Officer Baker, and found in good condition. Had a visit from Master TechSgt Manasse, who used to cook for me on Guadalcanal and on Cape Gloucester. He has volunteered to go across again, and is now in a draft which will leave very soon. If all my affairs were straightened out here, I might consider going across again also. I am very bored and uninterested here. Among the affairs that I have unsettled are: Bess's estate; my request for transfer to the east coast; my recommendation for promotion to the rank of Warrant Officer, Postal.

January 18, 1945 Thursday
H&S Co., 4th Infantry Training Regiment
Area 17-B-I, Camp Pendleton, Oceanside, Cal.

Have a bad head cold. I am taking quinine for it. The weather is chilly and sunless here. The work is light these days— so light that my clerks are becoming restless... In Europe, the English and Americans are making slow progress, while the Russians are moving ahead along a vast front in a push that is irresistibly rolling toward Berlin. I sure hope that Russia gets to Berlin before the English or the Americans, for they will take a greater revenge on the Nazis than would the Anglo-Americans. The progress of the war seems satisfactory, but I become discouraged when I think of all the problems that will confront the Allies in the post-war era. Will it be possible to prevent Germany from starting another World War in 20 or 30 years from now? There were a great many very nice people killed by those beasts, and there are many signs that they are thinking about another try at conquering the world in a third attempt at some future date... Very little is heard of the war in the Pacific, except McArthur's struggle in the Philippines. The news says nothing of Marine activity.

February 13, 1945 Tuesday
H&S Co., 4th Infantry Training Regiment
Area 17-B-I, Camp Pendleton, Oceanside, Cal.

Cool today. Read in the papers of the big snowstorms back east; and now of the thaws that threaten to flood some of the New England states. The papers also gave the first news of the meeting of Churchill, Stalin and Roosevelt in the Crimea. The results of the talks do not seem to be very concrete. It is foolish, I think, to hope for a clean-cut end to this war, and a satisfactory settlement of the political and economic problems of the post-war period. Nor do I believe that this will be the last war.

April 5, 1945 Thursday
Engr. Demo. Co., Spec. Schools Bn, Schools Regt.,
Area 16-B-3, Camp Pendleton, Oceanside, Cal.
      Did very little work all day. Read about three magazines. The present First Sergeant, Bell, is still doing all the work. He is an old-timer, and is called by his men "the bull of the woods." It is embarrassing to have him around, and I will be glad when he is finally relieved and I can take over. It should be a very simple matter to run this company... The food here is greatly inferior to that I have been getting on this post. In a way, this is of benefit to me, as I have been eating too much... Went to the movies tonight again, and then back to the barracks. Another reason I will be glad to see Bell go is that I will then be able to move into the office building and out of the crowded little room in which I am quartered at present. I am at loose ends. I have no specific aims or ambitions. I would like to get married again, but have not met the right girl, and do not know how to go about meeting her. I would like to be made a Warrant Officer, but do not know how to bring this about.

April 12, 1945 Thursday
Engr. Demo. Co., Spec. Schools Bn, Schools Regt.,
Area 16-B-3, Camp Pendleton, Oceanside, Cal.
      In the afternoon received the shocking news of President Franklin D. Roosevelt's death. This is a terrible loss for millions of small, ordinary people. He was a great humanitarian, and is assured of a prominent place in history. The progress of the world toward peace and universal democracy has received a set-back in his loss. It is a very depressing event.

May 3, 1945 Thursday
Engr. Demo. Co., Spec. Schools Bn, Schools Regt.,
Area 16-B-3, Camp Pendleton, Oceanside, Cal.
      Felt pretty sleepy today. The papers and the radio are full of guesses and predictions as to when Germany would be officially declared conquered and victory in Europe announced. I do not see why the big press associations are making such desperate efforts to announce the end of the European phase of the war at the exact instant it occurs. To the great majority of people it would make no difference even if the result was announced two or three days later. To the men fighting, I can see where every minute might mean the difference between life and death.

May 31, 1945 Thursday
Engr. Demo. Co., Spec. Schools Bn., Schools Regt.,
Area 16-B-3, Camp Pendleton, Oceanside, Cal.

Was kept busy all day getting out the first of the month reports. There is much news of the terrible bombing that is being given to Japan, and it looks as though Japan will not be able to last very long under it. It will not surprise me to see Japan defeated before the end of the year. Perhaps I have had my last trip out of this country for this war... Today a Marine Corps dispatch was received canceling the Letter of Instruction under which I was recommended to Marine Corps Schools. I do not know how this will affect my recommendation, as nothing was said about those recommendations already made. I sure wish I knew one way or the other about this matter.

June 12, 1945 Tuesday
Engr. Demo. Co., Spec. Schools Bn., Schools Regt.,
Area 16-B-3, Camp Pendleton, Oceanside, Cal.

Felt better today. Heard rumors that there had been a conference in Washington attended by the heads of the Marine Corps; and that it had been decided to form a new Division — the 7th. As if in support of this rumor, an order came out canceling the disbanding of four Training Battalions which had been set for June 16th. The revoking of this order for disbanding would indicate that there will be a lot of training going on. Perhaps there is some foundation for the rumor of the formation of a 7th Division... One of the officers in Headquarters Company was promoted today. This was all the new business accomplished. I sent the car into town and the horn is now fixed. In the past few weeks I have accumulated quite a few scratches and some dents in the fenders of the car. I will have to send it into town to have it retouched soon.

July 12, 1945 Thursday
Range Co., Hq. Battalion, Marine Training Command,
Area 16-B-3, Camp Pendleton, Oceanside, Cal.

A dispatch was received from Headquarters of the Marine Corps, addressed to the Commanding General of this area, notifying him that six men had been accepted for Marine Corps Schools at Quantico, Va., including Platoon Sergeant Hardman, the fellow who took the examination with me. This dispatch also said that action on my application was being held up pending receipt of the report of my physical examination. By now they must have received this report, and I should hear from them very soon. I hope they let me know very soon. I am very desirous of being ordered to the east coast. Now I have some purpose in life. I have something to strive for. I will work very hard to become an officer, just for something to aim for. My studies will keep me occupied, and prevent me from continually mulling over my position... In the evening I wrote a letter to Fred Bove telling him how things stood with me. I also wrote a letter to Gladys Poindexter in Florida, telling her to go ahead and get married if she has the opportunity, and not to wait for me.

July 23, 1945 Monday
Range Co., Hq. Battalion, Marine Training Command,
Area 16-B-3, Camp Pendleton, Oceanside, Cal.
     Hurrah! Hurrah! Hurrah! Received a telephone call today telling me to "stand by" for transfer to the east coast to the Marine Corps Schools at Quantico. The tentative date is Wednesday the 25th. Gee, I am glad. Most of my wishes are being granted. My only other wishes now are that I meet some very nice girl that I can make my wife, and that I have several children with her quickly. Then life will be complete for me... The Range Company moved into the barracks today. They are a disorderly lot. They lack firm control. We received the official orders for the disbanding of the entire Schools Regiment, of which the Special Schools Battalion is a unit. If my transfer becomes effective on Wednesday, I will be saved a lot of work in connection with the disbanding, which is scheduled for the 31st. Packed some of my stuff and went into town to try to ship it by railway express, but the office was closed when I got there. Received a letter from my brother Jack, acknowledging the letter I sent him recently. Also received a letter from Anita, Pat's wife, chiding me for not writing.

July 26, 1945 Thursday
En route to Quantico, Va.
     Felt quite rested after five hours sleep. Rose at 0700. Spent the day in the club car, talking with passengers and playing cards. Learned the game of hearts, and played for a penny a point, losing a dollar and a half... Now that I am leaving California, I am regretful that I didn't take more advantage of my stay there. I should have looked around and considered getting some property or land, and I should have made more trips. But I had been resentful at being stationed there; and with Bess along, I had had other ideas. Bess's illness and passing took up a lot of time, and then the emotional readjustment afterward consumed more time. I had always planned to stay on the east coast, near New York, to live. But if conditions were right, I would move to the west coast to live — preferably at Los Angeles

or somewhere south of that city, along the coast. I may yet come back to the west coast. My health has been very good, and there has been a very considerable improvement in my eyesight here, with the wide open spaces... I stayed up until 2000, then to my berth.

August 7, 1945 Tuesday
Barracks 3134, Screening Detachment,
Marine Corps Schools, Quantico, Va.
The morning was spent in schools on the M-1 rifle and Interior Guard Duty. In the afternoon we saw a movie, a training film. After that we had an hour of physical drill, followed by two trips over the obstacle course. I am very much out of condition, but I am doing as well as most of the class. This training is very good for me in view of the way I have permitted myself to become soft and flabby. The radio and the newspapers are full of the effects of the new atomic bomb that was dropped on Japan. The possibilities of this new discovery stagger the imagination. Its power for evil is so terrible. A notice was posted on the bulletin board for me and eight others to take our "Y" Form examination tomorrow morning. I guess this is it. I seriously doubt whether I can pass that eye test.

August 8, 1945 Wednesday
Barracks 3134, Screening Detachment,
Marine Corps Schools, Quantico, Va.
In the morning with the others to take my "Y" Form examination, and I in great trepidation over my eye examination. But that was one of the easiest parts of the examination. I came out with 17/20 in both eyes. I am now set as far as physical examinations are concerned until just before graduation. They gave me a height of 5 feet, 6 inches, which just passes me. I didn't know that there was a minimum on height; but I will have to be careful that they do not give me less than the 5' 6 when I get the final examination. In the afternoon everybody got excited about the news that Russia had declared war on Japan. With the advent of the atomic bomb, and with Russia's entry into the war against her, Japan should quit fairly soon. They may not even make another class for Platoon Commanders School. If I do not go ahead with my officer's course, I may get out of the service.

August 9, 1945 Thursday
Spent the morning with classes. In the afternoon we had Close Order Drill, Physical Drill, and ran the obstacle course two times. The whole

place excited over news that Japan was suing for peace. Of course, it is the finest thing that could happen for this war to be over, but it will have a bad effect on my efforts to become an officer. If I had any brains, I would get out right now and try to get a good Civil Service job before they begin releasing the millions of service men they will have to turn loose after the war. If I thought I was going to be successful, I would stay and become a Second Lieutenant, just so I could say I was an officer in this war. The fact that I had been an officer will have certain definite advantages on my applications for preferred positions.

August 14, 1945 Tuesday
Barracks 3134, Screening Detachment,
Marine Corps Schools, Quantico, Va.

Spent the day in classes and in drilling. The radio promised to have the official surrender announcements this evening, and after supper they began giving us the details of the surrender. Most of the men took off for the various nearby towns. The radio gave snatches of the celebrations in the different cities. I stayed in the barracks, and to bed early.

August 15, 1945 Wednesday

A very hot day today. The whole class sweated profusely. Part of the post is being given the day off. We were promised the day off tomorrow. We were also told that we were not to be sent on to the next phase of our training — the Candidates Refresher Course — on August 28th as originally scheduled, but on October 1st. This is the beginning of the shake-out process, I fear. This the first of many delays that will be presented to us. I would have stayed in for the six months that the former schedule required, just to become an officer; but I am almost certain that now they will make it for at least a year — maybe two years. That is longer than I can spare from my life, and longer than I can arrange for. It looks as though I have missed the boat again.

August 26, 1945 Sunday
Barracks 3127 Screening Detachment,
Marine Corps Schools, Quantico, Va.

Rose at 0800. It was quite cool. Dressed, had breakfast, and over to Newark. To the cemetery where Bess lies, and tried to find her grave, but the place was so overgrown that I could not locate it. Finally got some help from the cemetery staff, and found it. The weeds were waist high, and nothing had been done on the place for sometime. I arranged to have the weeds cleared from the grave, to have a temporary cement bed placed on it, and to have the plot planted... Returned to camp in the evening.

September 23, 1945 Sunday
Barracks 3132, Screening Detachment,
Marine Corps Schools, Quantico, Va.

Up at 0800, and felt good despite all the drinking I had done last night. To Pat's after breakfast, and in his car to the cemetery to visit Bess's grave. It was raining all morning. We got in touch with a dealer in tombstones and got some estimates on stones for Bess's grave. Had Pat drive me to Bill Panitch's house, and visited Bill for about half an hour. I told him I was planning to arrange for a tombstone for Bess, and we drove to the cemetery and we discussed stone styles and inscriptions. I suggested he talk to the rest of the family of Bess's, and see if any of them had any ideas in the matter; and that I would be up again next week and would put in the final order for the stone... Had lunch at Pat's. Called this Honey girl whom I had been reminded about yesterday. I had been told yesterday that she was doing very well — that she had a car and expensive furs and a good job. When I called her house today, her mother told me that Honey was feeling very poorly, had threatened suicide, and had left for some place unknown to her mother for a rest. Her mother suggested that I call in a week, and she would know more... I took the 1745 out of Newark, and stood all the way to Washington.

October 5, 1945 Friday
Barracks 3132, Screening Detachment,
Marine Corps Schools, Quantico, Va.

In the morning drove to Washington with another fellow and his wife. The town was crowded, and a big parade was going on in honor of Admiral Nimitz, the Admiral who did so much in the Pacific. The skies were filled with more planes than I had ever seen before... This fellow with me and I went to the Navy Annex, and we looked at our file jackets. I found that my request for assignment to the Officer Training class at Camp Lejeune had been forwarded from the Schools on the post with a recommendation for disapproval. This was quite a shock to me. I can't figure why this should have been done. I will try to find out... Came back to camp in the evening and called Freda Borok and we had dinner and spent the evening together. We got along very well. We danced and went to the movies. One of the actors in the picture was Charles Waggenheim, whom I knew in Hollywood.

October 11, 1945 Thursday
Barracks 3133, Screening Detachment,
Marine Corps Schools, Quantico, Va.

Received a letter from Bove scolding me for not having written to him sooner. He makes inquiry as to what has happened to me, and what my plans are. In the afternoon I to Washington to see if any action had been taken on my letter requesting transfer to Washington for duty. I got quite a shock when I found out what action had been taken — they had issued orders transferring me to Chicago, Illinois, where they were establishing a big separation center. They told me that there was no need for a First Sergeant in Washington, and that they could use me in Chicago. The thought came to me that Chicago was going to be a very cold place this winter, and that I detested cold. Also, if I should be discharged from Chicago, I would receive much less travel pay, and would have to bear the expense of traveling to New Jersey. However, I decided that any change was interesting, and told them that I would accept the job. We got to talking, and I mentioned that there was a job waiting for me at Quantico; whereupon they asked me if I would prefer that to Chicago. I thought it over and decided to take Quantico; and the officer-in-charge ordered my transfer to Chicago revoked... I out and took in a newsreel movie, and home early. I was downcast and dispirited at the disappointment of not getting to Washington, and at the casual manner in which they shift me around after the long and faithful service I have performed. Home early and to bed.

October 24, 1945 Wednesday
Barracks 3088, Hq. Co., Training Bn.,
Marine Corps Schools, Quantico, Va.

During the last couple of days notice has been received that two new ribbons have been authorized for which I am eligible. One of them is the American Campaign ribbon, which requires only a year's service in the United States since Pearl Harbor; and the other is the Victory Medal for the Second World War. The award of medals so easily earned cheapens all the rest of them. Even the Congressional Medal of Honor has been awarded too liberally in this war... As of November 1st, the point requirement for discharge has been lowered to 50 points. Everybody eligible in this Company for discharge wishes to be discharged just as soon as possible... I would like to get a furlough in before I get out. Furloughs have been increased just recently from 15 to 30 days annually.

November 11, 1945 Sunday
Barracks 3088, Hq. Co., Training Bn.,
Marine Corps Schools, Quantico, Va.

Up, and felt good after last night's drinking. To Newark and called the gravestone maker and he said he had not received the Jewish inscription for the stone from Bill Panitch. I called Bill, and he made some lame excuses, and said I would have the inscription by tomorrow. I gave the stone cutters the English part of the inscription. I to Rabbi Silberfeld, the rabbi who had married Bess and me, and who had officiated at her burial, and arranged for him to officiate at the unveiling of her stone. I made the date for three weeks from today, on December 2nd. I called Pat at his home, and could not get him. I was about to leave for New York when I took a last chance and called at his father-in-law's house. There I found him. I went over there and asked him to see that Bill gets that inscription to the man tomorrow. Also asked him to arrange to get me the cards announcing the unveiling, and to mail them out to all our relatives. Left early in the evening, and to New York. Fiddled around getting dinner, and took in a newsreel. Took a late train out, and got to camp at 0400 in the morning.

December 9, 1945 Sunday
Barracks 3088, Hq. Co., Training Bn., Marine Corps Schools, Quantico, Va.

Up and had breakfast. Pat called for me, and we to the railroad station and picked up Henrietta and her three children. Took them to Pat's house, and I and Pat to the cemetery. The stone was up, and covered with a cloth. The stone looked small to me, in comparison with the double stones around it. But it is a nice stone. The grave had been fixed up. I had lunch at Pat's, and then we all to the cemetery. It was a very nice

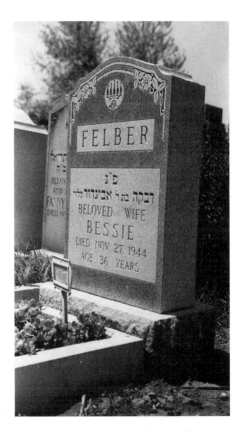

Headstone for Bess Panitch Felber, Hebrew Cemetery, Newark, N.J. Photograph made Dec. 9, 1945.

day for this time of the year. There was a large turn-out of relatives, both from Bess's side and from mine. It was very embarrassing to meet Bess's relatives. I was very glad when the ordeal was over. The rabbi made a very dignified and respectful ceremony of the affair... After the ceremony, to Pat's with several of our relatives. Stayed there until after dinner. Pat drove me to Olga's house, where I stayed a short while and picked up some bonds and a check that had been addressed to the Avon Avenue address. Then to the train and back to Washington. Arrived at the barracks at 0100.

December 27, 1945 Thursday
3458 Chase Ave., Miami Beach, Fla.

It was 0330 when I arrived at downtown Miami. To Kay's place, and they were closing up the Singing Bar for the night. They drove me home, and I to bed after 0400. Slept until 1030. Up and had breakfast, and greeted Pat and Anita. They went swimming in the afternoon, and I went along and met Alex and Sylvia Goldberg. Did but very little swimming, and then back to the house. Took things easy. Pat and Anita went out in the afternoon, but I stayed in. Worked on a jigsaw puzzle for a while, then to bed at 2200.

December 30, 1945 Sunday
3458 Chase Ave., Miami Beach, Fla.

Took things easy around the house most of the day. Took a nap in the afternoon. In the evening to the Olympic Hotel where I met Freda and Eddie Levine, and Alex and Sylvia Goldberg. They introduced me to Sadie Ackerman, a school teacher in the Newark, N.J. schools. She is the sister of the husband of Rose Abend. She is a short girl about five feet two, with dark blond hair. The six of us to the Seven Seas Restaurant, where we had a very nice meal. At about 2100 we all to a night club called the Bowery, where we met Pat and Anita. The place was stifling hot and very noisy, and the entertainment was loud and coarse and vulgar. After a couple of drinks we all left. They couldn't make up their minds where to go, so Sadie and I left them and we to the beach and to a night club called the Five O' Clock Club. We had a couple of drinks and danced and had a rather nice time. Saw the show, and left after 0100. We stopped in the park near her hotel, and sat and talked a while. It was 0200 when I brought her home. Back to the hotel, and to bed at 0300.

December 31, 1945 Monday
3458 Chase Ave., Miami Beach, Fla.

Rose late and had breakfast. Took things easy in the afternoon, and had a little nap. In the evening bathed and dressed. Presented Marcia with a nice bracelet, and Buddy with a good fountain pen. They were very pleased with their gifts. Out and to the Olympic Hotel and met Sadie. We to the Park Avenue Restaurant, where we had an excellent dinner, after having to wait in line. After dinner we out to a movie to let our dinner settle, and to pass the shank of the evening. After the movie we tried a couple of places, but they were either too full of New Year's Eve guests, or the prices were prohibitive. We finally wound up in Miami at a place called the Clover Club, where the evening was spent drinking and dancing. We had rather a nice time there. At

Abraham Felber with Sadie Ackerman on their wedding day, February 24, 1946.

about 0230 we left, and I took Sadie to her hotel. We said affectionate goodbyes, and I made a tentative date for January 12 with her in New York. Back to the house, and was told that my train reservation was for 0815 that morning. It was 0400 then. I packed in about fifteen minutes, and to bed for a couple of hours.

Afterword

On February 24, 1946, my father, the author of this diary, married Sarah (Sadie) Ackerman. Shortly thereafter he had the family he wanted, a son and two daughters.

During the Korean War, my father trained Marines at Camp Lejeune, North Carolina. He retired from the Marines as a Warrant Officer.

My father retired from the Newark, N.J., post office after 46 years of service. My mother was a schoolteacher for more than 30 years. Today, my father and mother live close to their daughters in New Jersey. Now in their nineties, they have six grandchildren.

When my sisters and I read this diary, we are awed by the "greatest generation." We can never repay the debt we owe to these ordinary men and women for their extraordinary deeds, except perhaps through our own children. May their sacrifices for us always be remembered.

Franklin Felber
San Diego, Calif.
January 2002

Annotations

by William H. Bartsch

March 1, 1941   Felber uses the old designation, the 1st Marine Brigade, for the 1st Marine Division. On this day, Headquarters and Service Battery, 11th Marines was activated, with Col. Pedro del Valle assuming command of the Regiment. (Emmet, p. 7.)

April 14, 1941   The USS *McCawley*, at 7,858 tons and 466-foot length, was indeed smaller than the USS *Wharton*, at 13,788 tons and 535-foot length. The *McCawley*, built in 1928 as the M.S. *Santa Barbara*, was commissioned as a transport in the Navy in 1940. (Fahey, p. 52; Charles, p. 147.)

April 15, 1941   The USS *Elliot* was the transport USS *George F. Elliott* (AP 13), built in 1940 as the *DelBrasil*. (Charles, p. 126.)

May 27, 1941   The *Barnett* was the transport USS *Barnett* (AP 11), commissioned in 1940. (Fahey, p. 37.) President Roosevelt delivered "an emotionally-charged radio speech" before a group of Latin American diplomats at the White House in which he proclaimed "an unlimited national emergency" and called for accelerated defensive measures against the threat of German aggression. (Gellman, p. 255.)

July 6, 1941   Shipboard conditions on Navy transports at the time were roundly criticized by the Marines. The USS *McCawley* (AP 10) was regarded as "overcrowded," with troop spaces, washrooms, and toilet facilities in "such a deplorable condition as to cause a general depressing effect on the troops." (Isely and Crowl, p. 63.)

July 11, 1941   What Felber refers to as Hurst Beach was commonly known as Onslow Beach. The men of the 1st Marine Division made their first landings on

Onslow Beach, a stretch of sand extending fourteen miles, which was to become very familiar to them in intensive amphibious landing training prior to joint training exercises with the Army the following month. (McMillan, p. 8.)

August 3, 1941   This massive exercise would involve the participation of the 1st Marine Division jointly with the 1st Army Division in a "full dress" landing. (McMillan, p. 8; Isely and Crowl, p. 63.)

August 4, 1941   This day commenced the weeklong exercises of the 1st Joint Training Force, involving the participation of 16,500 officers and men of the 1st Army Division and the 1st Marine Division. They were the largest amphibious landing exercises ever held in the United States to date, employing 42 naval vessels, four aircraft carriers and their four Marine aircraft squadrons, plus the new Higgins landing craft. (McMillan, p. 8; Isely and Crowl, p. 63; Smith, p. 81.)

September 27, 1941   An 11,000-acre tract of land near New River, N.C., had been purchased by the War Department in 1941 to meet the Marines' need for an East Coast amphibious training facility. When units of the 1st Marine Division began arriving in late September 1941, it was largely a wasteland. They immediately began setting up a "Tent City" that was at that time called "Marine Barracks, New River, N.C." In late 1942 it was re-designated "Camp Lejeune." (McMillan, p.8; Vandegrift, p. 99; "History of Camp Lejeune," www.lejeune.usmc.mil/history.html.)

October 19, 1941   On October 22, 1941, a fourth battalion was added to the 11th Marines as a 105mm howitzer battalion. The other three were 75mm pack howitzer battalions. (Emmet, p. 7.)

October 30, 1941   Felber and the others in their new camp on the edge of a coastal swamp faced a bitterly cold winter in their tents, heated with kerosene stoves that risked setting their tents on fire. The New River base was isolated, far from railroad connections and inadequately served by buses. (McMillan, p. 9.)

June 9, 1942   The 11th Marines left New River with the 1st Marines this day by train for San Francisco. The regiment now had a 5th battalion equipped with 105mm howitzers. (Emmet, p. 7.) Earlier, on May 1st, the advance echelon of the 1st Marine Division, mainly comprising the 5th Marines, had boarded trains at New River for Norfolk, Virginia, the port of embarkation for its transfer overseas. (McMillan, p. 15.)

June 14, 1942   As the *Kungsholm*, the *John Ericsson*, built in 1928, had been obtained by the War Shipping Administration shortly before December 7, 1941 to transport troops. (Charles, p. 291.) Most of the 1st Marines boarded the *Barnett* and the *George F. Elliott*. (Merillat, p. 32.)

June 22, 1942   The official history of the 11th Marines (Emmet, pp. 7–8) indicates that the Regiment boarded the *John Ericsson* on June 22 and sailed the same day, but Felber's diary documents that the men boarded her on arrival in San Francisco on June 14, remaining on board, except for liberty in town, until the sailing date.

Sailing with the 11th Marines this day was the 1st Marine Regiment, mainly embarked on the USS *Barnett* and USS *George F. Elliott,* leaving San Francisco the same day. The two regiments were considered the rear echelon of the 1st Marine Division being transferred overseas. The forward echelon, comprising Division headquarters, the 5th Marine Regiment, and some divisional units, had sailed from Norfolk on the *Wakefield* on May 20 and arrived in Wellington on June 14. (Johnstone, p. 14; Merillat, pp. 10–11, 31, 32; Frank, p. 48.)

July 11, 1942   1st Marine Division Press Officer 2nd Lt. Herbert C. Merillat watched the *John Ericsson* coming into the docks about 13:00 this day, followed by the *Barnett* and the *George F. Elliott.* (Merillat, p. 32.)

July 12, 1942   Yet unknown to Felber and the others, they were being ordered into combat in the Solomon Islands. On June 26, Vice Admiral Robert L. Ghormley, Commander South Pacific (COMSOPAC) in Auckland had informed Maj. Gen. Alexander A. Vandegrift that his 1st Marine Division was to seize Japanese-held "Tulagi and adjacent positions" in the Solomon Islands plus Ndeni in the Santa Cruz Islands to the east, with D-Day set at August 1. The orders came as a shock to Vandegrift, who had been informed before departing the U.S. that his troops would have at least six months in New Zealand to complete training begun at New River. Now the 11th and the 1st Marines that had just arrived in Wellington with the second echelon hurriedly had to board the transports that were being combat-loaded for the voyage to the Solomons. (Frank, p. 48; Vandegrift, p. 17; McMillan, pp. 17–18.)

Brig. Gen. Vandegrift had been promoted to Major General and assumed command of the 1st Marine Division on March 23, 1942, replacing Maj. Gen. Philip H. Torrey. (Vandegrift, p. 99.) Vandegrift had been ordered to prepare an infantry regiment for shipment to Samoa and, anticipating it would be facing combat shortly after its arrival, had stripped his other infantry regiments of their most experienced officers and NCOs for reassignment to the 7th Marines before its departure. On March 21, 1942, the 1st Battalion was attached to the 3rd Marine Brigade to leave for Samoa with the 7th Marine Regiment of the 1st Marine Division on April 10, 1942. (Emmet, p. 7; Frank, p. 46.)

July 14, 1942   According to the July 1942 muster roll of H&S Battery, 11th Marines, 1st Lt. Charles D. Harris was now Regimental Reconnaissance Officer, and Captain Philip L. Mossburg was Regimental Communications Officer.

July 17, 1942   "Lt. Tatsch" was 1st Lt. James H. Tatsch, at this time the commanding officer of Felber's H&S Battery. (July 1942 muster roll for H&S Battery, 11th Marines.)

July 21, 1942   Embarked on the *Hunter Liggett* were Felber's H&S Battery, the Special Weapons Battery, and the 5th Battalion, totaling 951 officers and men of the 11th Marines, plus 660 personnel from other units. Other Batteries of the 11th Marines were embarked on seven other transports and the cargo ship *Libra* in line with combat loading needs. (Secret Memo.)

July 26, 1942   Press Officer Merillat, now embarked on the *Hunter Liggett* with Felber, first spotted seven warships joining his group, including an aircraft carrier, followed an hour later by ten more ships, including another carrier, and finally eight more vessels, including a third carrier. He was impressed with this "most powerful invasion armada the United States had ever put to sea up to that time." Of the Navy's four carriers, three had been committed to support the Guadalcanal landings. (Merillat, pp. 37–38.)

July 27, 1942   There were reportedly 82 ships in the armada, divided into an Amphibious Force under Rear Admiral Richard Kelly Turner and Air Support Force under Rear Admiral Leigh Noyes. The *Ranger,* operating with the Atlantic Fleet, was not one of the carriers in the Force, which included the three carriers *Enterprise*, *Saratoga*, and *Wasp*. (Frank, p. 51; Merillat, p. 38.)

July 28, 1942   For a detailed description of the four-day practice landing off Koro Island in the Fijis, see Bartsch.

July 29, 1942   The day before, Lt. Tatsch was "placed under arrest pending investigation of discharge of a firearm and wounding of 1st Lt. John D. Jones, USMC," as noted in the July 1942 muster roll of H&S Battery, 11th Marines. Marine Gunner Charles E. Stuart was the Assistant R-1 at the time.

July 30, 1942   Maj. Gen. Vandegrift's staff had estimated the number of Japanese on Guadalcanal at 8,400, but Admiral Turner reduced the number to 7,124. The number is later reported to be 2,571. The Marines totaled about 14,300 men, including 11,300 slated for the Guadalcanal landing. (Frank, pp. 50, 51.)

August 4, 1942   The message read to the troops was apparently from Vice Admiral Ghormley, whom Admiral Ernest J. King, Commander-in-Chief of the U.S. Fleet, had originally designated to "command in person in the operating area." Ghormley decided to command the operation from his headquarters at Noumea, New Caledonia, instead. (Frank, pp. 55–56.)

August 7, 1942   Not mentioned is an attack by nine Japanese Aichi "Val" dive bombers on the ships offshore that commenced about 15:00. Only one hit was scored, on the destroyer *Mugford*, but it killed nineteen men and wounded 32. Intercepted by Navy Grumman Wildcats off the carriers, only three of the Japanese crews survived. (Frank, p. 69.)

August 8, 1942   Felber did not witness the most spectacular event of the day. Twenty-three "Betty" twin-engine bombers from the Japanese naval base at Rabaul appeared shortly before noon off the coast and went after the ships at wave-top height in torpedo attack runs. Before most could launch their torpedoes, the bombers were hit by withering anti-aircraft fire from the screening force of cruisers and destroyers, eight falling into the sea. Only one torpedo scored a hit, striking the destroyer *Jarvis* and killing fifteen of its crew. However, a damaged Betty deliberately crashed into the superstructure of the *George F. Elliott,* setting the transport on fire and resulting in her being scuttled with most of the supplies of the 2nd Battalion, 1st Marines lost. Attacked by Navy Wildcats as they limped back to Rabaul, only five of the Japanese bombers managed to return to base. It was the worst single loss of the *rikko* bombers in the Guadalcanal campaign. (Tagaya, pp. 45–46; Frank, p. 80; Pollock, p. 126.)

August 9, 1942   In the first of a succession of critical naval battles in the Guadalcanal campaign, seven Japanese cruisers and a destroyer engaged in a ferocious battle with a force of five American and Australian cruisers plus a few destroyers off Savo Island after 01:00 on August 9, resulting in the loss of one Australian and three American cruisers and the death of 1,023 men, against only moderate damage to three of the Japanese cruisers and 38 men killed. It was the worst defeat in the history of the U.S. Navy. (Dull, pp. 187–92.)

August 11, 1942   Casey was Sgt. James P. Casey, a mechanic in H&S Battery. Pvt. Leland W. Mattice was a welder in the Battery. (July 1942 muster roll for H&S Battery, 11th Marines.)

August 12, 1942   Kelly was Assistant Cook Joseph A. Kelley in H&S Battery. Lt. Cdr. Charles A. Dittmar, USN, was serving as Regimental and Divisional Chaplain. (July 1942 muster roll for H&S Battery, 11th Marines.)

August 21, 1942   In the first attempt of the Japanese Army to re-take the airfield, 917 officers and men of Col. Kiyonao Ichiki's first echelon that had landed to the east at Taivu Point at 01:00 on August 19 streamed across the sandspit of the "Tenaru River" (actually, Alligator Creek) during the small hours of August 21 against Marines of the 2nd Battalion, 1st Marines, who were supported by a battery of the 1st Special Weapons Battalion. Machine gun, 37mm cannon, and rifle fire, plus artillery fire from the 75mm pack howitzers of the 3rd Battalion, 11th Marines, mowed the Japanese down. Following the mopping-up operations of the 1st Battalion, 1st Marines and a company of the 1st Tank Battalion the following afternoon, the bodies of at least 777 Japanese were found left on the field of battle. (Frank, pp. 147–56.)

August 23, 1942   The information gleaned from the Japanese notebooks that the Japanese killed in the Battle of the Tenaru were the same ones "who had taken the island of Guam and killed all the Marines there" may have been wrong. Guam had been seized (on December 10, 1941) by units of the South Seas Detachment, which comprised the 144th Infantry Regiment and units of the 55th Division, not the 1st echelon of the Ichiki Detachment (of the 28th Infantry Regiment) that the Marines had faced at the Tenaru River. However, following their defeat at the Battle of Midway in early June 1942, the Japanese dropped the plan for the Ichiki Detachment to occupy Midway Island, the Detachment falling back on Guam and coming under the direct control of Imperial General Headquarters, which subsequently ordered it to Guadalcanal. Thus the men of the Detachment had indeed come from Guam, but only after it was already in Japanese hands. (Hough, Ludwig, and Shaw, pp. 77–78; Hayashi, pp. 32, 39; Merillat, p. 88.)

August 24, 1942   A submarine was believed to have been the warship that lobbed shells on the island at 02:00. Reportedly, it was the cargo ship *Fomalhaut* (AK-22), against which was fired the torpedo that missed and ended up on the beach at Kukum as "an object of much curiosity" for the Marines. (Merillat, p. 97.)

August 25, 1942   Three destroyers, arriving off Lunga Point at midnight and unable to establish the location of the airfield, fired their 4.7" guns blindly in the general area, killing two Marines and wounding three. (Frank, p. 189; Watts and Gordon, pp. 265–67.) The air raid that Felber describes was mounted by 23 Betty bombers that hit Henderson Field from 27,000 feet without opposition, as the recently arrived (August 20) Wildcats of Marine Fighting Squadron 223 could not reach them in time. There were no losses on either side. (Tagaya, p. 47; T. Miller, pp. 57, 211.)

August 26, 1942   Sixteen (Betty) bombers unloaded on Henderson Field, burning 2,000 gallons of scarce aviation fuel and damaging planes on the strip. Intercepted by VMF-223 Wildcats waiting for them, two were shot down and a third forced to ditch. In separate dogfights during the raid, three Zeros were shot down. (Tagaya, p. 47; T. Miller, p. 58; Hata and Izawa, p. 379.) The 90mm guns firing at the bombers were of the Marine 3rd Defense Battalion. These 90mm guns could reach to a maximum 39,500 feet. (Updegraph, p. 72.)

August 27, 1942   Lt. Col. William E. Maxwell, who was relieved of his command, had been the CO of the 1st Battalion, 5th Marines. Maxwell had asked to withdraw his men in the early afternoon from a difficult situation in which he was supposed to attack the Japanese west of Kokumbona and return by nightfall. Incensed by Maxwell's request, Maj. Gen. Vandegrift ordered Col. Leroy P. Hunt, the CO of the 5th Marines, to relieve him. (Frank, pp. 195–97.)

August 28, 1942   The press item that Felber read referred to the Battle of the Eastern Solomons, August 24-25, 1942. In this second major naval battle of the Guadalcanal campaign, the Japanese lost the carrier *Ryujo*, the destroyer *Mutsuki*, and the transport *Kinryu Maru,* with the cruiser *Jintsu* suffering major damage, plus 75 aircraft destroyed. On the American side, the carrier *Enterprise* was heavily damaged and 25 aircraft lost. (Frank, pp. 191–93.) The engagement was considered a clear American victory, although Ghormley's claims were greatly exaggerated.

August 29, 1942   The 0045 raid was carried out by three bombers, but is not documented in Japanese records. War correspondent Richard Tregaskis was informed that the unwelcome visitors were "some Jap float planes," individual ones of which would later be dubbed "Louie the Louse." (Tregaskis, p. 174; Merillat, p. 720.) The daylight attack this day was mounted by eighteen Betty bombers, of which one was shot down by VMF 223 Wildcats directly over the area and a second crash-landed at Buka in the western Solomons. There is no record of one crashing into a hangar at Henderson Field, although Felber visited the burning hangar. The raid destroyed two Wildcats and a Dauntless dive-bomber on the field. (Tagaya, p. 47; T. Miller, p. 60; Frank, p. 200; Tregaskis, p. 174.) The supply ship *Burrows* that Felber mentions visiting was the transport *William Ward Burrows* (AP-6) that had arrived with ground personnel for VMF 223 and VMSB 232 and equipment, including aviation gas trucks. (Jones, p. 48; T. Miller, p. 61.)

August 30, 1942   Eighteen Betty bombers attacked shipping in the harbor and sank the converted destroyer-transport USS *Colhoun* (APD-2), not, as the news was rumored, the USS *Gregory* (APD-3), with a perfect pattern of bombs before returning to Rabaul with no losses. The sister destroyer-transport *Gregory* was sunk on September 5 by Japanese destroyers. (Tagaya, p. 47; Frank, p. 202; Roscoe, p. 177.) The new Marine aircraft coming to Guadalcanal arrived during the air raid alert that followed the sinking of the *Colhoun*. They were nineteen Wildcats of VMF-224 and twelve SBD Dauntless dive-bombers of VMSB-231. (T. Miller, pp. 64, 214–15; Frank, p. 202.)

August 31, 1942   The Japanese warships sighted the night before were ferrying troops to Taivu Point to the east to build up forces for a new attempt to seize Henderson Field. (Dull, p. 211.) The vessels were involved in what became known as the "Tokyo Express." The false alarm scramble, to which Felber refers, resulted in the "mysterious disappearance" of three Wildcats of newly arrived VMF-224, one of whose pilots eventually made it back to base. (Frank, p. 203; T. Miller, pp. 214–15.)

September 1, 1942   Lt. Appleton was 1st Lt. Maurice L. Appleton, Jr., the Intelligence Officer of the 11th Marines (R-2). (July 1942 muster roll, H&S Battery, 11th Marines.)

September 2, 1942   Col. Bemis was Lt. Col. John A. Bemis, Executive Officer of the 11th Marines. (July 1942 muster roll, H&S Battery, 11th Marines.) The pre-noon air raid that Felber describes in such detail was mounted by eighteen Betty bombers, which managed to return to Rabaul without loss despite being intercepted by Wildcats. However, two of the twenty escorting Zeros were shot down in dogfights with VMF-223 pilots. (Tagaya, p. 48; Frank, p. 205; Hata & Izawa, p. 379.) The bombing was also a scary experience for Merillat and for a war correspondent sheltering in a hillside trench; bombs fell near them on both sides of Vandegrift's command post, nearly collapsing the whole hillside. (Merillat, p. 109.)

September 3, 1942   The early morning shelling was possibly from the two destroyers of the "Tokyo Express" that had ferried troops and anti-aircraft guns to Taivu

Point late that night and were returning to their base in the Shortland Islands in the western Solomons. War correspondent Tregaskis had been informed, however, that it was a submarine that had shelled them. (Frank, pp. 205–06; Tregaskis, pp. 186–87.)

September 5, 1942   The destroyer-transports *Little* (APD-4) and *Gregory* (APD-3) had heard and seen gunfire about 01:00 from what they believed was a submarine shelling Guadalcanal, as described by Felber. In actuality, the firing was from three destroyers of the "Tokyo Express" that had escorted transports carrying more troops to the Taivu Point area. The *Little* and *Gregory* set out to investigate, but when they neared the Japanese, a PBY inadvertently dropped flares that illuminated both destroyer transports for the destroyers. The *Yudachi* opened fire with its five 5" guns and sank both in a short engagement, with a loss of 22 killed on the *Little* and eleven on the *Gregory*. (Dull, p. 212; Frank, pp. 211–12.) The air raid Felber mentions was mounted by 27 Betty bombers escorted by fifteen Zeros that bombed positions east of the Lunga River. They were intercepted by eighteen Wildcats of VMF-223 and VMF-224, which claimed three bombers and a Zero shot down, but suffered the loss of two of their ships and one pilot. (Japanese Monograph No. 121, p. 19; T. Miller, p. 76; Olynyk.)

September 7, 1942   Following a month of errant bombs hitting near the command post of the 1st Marine Division, Vandegrift decided to shift it south about 1½ miles to a spur on a ridge, which would in a few days become known as "Edson's Ridge." At the same time, it was decided to move the command post of the 11th Marines to a point somewhat north of the new Divisional command post. Vandegrift expected that the next Japanese effort to seize Henderson Field would be along the coast, not from inland. (Merillat, p. 115; Twining, p. 95.)

September 8, 1942   Lt. Col. Stack was Lt. Col. Vincent E. Stack, Divisional Paymaster. Major Arthur B. Maas was Regimental Paymaster for the 11th Marines. (Muster rolls, August 1942, for Headquarters Company, 1st Marine Division and H&S Battery, 11th Marines.)

September 9, 1942   Some of the bombs during the aerial attack may have hit the beaches, but they were aimed at shipping in Sealark Channel. Twenty-five Bettys, escorted by thirteen Zeros, were intercepted by sixteen Wildcats of VMF-223 that had scrambled at 11:15 and caused the attack to be ineffectual, with two of the bombers shot down. (Tagaya, p. 62; T. Miller, p. 83; Olynyk; Japanese Monograph 121, p. 20.)

September 10, 1942   Positions on the east side of Henderson Field were bombed by 26 Bettys escorted by fifteen Zeros. Sixteen Wildcats of VMF-223 and VMF-224 intercepted them and shot down three of the bombers, against the loss of two Wildcats. (Tagaya, p. 62; Japanese Monograph 121, p. 20; T. Miller, p. 83.) The "new airfield," to which Felber refers, was located 2,000 yards east of Henderson Field, and was put into service on this day as "Fighter One." (T. Miller, p. 82.)

September 11, 1942 All twelve remaining Wildcats of the two Marine fighter squadrons took off at 12:10 to intercept 26 Bettys and fifteen Zeros. The bombers hit the eastern end of Henderson Field, killing or wounding 28 men and destroying a P-400 and a Wildcat. The Marine pilots claimed six bombers and one Zero, but only one of each was actually shot down, against a loss of one Wildcat that ditched without loss of life. (Japanese Monograph 121, p. 21; T. Miller, p. 84; Frank, p. 228; Hata and Izawa, p. 379.)

September 12, 1942 The 11:30 air raid Felber describes was mounted by 25 Bettys and fifteen Zeros that attacked the northwest section of Henderson Field. They were intercepted by eleven Wildcats of VMF-223 and VMF-224 and twenty Navy Wildcats of newly arrived VF-5, resulting in four Bettys and one Zero shot down. The VF-5 fighters were from the 24 that were flown in the night before off the carrier *Saratoga,* but reportedly no bombers arrived with them. (Tagaya, p. 62; T. Miller, pp. 85–86; Japanese Monograph 121, p. 21; Hata and Izawa, p. 379.) The night shelling that forced Felber to seek shelter was from the cruiser *Sendai* and three destroyers, which bombarded the perimeter, with most shells falling to the east of the newly established 1st Raider Battalion that had dug in on "Edson's Ridge" and killing three pilots. (Frank, p. 231.) "Major Clark" was Major James M. Clark, the R-4 of the 11th Marines. (July 1942 muster roll, H&S Battery, 11th Marines.)

September 13, 1942 The "24 fighter planes" that Felber was told had arrived in early morning were actually six Grumman Avenger torpedo bombers of VT-8 and twelve SBD Dauntless dive bombers of VS-3 that the Navy had assigned to bolster Guadalcanal's air strength. (T. Miller, pp. 91, 216, 218; Frank, pp. 234–35.) In the decisive Battle of Edson's Ridge that Felber describes from his vantage point, the 5th Battalion, 11th Marines, provided effective fire support with its 105mm howitzers for the 1st Raider Battalion and the 1st Parachute Battalion, which were dug in on the ridge and engaged in close combat with the Japanese under Major General Kawaguchi. (del Valle, pp. 728–29.)

September 14, 1942 Bryan, whom Felber selected to accompany him on his hunt for Japanese, was Pvt. Joseph D. Bryan, Jr., a carpenter in Felber's H&S Battery. (July 1942 muster roll, H&S Battery, 11th Marines.) The "3 American planes" that strafed the Japanese machine gun positions were three P-400s of the Army's 67th Fighter Squadron, which had flown their mission to strafe the ridge at dawn at very low altitude. Two were hit by ground fire. (T. Miller, p. 42.) Del Valle had positioned his Special Weapons Battery along the flank of the ridge south of his command post in order to provide security for it. During the evening of September 13-14, the Battery was overrun and fell back to take up a new position between Maj. Gen. Vandegrift's command post and his own command post, where the Battery was responsible for holding that line if the Raiders were completely overrun. (del Valle, p. 728). Records confirm that the Battery's Marine Gunner Paul R. Michael was killed on September 14, 1942. (*www.abmc.gov,* list of World War II dead.) The identity of the Raider Battalion man who shot him, and was in turn killed, has not been determined.

September 18, 1942 The 1st Battalion, 11th Marines, was equipped with 75mm pack howitzers and had been assigned as the artillery battalion supporting the 7th Marines. As Felber notes, it landed on Guadalcanal with the 4517 officers and men of the 7th Marines on September 18, providing a major increase in Vandegrift's force to hold Guadalcanal. (Frank, pp. 251, 252; del Valle, p. 730.)

September 19, 1942 A single cruiser, the *Sendai*, plus four destroyers were the warships that bombarded the Marines just after midnight, September 18-19. The *Sendai* fired shells from its 5.5" guns, while the destroyers shelled with 5" guns. (Frank, p. 252; Watts & Gordon, pp. 278, 284.)

September 21, 1942 The dead Japanese officer identified as a Lt. Col. might have been Major Yukichi Kokusho, commander of the 1st Battalion, 124th Regiment, who was killed on September 13 during the fighting that night. No higher ranked Japanese officer was reported killed in the Battle of Edson's Ridge. (Tani, 1991.)

September 24, 1942 Miller reported that there was no aerial activity on this day, due to continued bad flying conditions, a respite welcomed by the exhausted American aviators. (T. Miller, pp. 99, 100.)

September 26, 1942 The Marines who contacted the Japanese were those of the 1st Raider Battalion and the 1st Battalion, 7th Marines, who were in action in the area of the Matanikau River to the west. (Frank, p. 271.)

September 27, 1942 After a lull of nearly two weeks due to bad flying weather, Japanese bombing attacks were resumed. Eighteen Bettys with 38 Zeros were already over Henderson Field when they were intercepted by 35 Wildcats. Two of the Bettys and one Zero were shot down against no loss for the Marines. But six Wildcats, five SBD Dauntlesses, and five Grumman Avengers on the field were damaged by bombs and fires started in three places. (Tagaya, pp. 62–63; Japanese Monograph 121, p. 31; Hata and Izawa, p. 379; Frank, p. 272; T. Miller, pp. 100–01.) The withdrawal of the Marines Felber mentions was the conclusion of the so-called "Second Matanikau," an ill-fated engagement that had extended from September 24 to 27 and had cost 67 Marine lives and twelve wounded. (Frank, p. 274; Griffith, p. 137.)

September 28, 1942 Twenty-six Bettys escorted by 42 Zeros had been picked up by coastwatchers and were intercepted by 35 Wildcats far to the west of Henderson Field. Due to the ineffectual defense by the Zeros, the Japanese bomber formation was shredded. Five of the Bettys were shot down and another three crash-landed on their way back to base. No Wildcats were lost, though five were damaged. (Tagaya, p. 63; T. Miller, p.101; Frank, pp. 274–75.)

September 29, 1942 Due to the heavy bomber losses the day before, instead of the usual bombing raid, nine Bettys were used as decoys for a fighter sweep of Henderson Field by 27 Zeros. Sixty miles west of Henderson Field, over the Russell

Islands, the Bettys turned back as planned. As the Zeros approached the field, they were intercepted by eight Wildcats of VF-5 of the 33 that had been scrambled. One of the Marine pilots was shot down and killed. VF-5 claimed two Zeros, but none was actually lost. (Tagaya, p. 63; T. Miller, p. 102; Frank, p. 276; Hata and Izawa, p. 379.) Fowler was T/Sgt. Obert Fowler, the NCO in charge of the mess of the 11th Marines. (July 1942 muster roll of H&S Battery, 11th Marines.)

October 1, 1942 The night bombing by a single Betty implemented a new strategy by Japanese naval air officers at Rabaul, occasioned by the heavy losses of their bomber fleet during daylight attacks of Henderson Field. (Frank, p. 275; Japanese Monograph 121, p. 36; Tagaya, p. 63.)

October 2, 1942 Two Bettys bombed the western banks of the Lunga River in the late night attack, causing fires. (Japanese Monograph 121, p. 36.) "Everyone is cussing the radar this morning for not giving the alarm," Merillat noted in his diary. (Merillat, p. 140.) In late morning, the Japanese launched a fighter sweep of 36 Zeros led by nine Bettys, but the force became separated over northern Bougainville and all nine bombers plus nine of the Zeros prematurely returned to base. Not picked up by coastwatchers, the remaining 27 Zeros were intercepted late by 33 Wildcats before the Marines had reached attacking altitude. In the ensuing dogfights, the Japanese shot down six of the Marine fighters, with four pilots killed. The Americans claimed four Zeros shot down, but only one was lost. (T. Miller, pp. 103–04; Frank, pp. 278–79; Hata and Izawa, p. 379.)

October 3, 1942 At 09:00, one hour earlier than usual, fifteen Bettys took off from Rabaul to lead 27 Zeros to Guadalcanal, but this time were picked up by coastwatchers. The bombers turned back at the Russell Islands, but the Zeros continued eastward. With adequate alert time, however, 29 Wildcats, waiting for the Zeros to arrive over Henderson Field, pounced on the Japanese. American records indicate nine were shot down, but Japanese documentation acknowledges loss of only five, with all pilots killed. One Wildcat was shot down, but the pilot parachuted to safety. (T. Miller, pp. 104–05; Frank, pp. 279–80; Hata and Izawa, p. 379.)

October 5, 1942 Six destroyers of the "Tokyo Express" carrying troops to land on Guadalcanal had been hit in the afternoon by nine SBD Dauntlesses 150 miles west of Guadalcanal, with two ships damaged, one heavily. That night, Dauntlesses went after the remaining four destroyers, but failed to prevent them from unloading west of Lunga Point at midnight. Three Grumman Avengers attempted to bomb the landing area but became disoriented in the dark with two ditching in the water and only one crewmember surviving. (T. Miller, pp. 109–10; Frank, p. 281.)

October 7, 1942 The morning firing of the artillery opened the Marines' next Matanikau operation that would extend from October 7 to 9. (Frank, p. 284.) As reinforcements for the Army's 67th Fighter Squadron, eleven P-39 Airacobras arrived at Henderson Field, plus two more Grumman Avengers and two J2F amphibians. (Frank, p. 285; T. Miller, p. 213.)

October 8, 1942   During the three-day offensive against the Japanese in the so-called "3rd Matanikau," the 11th Marines fired 2,188 rounds of 75mm and 1,063 rounds of 105mm shells in support of the operation. It was successfully concluded with a loss to the Japanese of 690 men against a loss to the Marines of 65 killed and 125 wounded. (J. Miller, Jr., p. 134; Griffith, pp. 145–47; Frank, p. 289.)

October 9, 1942   In early September, the 3rd Defense Battalion had emplaced 5-inch coastal defense guns to challenge Japanese warships operating near the coast. (Frank, p. 231.)

October 11, 1942   The entire remaining air strength of the Rabaul base had been assigned to support a run of the Tokyo Express carrying a regiment of heavy artillery as part of a renewed attempt to seize Guadalcanal under Lt. General Maruyama. While missed by the coastwatchers, the incoming force was picked up by radar, but only seventeen Wildcats could make the interception in time. First over the area were seventeen Zeros in the usual fighter sweep, followed by a second group of 45 Bettys— the largest number to date — escorted by 30 Zeros. Hampered by bad weather, only eighteen of the *rikko* descended below the heavy clouds and released their bombs, all of which missed their target. Intercepted by the seventeen Wildcats, one was shot down and a second crash-landed at the new base at Buin on southern Bougainville. Five Zeros and their pilots were lost in the attack, including two that ditched at Buin. One Army pilot was reported missing and one of the Marines ditched his Wildcat, the only American losses. (Tagaya, p. 63; T. Miller, pp. 112–13; Hata and Izawa, pp. 379–80.)

October 12, 1942   The naval engagement to which Felber refers was the Battle of Cape Esperance of October 11-12, in which the Japanese lost one cruiser and three destroyers against one American destroyer sunk and a cruiser heavily damaged. While an American victory, the Japanese managed to land troops and heavy artillery for Maruyama's planned offensive. (Frank, pp. 309–12.)

October 13, 1942   The Army unit that arrived at 05:47 this morning was the 164th Infantry Regiment with 2,852 men. However, no Army artillery was landed. (J. Miller, Jr., p. 142.) In the first air raid, 25 Bettys escorted by eighteen Zeros eluded the coastwatchers' attention and radar pick-up, arriving over Henderson Field and Fighter One unchallenged. Bombs tore up the two airfields, destroyed a B-17, damaged a dozen other aircraft, and set ablaze 5,000 gallons of aviation gas. Finally intercepted on the homeward leg, one Betty was severely damaged and ditched at Rekata. In the afternoon raid, fourteen Bettys escorted by fourteen Zeros arrived while the Wildcats were being refueled on the ground. The Japanese force once again hit the two fields, inflicting less damage this time, and returned home without loss. During the day's attacks, a Zero was shot down and its pilot killed. (Tagaya, p. 63; T. Miller, pp. 116–17; Hata and Izawa, p. 380.) The first artillery shell to hit Henderson Field was fired at 18:30 from west of Kokumbona by a company of the newly landed 4th Field Heavy Artillery Regiment equipped with four 150mm howitzers. It was out of range for American counter battery fire. (Frank, p. 315; Tani, 1990.)

October 14, 1942 In "one of the most concentrated shellings in history," the battleships *Kongo* and *Haruna,* lying 17 miles offshore, each began firing their eight 14" guns at 01:34 a.m. at the Henderson Field area. Over the next hour and 22 minutes, 973 shells tore into the 14-square mile area, burning the whole stock of aviation fuel, rendering the field unusable, and destroying or damaging 30 of the 37 Dauntless dive-bombers, all the Grumman Avengers, and thirteen of the 42 Wildcats that were on Fighter One. Forty-one officers and men were killed, including five pilots. As recounted by Felber, one of the shells scored a direct hit on the command post of the 11th Marines, but caused no fatalities. (Frank, pp. 316–19; T. Miller, pp. 118–20.) The rumor about a PT boat counter-attack was confirmed, but the four newly arrived craft based at Tulagi failed to score a hit on the destroyers accompanying the two battleships. (Frank, p. 318.) To add to the Marines' woes, the four Japanese 150mm artillery pieces— whose operators were soon referred to as "Pistol Pete"— began firing on Henderson Field again in the early morning, as Felber records. (Frank, p. 319.)

Felber mentions a "morning raid" in passing. At about 10:30 a.m., 26 Bettys and eighteen Zeros attacked Henderson Field and Fighter One with no aerial opposition. In a follow-up raid an hour later that is not cited by Felber, twelve Bettys escorted by twenty Zeros were surprised to find Wildcats that had survived the night shelling waiting for them. Three of the *rikko* were shot down and a fourth had to ditch at Rekata. No Zeros were lost; one Wildcat was shot down and its pilot killed. (Tagaya, p. 64; T. Miller, pp. 120–21; Japanese Monograph 121, p. 42; Hata and Izawa, p. 380.)

October 15, 1942 From 01:47 to 02:17, the cruisers *Chokai* and *Kinugasa* fired 752 eight-inch shells into the Marines' defense perimeter. This bombardment was followed some three hours later by sixteen rounds from the 150mm "Pistol Petes" to the west that had disturbed the breakfast of Felber and his H&S Battery comrades. (Frank, p. 319; T. Miller, p. 123.) Joining in from 12:30 were the first rounds from four long-range 105mm cannon of the 2nd Company of the 7th Field Heavy Artillery Regiment that had been landed at Tassafaronga the day before. (Tani, 1990.) In the early afternoon air raid, 23 Bettys accompanied by nine Zeros arrived over Henderson Field at 12:45 without meeting any aerial opposition, but antiaircraft fire damaged fourteen of the bombers and caused one to ditch at Rabaul. One Wildcat was destroyed on the ground. (T. Miller, p. 129; Tagaya, p. 164; Frank, p. 323.) Unloading troops at Tassafaronga, ten miles west of Henderson Field, the Japanese lost three of their six transports to the few SBDs, Wildcats, P-39s, and B-17s the Americans could muster. (J. Miller, Jr., p. 151; T. Miller, pp. 122–29; Frank, p. 324.)

October 16, 1942 The cruisers *Myoko* and *Maya* fired 926 eight-inch shells, joined in by destroyers with 253 five-inch shells. Gasoline barges towed by two cargo ships and accompanied by two destroyers were not attacked by the cruisers, but later that morning 38 carrier aircraft pounced on the American ships, sinking the destroyer *Meredith.* (Frank, pp. 324–25.) The six transports that landed troops carried in total about 4,500 men. Vandegrift correctly estimated that there was a total of about 15,000 Japanese on the island after the latest landing, which was less than the number of Marine defenders. (Frank, pp. 315, 327.)

October 17, 1942   In the early morning raid, eighteen Val dive-bombers and eighteen Zeros, temporarily land-based from two Japanese carriers, attempted to hit two destroyers off the coast opposite Henderson Field. However, eight intercepting Wildcats tore into the formation and shot down six of the Vals and four of the Zeros, as acknowledged by the Japanese (though another authoritative Japanese source shows no Zero pilots killed this day), against the loss of only one Wildcat. (Japanese Monograph 121, p. 43; T. Miller, pp. 134–35; Hata and Izawa, p. 380.) Unopposed by Marine fighters in the midday attack, eighteen Bettys escorted by twelve Zeros attacked positions near Lunga River, evidently near the 11th Marines command post. One *rikko* had to ditch at Rekata on the return trip, apparently hit by anti-aircraft fire. The rumor that "15 out of 17" Japanese bombers had been shot down on the return was unconfirmed; no Marine claims were made in the second attack (Japanese Monograph 121, p. 43; Tagaya, p. 64; Olynyk, entry for October 17, 1942.)

October 18, 1942   The source of the shelling Felber describes as extending from 00:01 to 00:50 has not been identified. There is no record of a naval engagement that night. Felber was too far to the east to be aware of the air combat west of the Lunga River, where sixteen Wildcats, having been alerted by coastwatchers, were lying in wait for the fifteen Bettys and seven Zeros. In the ambush, two *rikko* were shot down and another crash-landed, while three Zeros were lost with their pilots. Two of the Wildcats were shot down, but the pilots were recovered. (T. Miller, p. 137; Frank, p. 329; Tagaya, p. 64; Hata and Izawa, p. 380.)

October 19, 1942   The two air raid alarms must have been for the seventeen Zeros that patrolled over Guadalcanal between 08:15 and 09:45 and again between 10:15 and 12:45. The ensuing combat resulted in two American planes shot down, according to Japanese records, or resulted in two Zeros shot down, according to Marine claims. An authoritative Japanese source on Zero pilots lost indicates a Zero shot down and its pilot killed this day over the Solomons. (Japanese Monograph 121, p. 42; Olynyk, October 19, 1942 entry; Hata and Izawa, p. 380.) Dr. Queen was Lt. William F. Queen, USN, the Regimental Surgeon for the 11th Marines, and PFC Routon was PFC Lloyd A. Routon, the orderly for H&S Battery. (July 1942 muster roll, H&S Battery, 11th Marines.)

October 20, 1942   In the second raid, nine Bettys accompanied by 25 Zeros attacked to the north of Henderson Field at 11:45, where they were intercepted by Wildcats. Earlier, fifteen Zeros conducted a fighter sweep over Guadalcanal. In the second attack, the Marines claimed nine Zeros and three bombers shot down, but in actuality no *rikko* were lost and just one Zero, its pilot killed. The Marines lost two fighters, one of whose pilots was killed. (Japanese Monograph 121, p. 44; Frank, p. 330; Tagaya, p. 64; Olynyk, October 20, 1942 entry; Hata and Izawa, p. 380.) Artillery fire from "Pistol Petes" firing 105mm and 150mm projectiles had forced the closure of Henderson Field for flight operations until October 23. Shells were even falling within 500 yards of Fighter One. (T. Miller, p. 139.)

October 21, 1942   Felber does not mention the two raids today in support of the Maruyama effort to seize Henderson Field. In the first attack, nine Bettys were escorted by fifteen Zeros. In the second attack, 20 Zeros conducted another fighter sweep. The Japanese were intercepted by fifteen Wildcats, whose pilots claimed to have shot down five Zeros, but only one was actually lost with its pilot against a loss of two Wildcats and one pilot. All the Bettys returned undamaged to their base. (Japanese Monograph 121, p. 44; Frank, p. 344; Tagaya, p. 64; Olynyk, entry for October 21, 1942; Hata and Izawa, p. 380.)

October 22, 1942   The rumors about Gen. Holcomb were correct. The Commandant of the Marine Corps arrived at Henderson Field on the evening of October 21 and on this day toured the front lines. (Frank, pp. 344–45.)

October 23, 1942   At 11:30, twelve Zeros arrived on a fighter sweep ahead of seventeen others escorting sixteen Bettys. They were intercepted by 24 Wildcats and four P-39s—the entire remaining fighter strength of the Americans—and, in the ensuing melee that Felber didn't see, one Betty and six Zeros were shot down. Seven Wildcats were damaged. (Frank, pp. 345–46; Tagaya, p. 64; T. Miller, pp. 139–40; Hata and Izawa, p. 380.) As part of the Marine response to the attack by the Maruyama force to seize Henderson Field beginning at 17:00, Col. del Valle emplaced everything he had—ten batteries of 75mm pack howitzers and three of 105mm howitzers—to face the Japanese west of the Matanikau River. In the massed fire of the 11th Marines that night, all threatened areas of attack were covered. (Frank, pp. 349–50; del Valle, pp. 730–31.)

October 24, 1942   All nine medium tanks that attempted to cross the mouth of the Matanikau River were hit and destroyed, eight by 37mm anti-tank guns and one by a 75mm gun. (J. Miller, Jr., p. 157; Frank, pp. 349–50.)

October 25, 1942   In order to determine if Maruyama's all-night attempt to seize Henderson Field had succeeded, a reconnaissance plane escorted by eight Zeros flew over the airfield at 08:00, but was shot down by anti-aircraft fire, though the news reached Rabaul that the Americans still held the field. This day was dubbed "Dugout Sunday," owing to the continuous and vicious air combat all day. In a raid by sixteen Bettys escorted by fifteen Zeros on the left bank of the Lunga River beginning at 14:30, the intercepting Wildcats claimed five bombers and seven Zeros shot down. In an earlier engagement from 11:00 to 12:30, four Zeros were claimed. Total victory claims for the day amounted to sixteen Zeros and five Bettys, plus the reconnaissance plane by anti-aircraft fire, against actual Japanese losses of ten Zeros and two Bettys. In this lopsided victory, only two Wildcats were shot down, with both pilots rescued. (Japanese Monograph 121, p. 44; Tagaya, p. 64; Olynyk, entry for October 25, 1942; T. Miller, pp. 142–47; Frank, p. 361; Hata and Izawa, p. 380.) In attacks on the Japanese warship to which Felber refers, an

SBD hit near the *Yura* with a 1,000-pound bomb, causing the cruiser to sink later in the day. Also, a near miss was scored on the destroyer *Akizuka*. (Frank, pp. 360–61.)

October 26, 1942	The ground action to which Felber refers ended Maruyama's attempt to take Henderson Field. His men had marched over 30 miles in the jungle to achieve surprise, but failed. On October 29, they would begin a general withdrawal. (Frank, p. 366; J. Miller, Jr., p. 165.) The corpsman whom Felber reported for insolence was Hospital Apprentice 1st Class Frank E. Notaro. (July 1942 muster roll, H&S Company, 11th Marines.)

October 27, 1942	Men of Weapons Company, 7th Marines, had fired canister from two 37mm guns into the Japanese, killing over 250 on the early morning of October 26th. (Frank, p. 362.) The Japanese were from the 16th Infantry Regiment, which had been based in the Dutch East Indies prior to its being assigned in late August 1942 to the Guadalcanal campaign. ("Digest of POW Interrogation Reports.") The Army unit participating with the Marines in this engagement was the 164th Infantry Regiment. (Frank, p. 363.) The naval engagement that Major Viall described to Felber was the Battle of Santa Cruz of October 25–27, 1942, deemed a tactical victory for the Japanese. The carrier *Hornet* was sunk and 81 aircraft lost against damage to two Japanese carriers and a cruiser plus 97 aircraft lost. (Morison, p. 224; Frank, pp. 400–01.)

October 30, 1942	The cruiser *Atlanta* and the destroyers *Aaron Ward*, *Benham*, *Fletcher*, and *Lardner* had escorted transports bringing in 155mm artillery for the 11th Marines. While the big guns were being unloaded after sunrise, the escort ships bombarded Japanese positions in the Point Cruz area in preparation for a new Marine offensive towards that objective. (Morison, p. 226.)

October 31, 1942	Felber refers to the renewed attempt to begin on the following day to extend the Marines' western defense perimeter beyond Kokumbona. The 11th Marines were to support this new offensive with mass fire. (J. Miller, Jr., p. 190.)

November 1, 1942	The bridge Felber observed under construction across the Matanikau was being built for vehicle traffic by the 1st Engineer Battalion about 500 yards from the mouth of the Matanikau. (J. Miller, Jr., p. 193.) The Marines who had run into heavy machine gun fire were those of the 1st Battalion, 5th Marines, who also were fired on by light artillery. One of its companies lost three officers. (Frank, p. 413.) The "small Jap field pieces" Felber saw were most likely Model 94 (1934) 37mm infantry rapid-fire guns.

November 2, 1942	The transports *Alchiba* and *Fuller* brought in F Battery of the Army's 244th Coast Artillery Battalion and another battery of the Marines' 5th Defense Battalion, each equipped with 155mm guns. Hours later, the 244th was firing on the "Pistol Petes" to the west. (J. Miller, Jr., pp. 177, 180.)

November 3, 1942   The rumors of Japanese landing to the east around Beach Red were correct, but the numbers involved may have been exaggerated. According to Frank, five destroyers landed 300 Japanese with two mountain guns and provisions at Koli late the night of November 2-3 to support troops of the Shoji Detachment heading from the east towards that point. (Frank, pp. 414–15.) According to Miller, "about 1,500" men (from the 230th Infantry Regiment) were landed. (J. Miller, Jr., p. 196.)

November 4, 1942   The bombardment of Japanese positions that Felber watched was by the cruisers *Helena* and *San Francisco* and the destroyers *Sterrett* and *Landsdowne*, all firing on the Japanese at Koli Point. (Frank, p. 420; J. Miller, Jr., p. 197.) Felber ended his day's trek to the front at the mouth of the Nalimbiu (not Malembui) River, which empties into Koli Point just to the west. (See Frank, pp. 414–24, for an account of the fighting in the Koli Point area, November 4–9, 1942.)

November 5, 1942   Twenty-seven Bettys escorted by 24 Zeros bombed Henderson Field. There was no opposition from Marine Wildcats, but anti-aircraft fire downed two of the Bettys. (Japanese Monograph No. 122, p. 6; Tagaya, p. 65.)

November 7, 1942   Japanese midget submarine #11 from the submarine I-20 had hit the auxiliary cargo ship *Majaba* off Lunga Point with a single torpedo at 09:29. Destroyers went after the midget with no success. The *Majaba* was later beached and salvaged. (Frank, p. 501; Morison, pp. 226–27.)

November 8, 1942   On the late afternoon of the day before, eleven troop-laden destroyers of the "Tokyo Express" protected by 10 floatplanes were attacked by seven SBD Dauntlesses, three Avengers, 21 Wildcats, and nine P-39s as the Japanese headed for Tassafaronga to the west. The Japanese force was barely scathed, with two destroyers slightly damaged, but seven of the floatplanes were shot down against a loss of one Wildcat, whose pilot (the celebrated Joe Foss) survived after ditching. Four-fifths of the troops were landed at Tassafaronga and Cape Esperance. (Frank, p. 422; Olynyk, entry for November 7, 1942.) The rumor of impending Army reinforcements was correct. The 182nd Regimental Combat Team would be arriving on November 12. (Frank, p. 430.)

November 10, 1942   The "big Jap gun," commonly thought to be of British origin, was probably either a Type 92 (1932) 105mm cannon of the four landed on October 14, or one of the twelve Type 96 (1936) 150mm howitzers landed October 11 and 14, both Japanese-made. (Tani, 1990.) On this day, the westward offensive towards Kokumbona was renewed. The 1st Battalion, 164th Infantry, the 8th Marines, and the 2nd Marines (less the 3rd Battalion), as supported by artillery fire of the 11th Marines, were executing a frontal attack on a wide front. (J. Miller, Jr., p. 200.)

November 11, 1942   The air raid was mounted by 25 Bettys and 26 Zeros attempting to attack Henderson Field about 11:40. They were met by seventeen Wildcats, which downed three of the *rikko*, but at a cost of three of the Grummans, with two pilots killed. Another of the bombers was lost in an operational accident. (T. Miller, p. 179; Tagaya, p. 65; Frank, p. 425.) On November 10, coastwatchers had reported 61 Japanese ships in the harbor in the Shortlands, from which it was surmised that big troop convoys could be expected to attempt to land on Guadalcanal in mid–November. Accordingly, Vandegrift decided to halt the offensive towards Kokumbona. (J. Miller, Jr., p. 202; Frank, p. 426.)

November 12, 1942   The transports and cargo ships were bringing in the Army's 182nd Infantry Regiment (minus its 3rd Battalion), the 4th Marine Replacement Battalion, and artillery. The air raid was against the ships. Nineteen Bettys carrying torpedoes escorted by 30 Zeros had been picked up by coastwatchers and, after splitting into two groups at 14:05, were intercepted by twenty Wildcats and eight P-39s. In an eight-minute engagement, all the Bettys missed with their torpedoes and were decimated by the fighters, fourteen of the nineteen *rikko* going down in flames. One Zero was also lost. Three of the Wildcats were shot down, their pilots surviving. A P-39 was shot down with its pilot. (Tagaya, p. 65; Frank, pp. 431–32; Hata and Izawa, p. 381.) The "new planes" that landed this day were eight Army P-38s of the newly formed 339th Fighter Squadron, preceded by three Wildcats, six Grumman Avengers, and ten SBD Dauntlesses. (T. Miller, pp. 181–82.)

November 13, 1942   A Japanese naval force planning another bombardment of Henderson Field in the small hours was set upon by five cruisers and eight destroyers immediately before the battleships *Hiei* and *Kirishima* could begin firing. In the vicious point-blank engagement—"one of the most furious naval battles ever fought" in Admiral King's words— one Japanese and two American destroyers were sunk and two American cruisers and the *Hiei* heavily damaged. (T. Miller, pp. 182–83; Frank, pp. 432–54.) In the second stage of what would be called "The Naval Battle of Guadalcanal," Henderson Field aircraft began taking off at 06:00 in the first of several strikes to inflict further damage on the Japanese, focusing on the *Hiei*. By the end of the day, the Americans had lost four destroyers and two cruisers, against Japanese losses of two destroyers and the *Hiei*. (Dull, pp. 241–42.) Contrary to the reports, no Japanese aircraft carriers had been involved, and no Japanese cruisers had been sunk.

November 14, 1942   From 01:30 to 02:01, the heavy cruisers *Suzuya* and *Maya* bombarded Guadalcanal with 8-inch fire, but missed Henderson Field, only hitting the area around Fighter One where two Wildcats and one SBD were destroyed. In the morning, five SBDs, six Avengers, and eight Wildcats went after the bombardment group, linked up with the main force, and claimed bomb and torpedo hits, as reported on the bulletin board Felber saw. Japanese records show no such results. (Frank, p. 434.) The report of a Japanese task force heading towards Guadalcanal was correct: a convoy of eleven transports and twelve escorts had left the Shortlands at 17:30 the day before, carrying 7,000 troops of the 38th Division scheduled for landings at Cape Esperance and Tassafaronga. (Frank, pp. 428, 465.) Beginning at 12:50, Henderson Field's aviators began their attack, leading off with eighteen SBDs and seven Avengers, and continuing through the day as they shuttled back and forth, joined in by aircraft from the carrier *Enterprise,* mentioned by Felber as landing afterwards on Henderson Field. By day's end, six of the eleven transports had been sunk or abandoned. (Frank, pp. 465–68.) The night firing Felber heard out to sea was the second round of fighting between naval forces that began at 23:17 and lasted until 01:40. In this "Part II Naval Battle of Guadalcanal" fought off the island of Savo and considered an American victory, the Japanese lost the battleship *Kirishima* and a destroyer against three American destroyers sunk. (Frank, pp. 472–87.)

November 15, 1942   Rather than five light cruisers, the SBDs off the *Enterprise* sank the heavy cruiser *Kinugasa* and damaged the light cruiser *Isuzu.* (T. Miller, pp. 192–94; Frank, pp. 464–65.) The four transports that had survived the previous day's attacks were lying off Tassafaronga in plain view. Three were beached and unloading, while the fourth was pulling out. A battery of the 244th Coast Artillery Battalion hit and burned one at 05:00. Following attacks by Henderson Field aircraft, all four were left burning hulks by noon, abandoned in shallow water. Only 4,000 of the troops embarked on the eleven transports were safely landed, and these without half of their supplies and rations. (J. Miller, Jr., p. 188, indicated there were "10,000 or more" troops embarked. Frank, p. 428, indicated there were about 7,000 troops embarked.)

November 18, 1942   The bombing mission for which Felber could not obtain information was by ten B-17s of the 11th Bomb Group that were escorted by twelve P-38s. The B-17s attacked Japanese shipping in Tonolei Harbor (in the Shortland Islands area), where at least fifteen Zeros jumped them and followed them as they returned to Henderson Field. One B-17, piloted by Major Allen J. Sewart, was hit over Buin, southern Bougainville by the Zeros, and Sewart and the co-pilot were killed. Flying the mission as an observer, the 11th Bomb Group CO, Col. Laverne Saunders, took over the controls and managed to continue 70 miles under attack by the Zeros before ditching in the waters off Baga Island. The surviving crew members were all rescued, including Saunders. (Salecker, pp. 294–96.) Final results of the three-day Naval Battle of Guadalcanal were ten transports, two battleships, one heavy cruiser, three destroyers, 40 planes, and 1,895 men lost by the Japanese against two light cruisers, seven destroyers, 26 aircraft, and 1,732 men lost by the Americans. The Japanese human losses exclude troops carried on the transports. It was a clear American victory. (Frank, p. 490.)

November 19, 1942   The news bulletin greatly exaggerated the number of Japanese troops drowned. A total of 1,895 Japanese sailors, soldiers, and airmen died, but this figure excludes an estimated 3,000 soldiers on the transports drowned of the 7,700 on board. About 3,000 landed and another 1,700 were rescued at sea. (J. Miller, Jr., footnote 46, p. 188; Frank, p. 490.) Frank maintains that only 2,000 Japanese got ashore of the 7,000 embarked on the transports. (Frank, pp. 428, 490.)

November 20, 1942   Although the Reising gun was lighter and more accurate than the Thompson machine gun and had twice its effective range, it would frequently malfunction, making it an undependable weapon for the Marines. (George, p. 396.)

November 21, 1942   After the naval victory of November 13–15, Maj. Gen. Vandegrift decided to renew the offensive towards Kokumbona. The 164th Infantry Regiment, the 8th Marines, and the 2nd Battalion of the 182nd Infantry Regiment, with artillery support from the 11th Marines, were committed to the operation. (J. Miller, Jr., pp. 202–09.)

November 24, 1942   "The fighting in the west" had been suspended the day before, as the frontal assault was proving too costly and reinforcements were needed. (J. Miller, Jr., pp. 208–09).

November 25, 1942   Three Bettys were responsible for the night raid on Henderson Field. (Japanese Monograph 122, p. 12.)

November 27, 1942   In this night attack, two Bettys dropped their bombs south of Lunga Point. (Japanese Monograph 122, p. 12.)

November 28, 1942   The air raid was indeed a false alarm. There was no attack by the Japanese bombers this night. (Japanese Monograph 122, p. 12.)

November 29, 1942   Japanese records do not indicate any attack this night. (Japanese Monograph 122, p. 12.)

November 30, 1942   On the morning of November 28, midget submarine No. 10 from the mother submarine I-16 fired a torpedo into the freighter *Alchiba,* loaded with ammunition, bombs, and gasoline. When the vessel caught fire, it was run aground west of Lunga, where part of the crew offloaded her lethal cargo. (Frank, p. 501.) The depressing rumors of eight Japanese troop transports headed for Guadalcanal were erroneous. Rather, six destroyers, escorted by three other destroyers, were headed in with heavy drums loaded with rice and barley to be released off Tassafaronga for the starving troops on shore. At 23:16, they were engaged by a greatly superior force of five cruisers and four destroyers, but in a "humiliating defeat," one American cruiser was sunk and three damaged against a Japanese loss of only one destroyer. All the food drums were successfully dropped. This engagement, which became known as the "Battle of Tassafaronga," demonstrated that the American naval crews were still not adequately trained for night engagements. (Frank, pp. 507–18; Dull, pp. 255–57.)

December 2, 1942   The frontal assault of the Army's 164th and 182nd Infantry Regiments west of the Matanikau was proving "costly." (J. Miller, Jr., pp. 208–09.) The rumors that the naval Battle of Tassafaronga had dealt a severe blow to the Japanese navy were wrong.

December 3, 1942   The reports Felber had heard of warships heading his way were generated by coastwatcher sightings of 10 destroyers moving towards Guadalcanal.

They were on another supply run and benefited from air cover by 12 floatplanes. As the sun set off the north coast of New Georgia 160 miles short of their destination, the "Rat Transportation" destroyers were attacked by eight SBDs and seven Avengers, but suffered only slight damage to one destroyer, while one Avenger and one SBD were shot down. Escorting Wildcats bagged five floatplanes at a cost of one Wildcat. (Morison, p. 318; Frank, pp. 519–20; Olynyk, December 3, 1942 entry.)

December 4, 1942   The "big gun" that the Marines destroyed was probably one of the 150mm howitzers, as the four 105mm cannons also used for firing on Henderson Field had been destroyed by the Japanese commander on November 18, when they had proven useless. ("Four Months on Hell Island," p. 35.)

December 7, 1942   The submarine that torpedoed the *Alchiba* for a second time was Midget No. 38 off the mother ship I-24. The torpedo struck the hapless cargo ship while it was aground. (Frank, p. 501.)

December 8, 1942   The Japanese ships engaged the previous night were twelve destroyers on yet another "Rat Transportation" run with barrels of provisions. At 18:40 the ships were set upon by thirteen SBDs, which only managed a near miss on one and slight damage to another. Escorting floatplanes shot down and killed the leader of the SBDs, the CO of VMSB-132. The other destroyers continued on and were met by eight PT boats off Guadalcanal just before midnight. In the ensuing skirmish, the destroyers had to abort their supply mission. (Frank, pp. 520–21.) Felber's hopes for a return to the U.S. were shared by all Vandegrift's Marines. On November 30, the Joint Chiefs of Staff had decided to relieve the 1st Marine Division and send in the Army's 25th Division. In the meantime, the Army's Americal Division already on Guadalcanal and engaged in the fighting was to take over, and by December 8, its staff had assumed full responsibility for Guadalcanal land operations. (J. Miller, Jr., pp. 212–13.)

December 9, 1942   On this day, Maj. Gen. Vandegrift formally turned over command to Maj. Gen. Alexander M. Patch of the U.S. Army. The first group of Marines, mainly from the 5th Regiment, began boarding transports for departure to Brisbane, Australia. (Frank, pp. 521–22; McMillan, pp. 135, 146.)

December 12, 1942   Eleven destroyers on another "Rat Transportation" mission with barrels of provisions were intercepted by fourteen SBDs at sunset the evening before. Despite having no floatplane protection, they suffered no damage from the attack and shot down one of the dive-bombers. After off-loading their drums at Cape Esperance and beginning their return journey at 01:15, they were attacked by three PT boats. The flagship destroyer was hit by a torpedo and had to be scuttled, but two other destroyers shelled and sank one of two other PT boats joining in the melee. Only one-fifth of the drums were recovered by the Japanese troops on land. It would be the last of the supply runs by Japanese destroyers to Guadalcanal. (Frank, pp. 523–24.)

January 8, 1943   The Marines had left Camp Cable the day before for the trip in Army trucks to Brisbane harbor. In 1942, the Navy had taken over the *America* and re-named it *West Point*. It was indeed a huge vessel, capable of carrying 8,175 passengers, or six times as many as the *Hunter Liggett*. (Charles, pp. 36, 146.) The *West Point* would be taking them to Melbourne, from where they would entrain 70 miles to the town of Ballarat and on to their camp one mile away. While on board the *West Point*, the 5th Battalion, 11th Marines, was disbanded. (Emmet, p. 12.)

March 8, 1943   The trial was of Pvt. Leland W. Mattice, who had shot Sgt. Casey on the night of August 11, 1942, as recorded in Felber's diary for that date.

April 17, 1943   According to records, Col. Pepper became Commanding Officer of the 11th Marines on March 29, 1943. (Emmet, p. 52.) He was formerly Commanding Officer of the 3rd Defense Battalion.

December 26, 1943   In September and October, the 11th Marines had sailed from Melbourne for New Guinea staging areas for the planned landing on Cape Gloucester, New Britain, set for December 26, 1943, where they were to support the troops of the 1st Marine Division initially charged with seizing the Japanese airdrome there. (Emmet, p. 12.) The capture and development of the Cape Gloucester airfield and the adjoining areas, defended by about 7,500 Japanese, was considered necessary to facilitate the isolation of Rabaul and support other operations in the Bismarck Archipelago. (U.S. Strategic Bombing Survey, p. 178.) Felber himself had arrived in LST-456 at Beach Yellow, about 5 miles east of Cape Gloucester. Going ashore with the 11th Marines were the 7th and the 1st Marines (less the 2nd Battalion), the latter moving west along the coast from the time of their morning landing to assault the airdrome. The 11th Marines' 1st Battalion was to provide close artillery support for the 7th Marines, while the 4th Battalion was to do likewise for the 1st Marines. (McMillan, pp. 182–83.) In the bombing mission to support the landing that Felber mentions, anti-aircraft guns on the American destroyers accidentally shot down two B-25s and damaged two others. (Craven and Cate, p. 341.) The "big squadrons of bombers" Felber saw overhead were 43 B-24s and 38 B-25s that were dropping 112 tons of bombs on the areas beyond the beaches. (Craven and Cate, p. 339.)

December 28, 1943   Felber's H&S Battery Commander was 23-year-old James Fairclough, at the time of the Guadalcanal landing a 2nd Lt. forward observer for G Battery, 3rd Battalion, 11th Marines. (July 1942 muster roll for G-3-11; Social Security Death Index for James Fairclough.)

December 31, 1943   The American flag was indeed raised over Cape Gloucester airfield this day, at noon. Both strips of the airfield had been seized on the day before at noon. (McMillan, p. 191; Craven and Cate, p. 342.)

January 1, 1944   The units of the Division that were to be shifted were the 7th Marines and the 3rd Battalion, 5th Marines, which on the following day moved forward into the interior off Borgen Bay across a heavily defended stream. (McMillan, p. 193.)

January 2, 1944   The night attack was flown by about eight Bettys of the 751 *kokutai* operating from Rabaul. Night-flying Bettys would harass the Americans from the time of the Cape Gloucester landing until the occupation of the area by the Marines was completed. (Navy Interrogation No. 97, p. 416.)

January 4, 1944   Things were not "quieting down" for the 7th Marines, which this day finally were able to cross "Suicide Creek" with the support of the 11th Marines' artillery and tanks and begin the assault on Hill 150, Aogiri Ridge, and Hill 660, possession of which was critical for the success of the Cape Gloucester campaign. (Emmet, p. 14.)

January 12, 1944   While the campaign was "very dull" for Felber's H&S Battery, it was not so for the batteries of the 1st and 4th Battalions, which had been pounding Hill 150 and Aogiri Ridge with 75mm and 105mm artillery fire. (Emmet, p. 14.)

January 14, 1944   On this day, apparently unreported to H&S Battery, the 3rd Battalion, 7th Marines, succeeded in capturing Hill 660, to the southeast of Aogiri Ridge, at 18:30, fighting through strong Japanese defenses and mud deep from incessant rain to reach the top of the ridge and consolidate its position there. The 1st and 4th Battalions of the 11th Marines provided support by pounding the Japanese positions during the two-day offensive. (Emmet, pp. 14–16; McMillan, pp. 199–205.)

January 16, 1944   Felber was unaware of the excitement at Hill 660, where at 05:30 the Japanese in a *banzai* attack tried to drive the 3rd Battalion, 7th Marines, off the ridge in a disastrous effort that represented the end of Japanese resistance in the area. (McMillan, pp. 199–205; Emmet, p. 16.)

January 22, 1944   The new H&S Battery Commander was Captain David R. Griffin, at the time of the Guadalcanal landing a 2nd Lt. serving as Assistant Executive Officer in I Battery, 3rd Battalion, 11th Marines. (July 1942 muster roll for I-3-11.)

January 25, 1944   Felber was now able to see for himself the terrain of Hill 660, where the 3rd Battalion, 7th Marines had fought under such difficult physical conditions to seize the strategic point.

February 6, 1944   Lt. Col. Edmund J. Buckley had succeeded Lt. Col. Frank Goettge as Division Intelligence Officer on August 14, 1942, following Goettge's death on an ill-fated Guadalcanal patrol on August 12. (Frank, pp. 130–32.)

June 2, 1944   Felber had remained at Cape Gloucester until April 24, when he was shifted with the rest of the Division to Pavuvu, the largest of the Russell

Islands, in the western Solomons, a "rest camp" and limited training area affording only primitive conditions. Felber was fortunate in that he was among those 260 officers and 4,600 enlisted men of the Division who were to be rotated home after having served 24 months. The remaining 264 officers and 5,750 enlisted men on Pavuvu would have to go into the Division's third campaign, the invasion of Peleliu. (McMillan, pp. 227, 250.)

September 3, 1944   Felber had returned to Camp Pendleton on August 24, following the end of his furlough.

April 5, 1945   Following the disbandment of his 4th Infantry Training Regiment at the end of March, Felber was assigned to the Engineer Demonstration Company, Special Schools Battalion, Schools Regiment, based near his previous location, where he replaced the Company's 42-year-old 1st Sergeant being assigned overseas.

October 24, 1945   On October 12, Felber had accepted the 1st Sergeant job in Headquarters Company, Training Battalion and was transferred to that position the following day. He had been informed on October 14 that his old job at the Newark, New Jersey, Post Office was open for him anytime up to 90 days after leaving the service.

December 27, 1945   Felber had been on furlough in Miami, Florida, from December 17 to 22 and in Havana, Cuba, from December 23 to 26, returning to Miami this day.

Bibliography

Bartsch, William H. "Operation Dovetail: Bungled Guadalcanal Rehearsal," *The Journal of Military History*, April 2002.

Charles, Roland W. *Troopships of World War II*. Washington, D.C.: Army Transport Association, 1947.

Craven, Wesley F., and James L. Cate, *The Army Air Forces in World War II*, Vol. 4. Chicago: University of Chicago Press, 1950.

del Valle, Brig. Gen. P. A. "Marine Field Artillery on Guadalcanal," *The Field Artillery Journal*, October 1943.

"Digest of POW Interrogation Reports of members of the 16th Infantry Regiment," SOPAC M-2 022807, at Marine Corps Historical Center, Washington, D.C.

Dull, Paul S. *A Battle History of the Imperial Japanese Navy (1941–1945)*. Annapolis: Naval Institute Press, 1978.

Emmet, Robert *A Brief History of the 11th Marines*. Washington, D.C.: U.S. Marine Corps, 1968.

Fahey, James C. *The Ships and Aircraft of the U.S. Fleet*, War Edition. Annapolis: Naval Institute Press, reprinted 1976.

"Four Months on Hell Island," *Military History*, December 1990.

Frank, Richard B. *Guadalcanal*. Random House: N.Y., 1990.

Gellman, Irwin F. *Secret Affairs: Franklin Roosevelt, Cordell Hull, and Sumner Welles*. Baltimore: Johns Hopkins University Press, 1995.

George, John. *Shots Fired in Anger*. Washington, D.C.: National Rifle Association of America, 1981.

Griffith, Samuel B., II. *The Battle for Guadalcanal*. J. B. Lippincott: Philadelphia, 1963.

Hata, Ikuhiki, and Yasuho Izawa, *Japanese Naval Aces and Fighter Units in World War II*. Annapolis: Naval Institute Press, 1989.

Hayashi, Saburo. *Kogun: The Japanese Army in the Pacific War*. Quantico, Va.: Marine Corps Association, 1959.

Hough, Frank, Verle Ludwig, and Henry Shaw. *History of U.S. Marine Corps Operations in World War II, Vol. 1, Pearl Harbor to Guadalcanal*. Washington, D.C.: Historical Branch, U.S. Marine Corps, 1958.

Isely, Jeter A., and Philip A. Crowl, *The U.S. Marines and Amphibious War*. Princeton, N.J.: Princeton University Press, 1951.

Japanese Monograph No. 121, "Outline of Southeast Area Naval Air Operations, Part II." Office of the Chief of Military History, Military History Section, Headquarters, Army Forces Far East, Washington, D.C.: Department of the Army, 1950.

Japanese Monograph No. 122, "Outline of Southeast Area Naval Air Operations, Part III, November 1942–June 1943." Office of the Chief of Military History, Military History Section, Headquarters, Army Forces Far East, Washington, D.C.: Department of the Army, 1950.

Johnstone, John H. *A Brief History of the First Marines*. Washington, D.C.: U.S. Marine Corps, 1962.

Jones, Arvil and Lulu. *Forgotten Warriors*. Paducah, Ky.: Turner Publishing Company, 1994.

McMillan, George. *The Old Breed: A History of the First Marine Division in World War II*. Washington, D.C.: Infantry Journal Inc., 1949.

Merillat, Herbert C. *Guadalcanal Remembered*. New York: Dodd, Mead & Co., 1982.

Miller, Jr., John. *Guadalcanal: The First Offensive*. Washington, D.C.: Department of the Army, 1949.

Miller, Thomas. *The Cactus Air Force*. New York: Harper and Row, 1969.

Morison, Samuel E. *The Struggle for Guadalcanal*. New York: Little, Brown and Co., 1949.

Navy Interrogation No. 97, "Interrogation of Captain Takahashi Miyazaki," in US Strategic Bombing Survey, *Interrogations of Japanese Officials*, Vol. II. USGPO: Washington, D.C., 1946?.

Olynyk, Frank J. *USMC Credits for the Destruction of Enemy Aircraft in Air-to-Air Combat, World War 2*. Aurora, April 1982.

Pollock, General Edwin A. Oral History Transcript. Washington, D.C.: U.S. Marine Corps, 1977.

Roscoe, Theodore. *United States Destroyer Operations in World War II*. Annapolis: Naval Institute Press, 1953.

Salecker, Gene E. *Fortress Against the Sun*. Conshohocken, Pa.: Combined Publishing, 2001.

Secret Memo, Hq., 1st Marine Division, "Combined Station List and Strength Report, Forward Echelon, 1st Marine Division, Fleet Marine Force, and Attached Units, Sunday, August 2d, 1942," in National Archives Record Group 127, Geographic File — Guadalcanal, Box 47, Folder E-1-1.

Smith, Holland M. *Coral and Brass*. New York: Scribner's, 1948.

Tagaya, Osamu. *Mitsubishi Type 1 Rikko "Betty" Units of World War 2*. Oxford: Osprey Publishing, 2001.

Tani, Akio. Letter to W. H. Bartsch, March 16, 1990.

Tani, Akio. Letter to W. H. Bartsch, May 22, 1991.

Tregaskis, Richard. *Guadalcanal Diary*. New York: Random House, 1943.

Twining, Merrill B. *No Bended Knee: The Battle for Guadalcanal*. Novato: Presidio Press, 1996.

U.S. Strategic Bombing Survey. *The Campaigns of the Pacific War*. Washington, D.C.: USGPO, 1946.

Updegraph, Charles L., Jr. *U.S. Marine Corps Special Units of World War II.* Washington, D.C.: U.S. Marine Corps, 1972.

Vandegrift, A. A. *Once a Marine.* New York: W.W. Norton, 1964.

Watts, A. J., and B. G. Gordon, *The Imperial Japanese Navy.* London: Macdonald, 1971.

Military Index

Japan

Imperial General Headquarters 220

IMPERIAL ARMY

Ichiki Detachment 70, 219, 220
Kawaguchi Brigade 70
Shoji Detachment 231
South Seas Detachment 219
38th Division 232
55th Division 219
4th Heavy Field Artillery Regiment 226
7th Heavy Field Artillery Regiment 227
16th Infantry Regiment 230
28th Infantry Regiment 219
124th Infantry Regiment 224
   1st Battalion of 224
144th Infantry Regiment 219
230th Infantry Regiment 231

IMPERIAL NAVY

Yokosuka 5th Special Landing Force 70

IMPERIAL NAVY AVIATION

751st *Kokutai* 237

IMPERIAL NAVY SHIPS

Akizuka 230
Chokai 227
Furutaka 117
Haruna 227
Hiei 146, 232
Isuzu 233
Jintsu 220
Kinryu Maru 220
Kinugasa 227, 233
Kirishima 232, 233
Kongo 227
Maya 227, 232
Midget submarine #10 234
Midget submarine #11 231
Midget submarine #38 235
Mutsuki 220
Myoko 227
Ryujo 220
Sendai 223, 224
Submarine *I-16* 234
Submarine *I-20* 231
Submarine *I-24* 235
Suzuya 232
Yamazuki Maru 146
Yudachi 222
Yura 230

United States

ARMY

Americal Division 235
   164th Infantry Regiment 139, 142,
     226, 230, 234
     1st Battalion of 231

182nd Infantry Regiment 231, 232, 234
   2nd Battalion of 234
   3rd Battalion of 232
244th Coast Artillery Battalion 230, 233
   F Battery 230
1st Infantry Division 216
25th Infantry Division 235

ARMY AVIATION

11th Bomb Group 233
67th Fighter Squadron 223, 225
339th Fighter Squadron 232

MARINE AVIATION

VMF-223 220–223
VMF-224 221–223
VMSB-132 235
VMSB-231 221
VMSB-232 221

MARINE CORPS

Headquarters 203
Marine Corps Schools 12, 130, 203–209
   Training Battalion 203, 208, 209, 238
      Headquarters Company 198, 203, 208–210, 238
   Marine Training Command 203, 204
      Headquarters Battalion 203, 204
         Range Company 203, 204
   Reserves
      Fleet Marine Corps 5
      19th Regiment 5
      2nd Battalion 5
      4th Battalion 5, 11, 15, 19, 180
         D Company of 19
      7th Battalion 6, 11, 15, 22
      8th Battalion 13, 15
   Schools Regiment 204
   Special Schools Battalion 203, 204
      Engineer Demonstration Company 202, 203, 238
      Headquarters Company 203
1st Marine Amphibious Corps 188, 189
1st Marine Brigade 6, 18, 215
1st Raider Battalion 96, 98, 101, 102, 108, 126, 154, 223, 224

2nd Raider Battalion 137, 138
3rd Defense Battalion 104, 115, 123, 125, 157, 220, 236
4th Marine Replacement Battalion 232
4th Infantry Training Regiment 200–202, 238
   H&S Company 200–202
5th Defense Battalion 134, 137, 230
12th Defense Battalion 174

1st Marine Division 6, 48, 70, 78, 215–217, 235–238
   D–2 Intelligence Section of 60, 96, 107
   Field Hospital of 89, 119, 120, 124, 125
   Headquarters of 83, 106, 114, 132, 186, 217
   Message Center of 89
   Military Police Company 79, 115, 127, 129
   Motor Transport 182
   Paymaster 147–149, 196, 222
   Photo Section 140
   Post Office 108
   Quartermaster 107, 119, 148, 187
   1st Amphibian Tractor Battalion of 72, 91, 143
   1st Engineer Battalion of 131, 185, 230
   1st Parachute Battalion of 103, 156, 223
   1st Pioneer Battalion of 95
   1st Special Weapons Battalion of 137, 219
   1st Tank Battalion of 219
   1st Regiment of 217
      1st Battalion of 219
      2nd Battalion of 219, 236
   5th Regiment of 21, 42, 84, 98, 102, 133, 156, 189, 216, 217, 220, 230, 235–237
      1st Battalion of 220
      3rd Battalion of 236, 237
   7th Regiment of 42, 104, 105, 108, 110, 137, 139, 189, 217, 224, 230, 236, 237
      Weapons Company 230
      1st Battalion of 224
      3rd Battalion of 237
   11th Regiment of 6, 13, 18, 29, 46–50,

51, 88, 104, 113, 125, 126, *174*, *176*, 188, 216–218, 226, 229–231, 236, 237

Communications Section 58, 84, 108, 118, 124

H&S Battery 48, 57, 60, 61, 63, 67, 71, 73, 75, 77–79, 81–83, 86, 87, 88, 89, 91–95, 97–99, 101, 102, 104, 106–108, 110, 112, 116, 117, 122–124, 126, *128*, 130, 131, 143, 144, 147, 149, 150, 152, 155, 156, 158–161, 165, 168, 169, 171, 177, 182, 184, 186, 215, 217–219, 221–223, 228, 236, 237

Mess Section 97, 112

Motor Transport Section 75, 76, 97, 108

Ordnance Section 75, 84, 96, 187

Plans and Training Section 188

Police Section 97, 112, 148, 153

Quartermaster 50, 75, 97

R-1 Section 218

R-2 Section 53, 89, 143, 221

R-3 Section 89, 118, 153

R-4 Section 223

Special Weapons Battery of 76, 82, 94, 101–103, 109, 123, 125, 135–137, 144, 153, 165, 217, 223

1st Battalion of 42, 104, 119, 124, 224, 236, 237

 A Battery 41

2nd Battalion of 6, 18, 19, 21, 41, 56, 84, 98

 D Battery 107, 176, *176*, 177

 E Battery 18, 19–21, 23, 24, 28–31, 36, 39–41, 43, 44, 48, 110

 F Battery 19, 24, 27, 28

 H&S Battery 98

3rd Battalion of 6, 14, 20, 27, 84, 94

 G Battery 39–44, 236

 H Battery 6, 13, 18, 20, 94

 H&S Battery 110

 I Battery 94, 101, 111, 237

4th Battalion of 6, 43, 216, 236, 237

5th Battalion of 6, 67, 85, 110, 114, 127, 139, 157, 174, 179, 216, 217, 223, 236

2nd Marine Division

 2nd Regiment, 3rd Battalion of 231

 8th Regiment 137, *140*, 141, 231, 234

7th Marine Division 137, 139, 189, 203

NAVAL AVIATION

VF-5 223, 225

VS-3 223

VT-8 223

NAVY SHIPS

Aaron Ward 230

Alchiba 151, 152, 155, 230, 234

American Legion 157, 161

Arcturus 30

Atlanta 230

Barnett 28, 30, 215–217

Bellatrix 93

Benham 230

Betelgeuse 88

Colhoun 221

Dewey 67

Elmore 9

Enterprise 145, 218, 220, 233

Fletcher 230

Fomalhaut 81, *82*, 220

Fuller 230

General Robert L. Howze 9, 197

George F. Elliott 23, 30, 74, 215–217, 219

Gregory 87, 221, 222

Helena 231

Hornet 230

Hull 67

Hunter Liggett 8, 9, 56–71, 74, 158–161, 217, 218, 236

Jarvis 219

Landsdowne 231

Lardner 230

Lee 30

Libra 218

Little 222

LST #456 9, 236

LST #470 9

Majaba 231

McCawley 7, 8, 22–24, 29–35, 38, 39, 215

Meredith 227

Mugford 218

Neville 30, 31

North Carolina 62

Ranger 62, 218
Sailfish 13
San Francisco 231
Saratoga 218, 223
Squalus 13
Sterrett 231

Wakefield 217
Wasp 62, 218
West Point 9, 164, 165, 236
Wharton 6, 7, 12, 13, 23, 215
William Ward Burrows 85, 86, 221

General Index

Notes: Military rank is at time of first citation.
Page numbers in *italics* refer to figure captions.

Abend, Max 26; Morris 27, 179, 200;
    Rose 210
Accidental woundings 135
Ackerman, Sarah (Sadie) 210, 211, 213
Adelaide Street, Brisbane 164
Advance echelon, 1st Marine Division
    216
Aerial attacks: American 173; Japanese,
    daylight 74, 78, 83–91, 94–97, 105,
    108, 109, 116, 117, 120–122, 124–126,
    138, 143, 175, 218–222, 224–229, 231,
    232; night 110–112, 114, 117, 118, 121,
    123, 124, 127, 130, 138, 149–151, 157,
    177, 180–182, 186, 192, 195, 196, 220,
    223, 225, 234, 237
Aerial reconnaissance: Japanese 183
Air raid alarms 85, 86, 88, 90–92, 94,
    95, 97, 109, 111–117, 120–127, 129, 130,
    138, 141, 143, 145, 149, 152, 153, 156,
    157, 182–184, 186, 187, 192, 195, 221,
    228, 234
Air raid shelters 75, 82, 88–91, 96, 97,
    102, 103, 108, 109, 111, 112, 114,
    117–119, 121–124, 126, 141, 144, 164
Air Support Force 218
Aircraft carriers: American 45, 62, 143,
    145, 216, 218; Japanese 144, 155, 228,
    230, 232
Airfields: Cape Gloucester 171, 175,
    177–179, 182, 184, 186, 188, 189, 236;
    Guadalcanal 70, 83, 85, 94, 96–98,
    103, 104, 106, 110, 111, 116–121, 124,
    131, 138, 142, 145, 149, *151*, 152

Airplanes, American 36, 37, 131
Aleutian Islands 115
Allies 201
Alligators 94
America 164, 236
American Campaign ribbon 208
Americans 164, 173, 201
Ammunition dumps, Guadalcanal 85,
    87, 89, 121, 151
Amphibious Force 218
Amphibious landing exercises: Hurst
    Beach, N.C. 30–32, 34–39, 216; Joint
    Army-Marine 34–39, 216; Koro, Fiji
    60–66, 218
Amphibious tractors ("Alligators") 71,
    72, 105, 135, 139, 174, *175*, 176, 179,
    184, 185
Anglo-Americans 201
Anti-aircraft fire, American 74, 83,
    95–97, 108, 109, 111, 120, 122–124,
    126, 130, 138, 143, 152, 157, 173,
    180–182, 187, 219, 220, 227–229, 231,
    236
Anti-aircraft guns, American, 20mm
    60, *61*, 97, 180
Anti-tank guns: American 37mm 40,
    41, 71, 81, 96, 98, 127, 219, 229, 230;
    Japanese 30mm 132
Aogiri Ridge, Cape Gloucester 237
APDs 91, 222
Apia, Samoa 104
Appleton, Lt. Maurice L., Jr. 88, 130,
    221

Armillita (toreador) 198
Army, American 116, 122, 126, 128, 132, 134, 140, 148, 149, 153, 154, 157, 158, 162, 163, 166, 168, 179, 184, 216, 226, 230, 231, 235
Army engineers 36
Army Military Police 161
Army soldiers 30, 31
Artillery and artillery fire: American 76–78, 84, 94, 130, 132, 140, 145, 147–149, 153, 155, 177, 189, 226, 230, 231; 75mm pack howitzer 19, 30, 31, 35–42, 44, 45, 47, 51, 66, 71, 98, 108, 110, 113, 114, 155, 176, 216, 219, 224, 226, 229, 237; 90mm anti-aircraft 83, 95, 96, 108, 109, 111, 123, 124, 138, 143, 152, 157, 180, 220; 105mm howitzer 62, 97, 98, 109, 112, 155, 216, 223, 226, 227, 229, 237; 155mm cannon 134, 135, 137, 154, 155; 155mm howitzer 21, 42, 98, 230
Artillery, Japanese 108, 117–121, 124–127, 129, 132, 133, 141, 142, 151, 154, 155, 226–230; 105mm cannon 151, 227, 228, 231, 235; 150mm howitzer 226–228, 231, 235
Artillery aerial observers 188
Artillery shells: American 39, 41, 44, 45; HE (high explosive) 39, 41, 44
Ashman, Pvt. Lawrence 143, 179
Atlantic City, N.J. 28
Atlantic Marine Force 20
Atomic bomb 205
Auckland, New Zealand 217
Australia 156, 160–171
Australian Women's Army Service (AWAS) 166
Australians 167, 173
Aviation gasoline, Guadalcanal 220, 221, 226, 227
Avon Avenue, Newark, N.J. 173, 197, 210
AWOL 50, 61

B-17 Flying Fortresses 92, 116, 117, 120, 147, 226, 227, 233
B-24s 236
B-25s 236
Bachelor Officers Quarters (BOQ), Parris Island 42
Baga Island, Solomon Islands 233

Baker, Warrant Officer 201
Ballarat, Victoria, Australia 9, 165, 167–173, 236
Banzai attacks 237
Barracks: Headquarters Company, Training Battalion #3088 208–210; Screening Detachment #3127 206; #3132 207; #3133 208; #3134 205, 206
Barrier Reef, Australia 161
Battery Commanders, 11th Marines: E Battery 18–20, 23, 27, 28, 30, 34; H&S Battery 57, 63, 64, 67, 71, 97, 98, 100–102, 110, 127, 149, 152, 153, 169, 171, 173, 176, 177, 179, 183–185, 188, 189, 192, 193, 195, 236, 237; Special Weapons Battery 94, 101
"Battle Hill," Guadalcanal 126, 127
Battle of "Bloody Ridge" ("Edson's Ridge") 70, 96–103, 105, 222–224
Battle of Cape Esperance 117, 226
Battle of Midway 219
Battle of Santa Cruz 230
"Battle of Tassafaronga" 234
Battle of the Eastern Solomons 220
Battle of the Tenaru 70, 78–81, 219
"Battle of 23 October" 125–129, 129, 132, 134
Battleships: American 45, 62; Japanese 119, 140, 144, 146, 147, 155, 227, 232, 233
Bayonet charges, Japanese 99, 103
Bayonets, Japanese 103, 128
Beach Red, Guadalcanal 69–74, 78, 116, 135, 231
Beach Yellow, Cape Gloucester 171, 236
Beaching stations 171
Bear Inlet, N.C. 31
Beli Beli, Goodenough Island, New Guinea 9
Bell, 1st Sgt. 202
Bemis, Col. John A. 88, 221
Berlin 201
Bess see Felber, Bess
Bethlehem Shipbuilding Company 61
Bismarck Archipelago 236
Black, TSgt 177, 179
Blackout 164
Boland, Lt. 183
Bombers: G4M "Betty" 154, 218–229, 231, 232, 234, 237; Japanese 83, 85, 87, 89, 92, 94–96, 108, 109, 111, 116, 120, 122, 124, 126, 143

Bombs, American: 500 pound 85, 86, 139; 1000 pound 127, 139, 144, 151, 230

Bombs, Japanese 83, 85, 86, 88–90, 94, 95, 97, 105, 108–111, 116, 118, 120, 122–125, 127, 149, 150, 157, 174, 177, 180, 182, 186, 221, 222, 224, 226; 100-pound 90; 500-pound 89, 92; personnel 180

Bonne *see* Gilsenan, Bonne

Boqueron, Cuba 17, 19

Borgen Bay 189, 237

Borok, Freda 207

Bougainville 225, 226, 233

Bove, 1st Sgt Frederick 12, 18–20, 22, 28, 29, 33, 39–41, 44, 48, 49, 104, 106, 110, 111, 113, 133, 139, 147, 153–155, 157, 166, 171, 199, 204, 208

Braddock, Cpl. Wilbur R. 119, 123

Brisbane, Australia 9, 156, 158, 160–164, 235, 236

British Isles 83

British Solomon Islands 197

Bromfield, Louis 62

Brooklyn Navy Yard 12

"Brown-out" 164

Browning Automatic Rifle 22, 73

Brush, Capt. Charles H., Jr. 70

Bryan, Pvt. Joseph D. 99, 100, 223

Buckley, Major Edmund J. 46, 194, 237

Buddy Rutkin 47

Buin, Bougainville 226, 233

Buka, Bougainville 221

Buna, Papua 150

Burials: American 76, 77; Japanese *80*, 103, 105, 129, 177, 179, 190

Burnett, Pvt. W. E., Jr. 192, 193

Butler, PlSgt 15, 19

Caimanera, Cuba 14, 17

California 52, 197, 204

Camouflage suit, 172, *173*

Camp Cable, Australia 9, 161, 162, 236

Camp Davis, N.C. 51

Camp Lejeune, N.C. 8, 207, 213, 216

Camp Paikakeriki, New Zealand 60

Camp Pendleton, Cal. 10, 198–204, 238; *Area 16-B-3* 202–204; *Area 17* 199; *Area 17-B-1* 200

Camp Victoria Park, Australia 9, *172*, 173

Candidates' Refresher Course 206

Canister 127, 230

Cape Cretin, Papua 9, 190

Cape Esperance, Solomon Islands 231, 232, 235

Cape Gloucester, New Britain 9, 171–196, 201, 236, 237

Cape Lookout, N.C. 8

Caravela Point, Cuba 7, 13–19

Cardozo Hotel, Miami Beach, Fla. 33

Cargo ships: American 85, 134, 139, 140, 143, 217, 227, 231, 232; Japanese 143, 147

Carver 95

Casey, Sgt. James P. 76, 77, 83, 92, 167–169, 219, 236

Castle Hill Point, Cuba 7, 18–22

Casualties: American 82, 94, 95, 103, 108, 109, 114, 115, 118, 121, 124, 125, 128, 132, 135, 150, 155, 173, 175, 177, 180, 186, 218, 219, 222, 224, 226, 227, 230, 232, 233; Japanese 79, 105, 147, 219, 230–233

Caterpillar tractors 175

Cemeteries, Guadalcanal 76, 115, 156, 206, 207

Censorship 47, 108

Change Sheet 67, 165, 177

Charleston, S.C. 7, 8, 12, 24, 29, 32, 33, 39, 44

Charleston Navy Yard 23, 24, 31, 32

Charleston Ordnance Department 32

"Charley" *174*

Chase Avenue, Miami Beach, Fla. 210

Chicago, Il. 208

Churchill, Winston 201

Civil Service 206

Close Order Drill 205

Clover Club, Miami, Fla. 211

Coast Guard 67

Coconut Grove, Brisbane 164, 168

Coffey, Battery Police & Property Sgt. Cornelius W. 84

Coleman, Sgt. 14

College Hill, N.C. 33

Colored troops 184

Commandant, U.S. Marine Corps 18, 49, 229

Commander, South Pacific Force and Area 148, 217

Commander-in-Chief, U.S. Fleet 218
Commanding General: 1st Marine Division 53, 126, *170;* 11th Marine Regiment 126; Marine Training Command 203
Commanding Officer, 3rd Defense Battalion 236
Commissary stores 183
Company Commander, H&S Company, 4th Infantry Training Regiment 201
Congressional Medal of Honor 208
Conley, PFC William J. 114
Conrad, Joseph 149
Construction Battalion men 186
Cook Straits 60
Corpsmen 106, 109, 132, 183, 230
Court martial 15, 17, 46, 58, 78, 83, 91, 114, 127, 129, 167, 186
Crete 28
Crimea 201
Cruisers: American 60, 62, 65, 130, 135, 143, 147, 219, 231, 232, 234; Australian 61; Japanese 87, 91, 96, 104, 112, 113, 116, *117*, 127, 139, 140, 144, 145, 147, 219, 226, 227, 230, 232, 233
Cunningham, Denver 18

D-Day 217
D-Section Map: *#101* 78–104; *#104* 112
Dalglish, Quartermaster Clerk Gordon R. 91
Dauntless SBD dive-bombers 221, 223–225, 227, 230–233, 235
"Davy Jones" 53, *54*
Daylight Saving Time 40
Dead, Japanese 79, 80, *80, 81,* 102, 103, 114, 115, 127–129, *129,* 141, 147, 173, 177, 179, 190, 219
Decoration Day 28
DelBrasil 215
Del Valle, Col. Pedro 43, *49,* 53, 57, 58, 67, 73, 78, 79, 84, 88, 90, 91, 93, 109, 114, 118, 119, 122, 126, 127, 144, 145, 155, *169,* 170, 215, 223, 229
D'Entrecasteaux Group 9, *174*
Depth charges, 139, 143, 151, 155, 159
Destroyers: American 23, 30, 31, 34, 60, 62, 65, 67, 69, 87, 116, 130, 134, 139, 143, 144, 147, 159, 161, 218, 219, 227, 228, 231–234, 236; British 87; Japanese 79, 81, 82, 84, 87, 91, 98,

104, 116, 119, 137, 139, 140, 144, 147, 152, 157, 219–227, 230–235
Diary: Felber 68, 78, 103, 107, 109, 188, 213, 217, 236; Merillat 225, 240
"Dim-out" 164
Dittmar, Chaplain Lt. Cdr. Charles A. 76, 77, 86, 93, 105, 109, 119, 123, 124, 129, 156, 219
Dive-bombers: American 87, 95, 128, 223; Japanese 218, 228
Division Brig 129
Division Command Post 221–223
Division Intelligence Officer 194, 237
Division of Public Relations 173
Divisional Chaplain 219
Divisional Paymaster 222
Dog-fighting 83, 220, 221, 225
Doma Cove, Guadalcanal *146*
Dual purpose guns, Japanese *141*
"Duds" 82, 118
"Dugout Doug" McArthur 152
"Dugout Sunday" 229
Dugouts: American 142, 173, 185, 186, 193; Japanese 142, 173, 179, 186, 187, 189
Dutch East Indies 128, 230
Dwyer, 2nd Lt. James J., Jr. 17
Dzizynski, Sgt. John, Jr. 123

Earthquakes 179
Eaton, Lt. 137
"Edson's Ridge" 222–224
Eggers, Pay Clerk 196
Elizabeth, N.J. 29
Ellison, Lt. 19
Embarkation rosters 156, 157
Emerson, Hannah (Gross) 26
England 28
English 201
Ennis, Major Louis A. 177, 178, 184, 192
Equator 53, *54, 55*
Ernest, PFC 186
Essex County Building and Loan 47
Europe 201, 202
Executive Officer, 11th Marine Regiment *170,* 221
Executive Order 8244 5

Fairclough, Captain James 176, 188, 189, 236
False alarm 109, 111, 221, 234

Felber, Anita 204, 210
Felber, Bess 3, 13–16, 18–25, *25*, 26–29, 32, 33, 39–44, 46–50, *50*, 65, 88, 90, 95, 105, 125, 130, 144, 145, 154–157, 168, 171, 191, 192, 197–201, 204, 206, 207, 209, 210
Felber, Jack *16*, 22, 90, 140, 199, 204
Felber, Joseph *16*, 156
Felber, Pat *16*, 207, 209, 210
Felber, Rose *16*
Felber, Sadie Ackerman 213
Fighter One airfield, Guadalcanal 94, 222, 226, 227, 229, 232
Fighter squadron, American 87
Fighters: American 87, 95, 97, 109, 111, 126; F4F Wildcats 97, *158*, 218–229, 231, 232, 235; P-38s 143, 232, 233; P-39 Airacobras 113, 225, 227, 229, 231, 232; P-400s 223; Japanese 83, 108, 120, 122, 126; Zeros 83, 96, 109, 111, 116, 173, 187, 220–229, 231–233, 238
Fiji Islands 60–66
First Battle of the Matanikau River 70
First Echelon, Ichiki Detachment 219
First Joint Training Force 216
First Sergeant: 4th Infantry Training Regiment, H&S Company 200; 11th Marine Regiment, Headquarters 27, 49, 88, 104; H&S Battery, 3rd Battalion 110
Fitness Reports 106, 110, 188
Fitzgerald, Lt. (J.G.) James J. 156, 157
Five O'Clock Club, Miami Beach, Fla. 210
Flame throwers, Japanese 79
Flares, Japanese 97, 104, 117, 118, 120, 121, 138, 144
Floatplanes, Japanese 231, 235
Florida 204
Food, Japanese 85
Formal Guard Mount 41
Fort Hamilton, N.Y. 179
Forward Echelon, 1st Marine Division 149, 150, 156, 217
Forward observers 132, 142
Foss, Joe 231
Fowler, TSgt(Mess) Obert 110, 111, 225
Foxholes: American 75, 103, 124, *128*, 173, 176, 178, 180; Japanese 114, 142
Fredericksburg, Va. 29
Funeral services 76, 77, 209, 210

Gas masks 141, 144, 152
Gasoline 121, 173
Gasoline dump, Guadalcanal 95
Gelfo(u)nd, Max 19, 20, 23, 42, 44, 47, 48, 157
General Court Martial 78, 83, 91, 127, 129, 167, 186
General Quarters 60, 61, 67, 68, 159
Germany 201, 202, 215
Ghormley, Rear Admiral Robert L. 84, 217, 218, 220
Gibson, Quartermaster Sgt George G. 91, 114
Gilsenan, Bonne 168, 169
Goettge, Lt. Col. Frank B. 70, 237
Goldberg, Alex and Silvia 210
Goldberg, Bertie 27
Goodenough Island 9, *174*, 182, 193
Goodheart 167
Greece 26
Grenade throwers, Japanese 79
Grenadilla Point, Cuba 7, 17, 18
Griffin, Capt. David R. 188, 237
Gross, Kay 15, *16*
Grosvenor Hotel, Brisbane 163
Guadalcanal 9, *61*, *62*, *64*, 65, 66, 69–155, 163, 166, *169*, 174, 179, 181, 189, 197, 201, 218–236
Guam 79, 219, 220
Guantanamo Bay, Cuba 5–7, 11, 13–23
Guantanamo City, Cuba 16, 19, 21
Guard Book 17
Gunnery Sergeant 182, 188

Haines, Sgt. 27
Hallo, John 166
Halsey, Admiral William F. 148, 152
Hand grenades: American 67, 173; Japanese 99
Hardman, PlSgt 203
Harrington, TSgt Howard W. 108
Harris, Lt. Charles D. 57, 59, 64, 67, 97, 98, 115, 145, 217
Harrison, Col. 192, 193
Haryan, PFC George H. 108
Havana, Cuba 10, 15, 238
Haw Run, N.C. 44, 45
Hawaii 168
Hebrew Cemetery, Newark, N.J. 200, *209*

Hemingway, Ernest 2
Henderson Field, Guadalcanal 219–235
Higgins boats 29, 30, *63*, 65, 66, 69, 71, 74, 85, 132, 216
Hill 150, Cape Gloucester 237
Hill 450, Cape Gloucester 189
Hill 660, Cape Gloucester 189, 190, *190*, 192, 237
Hirt, Cpl. Paul L. 108
Hodge, Pvt. Wilmouth C. 93
Holcomb, MajGen Thomas *49*, 125, 229
Holden, SSgt. Edward C. 119
Holt, SgtMajor 198, 199
Honolulu, Hawaii 46, 155
Hood, Lt. 36
Horse Island, S.C. 40
Hotel Australia, Melbourne 166
Hotel Cecil, Wellington, N.Z. 58
Hour Glass Café, Newark, N.J. 197
Hughes, Major Thomas B. 74, 91, *170*
Hunt, Col. Leroy P. 220
Hurst Beach, N.C. 8, 30–32, 34–38, 215

Ice making machinery, Japanese 95
Ichiki, Col. Kiyonao *70*
Ilu River 135, 136
Infantry, Marine 94, 102, 131
Interior Guard Duty 205
International Date Line 56
Italians 165

J2F amphibian 225
Jack Dempsey's Restaurant, Miami Beach, Fla. 33
Jacksonville, N.C. 8
Japan 46, 47, 107, 203, 205, 206
Jasinski, Carl E. 33, 43, 44, 49, 57, 58, 110, 127–130, 139, 147, 148, 153, 157, 175, 184
Jeeps *64*, 107–109, 114, 126, 148, 153
John Carroll 9
John Ericsson 8, 52–58, 216, 217
Joint Chiefs of Staff 235
Jones, 1st Lt. John D. 64–67, 218
Jungle conditions 94, 110, 173, 175–177, 181, 185–187, 190

Karlage, 1stSgt 19
Kawaguchi, MajGen Kiyotaki 223
Kay *see* Gross, Kay

Kelly (Kelley), Asst Cook Joseph A. 76
Kendall, Lt. Lane C. 19
Kennedy, Cpl. 20
Kennedy home 48
King, Admiral Ernest J. 218, 232
King Neptune 53, 54, *54*
Kinston, N.C. 48
Klein, Pvt. 95, 106
Kokumbona, Guadalcanal *140*, *151*, 220, 226, 230–232, 234
Kokusho, Major Yukichi 224
Koli, Guadalcanal 231
Koli Point, Guadalcanal 70, 231
Korean War 213
Koro, Fiji Islands 8, 60–65, 218
Kuboff, PFC Stephen E. 108
Kukum, Guadalcanal 81, 104, 132, *141*
Kungsholm 52, 216
Kuntze, Bill 19, 157, 166, 168, 199

Landing barges, Japanese 190
Landings: American 69–72, 104, 116, 133–135, 137, 138, *138*, 171, 173; Japanese 78, 79, 120, 121, 135, 137, 144, 145, 147, 226, 227, 231–233
Latrines 14, 37, 87, 90
Letiziano, Cpl. 22
Letter of Instruction 203
Levine, Eddie 210
Lewis, Sarah 90
Life magazine 191
Limited National Emergency 5
Lincoln Road, Miami Beach 25
Listening posts, Guadalcanal 117, 176
Long Island, N.Y. 48
Looting, Guadalcanal 73
Los Angeles, Calif. 10, 204
"Louie the Louse" 220, 221
Love, 2nd Lt. Donald 17
Loveland 108
LSTs 174, 190
Lummus Park, Miami Beach, Fla. 25
Lunga, Guadalcanal 234
Lunga Point, Guadalcanal 220, 225, 231, 234
Lunga River, Guadalcanal 75, 81, 83, 101, 102, 104, 110, 113, 116, 117, 122, 123, 135, 138, 141, 225, 228, 229
Lunga River bridge 73–77, 81–94, 99, 101, 102, 104–108, 116, 123

Maas, Major Arthur B. 93, 222

Machine guns, American 80, 103, 105, 135, 142, 143, 176–179, 219; .50 caliber 38, 44, 60, 66, 71, 96, 98–101

Machine guns, Japanese 69, 79, 99–101, 103, 127, 132, 189; .25 caliber 99–101

Mail 16, 24, 30, 47, 88, 90, 108, 125, 143, 144, 145, 153, 157, 171, 178, 179, 190, 191, 193, 199

Malaria 106, 113, 119, 120, 123–125, 160, 165, 197–200

Malarial meningitis 165

Malembui (Nalimbui) River 137, 139, 231

Maloyd, PFC Joseph S. 119, 123

Manasse, MessSgt Adolph 112, 201

Maneuvers, Marine Corps 21, 27, 33, 37, 42, 44, 45, 48

Maps, Japanese 105

Marcus, Sam 48

Marine Barracks, New River, N.C. 216

Marine Corps Institute (M.C.I.) 43

Marine Corps Reserve 40

Marine Corps Schools 11, 50, 130, 203–209

Marine Gunner 64, 101, 107, 171, 184, 218, 223

Maruyama, Lt. Gen. Masao 226, 229, 230

Mason, PFC George 83

Matanikau River 125, 126, 128, 130–135, 140–143, 147, 148, 153, 224–226, 229, 230, 234

Matsonia 53

Mattice, Pvt. Leland W. 76, 83, 92, 167–169, 219, 236

Maxwell, Lt. Col. William F. 84, 220

McArthur, Lt. Gen. Douglas 152, 201

McCallon, PFC H. D. 108

McDonough, Pvt. 112

Meals 39, 52, 57, 60, 61, 73, 75, 78, 85, 94, 102, 120–122, 130, 159–161, 165

Melanesian natives *138*

Melbourne, Australia 9, 165–169, 186, 236

Merillat, 2nd Lt Herbert C. 217, 218, 221

Mess hall 32, 39, 169, *174*, 185, 186

Mexico 166, 198

Meyers, Mrs. 198

Miami, Fla. 24–26, 33, 34, 39, 210, 211, 238

Miami Beach, Fla. 7, 8, 10, 24–26, 33, 210, 211

Michael, Marine Gunner Paul R. 101, 223

Miles, PFC Talmadge L. 84, 91

Militano, Sgt. 57, 58, 101

Military Police 79, 115, 127, 129, 161, 167, 173

Mollenhauer, Sgt. Rudy 43

Morale, American 30, 121, 124

Morgan's Bridge, Savannah, Ga. 27

Morning Report 156, 165, 177

Mortars: American 131, 132, *133;* 81mm *133*

Mortars: Japanese 97, 99, 126, 127, 154

Moscow 150

Mossburg, Capt. Philip L., Jr. 57–59, 112, 217

Mt. Martha, Victoria, Australia 166

Munson Line 12

Murphy, PFC 35

Murray, Cpl. Carl W.D. 50, 60, 110, 130

Muster Roll, H&S Battery, 11th Marines 217–219, 221–223, 225, 228, 230, 236, 237

Muster Roll Report 109, 130

Muster rolls 166, 167

Nalimbiu River, Guadalcanal 70, 231

Natamo Point, New Britain 189, 190

National Service Life Insurance 27

Native villages 136, 137, 188, 194

Natives, New Guinea 174, 183, 187, 188, 194, *195*

Naval Battle of Guadalcanal 232–234

Naval bombardment: American 130, 135, 171, 230, 231; Japanese 81–83, 90–92, 96, 104, 110, 115–121, 123, 127, *131*, 140, 144, 181, 219, 221, 223, 227, 232

Naval engagements 73, 84, 85, 87, 116, 119, 121, 123, 127, 128, 139, 143–147, 152, 153, 155, 219, 220, 226, 228, 230, 232–234

Naval guns: American 115, 226; Japanese 118–120, 224, 227, 232

Navy, American 34, 35, 41, 84, 121, 128, 148, 152, 164, 215, 218, 223, 236

Navy Annex 207

Nazis 201

Ndeni, Santa Cruz Islands 217
Nees, Major Charles M. 130
Netherland Hotel, Miami, Fla. 24–26, 33
Netherlands East Indies 103
Nevin, SgtMajor Donald D. 84
New Britain 171–196, 236
New Caledonia 93, 218
New England 201
New Georgia Island, Solomon Islands 127, 235
New Guinea 150, *174*, 236
New Jersey *173*, 208, 213, 238
New River, N.C. 8, 30, 31, 34–38, 42–50, *51*, 88, 107, 113, 162, 216, 217
New Year's Eve 164, 179, 211
New York, N.Y. 1, 10, 164, 200, 204, 209, 211
New Zealand 53–60, *61, 64, 66*, 161, 162, 217
Newark, N.J. 1, 5, 7, 8, 10, 11, 15, 19, 22, 26–29, 33, 40, 50, 106, 107, 147, 172, 188, 197, 198, 200, 206, 207, *209*, 210; Post Office 166, 168, 213, 238
Nicaragua 166
Nichols, Cpl. Robert L. 108, 109
Nimitz, Admiral Chester W. 207
Ninth Australian Division 167
North Carolina 28, 30, 133
North Island, New Zealand 60
Notaro, Hospital Apprentice 1st Class Frank E. 61, 127, 129, 130, 230
Noumea, New Caledonia 218
Noyes, Rear Admiral Leigh 218

Observation posts: American, Cape Gloucester 182, 189, *190;* Guadalcanal 106
Oceanside, Ca. 198–204
"Occupation money," Japanese 128
O'Connor, PlSgt John 48, 110
Officer of the Day 17, 49
Officer Training class 207
Official photographer, 11th Marine Regiment 79
Okeechee River, Ga. 27
Olympic Hotel, Miami Beach, Fla. 210, 211
Onslow Beach, N.C. 215, 216
Orderly, 11th Marine Regiment 93, 95, 228
Oro Point, New Britain 190

Panama, Canal Zone, Post Office Department 166
Panitch, Bill 144, 198–200, 207, 209
Panitch, Bob 29, 191
Pardi, Pvt. Peter A. 84
Park Avenue Restaurant, Miami Beach, Fla. 25, 211
Parris Island, S.C. 5–8, 11, 12, 20, 24, 27–29, 37, 39–44
Passwords 68
Patch, MajGen Alexander M. 235
Patrols: Cape Gloucester 178, 190, 237; Guadalcanal 70, 99, 154
Pavuvu, Russell Islands 9, 197, 237, 238
Payrolls 166
PBYs 222
Pearl Harbor attack 46, 155, 208
Peleliu 238
Pepper, Col. Robert H. 170, *170*, 186, 188, 191, 236
Perez (toreador) 198
Persinowski (Pierzynowski), Cpl. Charles 84
Pescatore, Lou 188
Philadelphia, PA 29
Philippines 201
Physical Drill 205
Pier 44, San Francisco, Calif. 52
Piper Cub aircraft 188
"Pistol Pete" *151*, 227, 228, 230
Pistol range, Parris Island, S.C. 42, 43
Pistols: American 43, 61, 64, 67, 69, 71, 76, 82, 99–101, 142; Japanese 103, 115, 128
Platoon Commanders school 205
Poindexter, Gladys 204
Point Cruz, Guadalcanal 132, 142, 154, 230
"Pollywogs" 53, 55
Pontoon bridges, 131
Port Royal, S.C. 12
Post exchanges, Guadalcanal 86, 88, 92, 93, 110, 129, 155
Post Office Department 153
Postal Money Order 155
Postmaster, Newark, N.J. 147
Press, Louis K. 200
Press Officer, 1st Marine Division 217, 218
Prisoners: Japanese 74, 78; Korean 74, 79, *80*, 115, 129

Promotions 88, 91, 112, 150
Propaganda, Japanese 173
Property Sergeant, H&S Battery, 11th Marine Regiment 185
PT boats 119, 139, 157, 227, 235

Quantico, Va. 10, 42, 203–209
Quarters, Col. Del Valle 109, 118, 122
Queen, Dr. (Lt.) William F. 124, 228
Queen's Wharf, Wellington, New Zealand 57–59
Quilter, Supply Sgt. 124
Quinine 67, 160, 161, 198, 199–201

Rabaul, New Britain *154*, 221, 225–227, 229, 236
Radar 225, 226
Radio shack 95
Raiders' Ridge 126, 127, *129*
Raleigh, N.C. 29
Ramp boat *64*, *65*, 86, 152, 171
Ramsey 193
Rapid fire gun, Japanese 230
Rasmussen, Sgt. 82
"Rat Transportation" 235
Ration Statement 165
Rear echelon: 1st Marine Division 165, 217; 11th Marines 182, 183, 188, 193
Reconnaissance planes, Japanese 178, 229
Record of Events, 11th Marines 78, 98, 105, 193
Red Cross 162–164
Regimental Chaplain, 11th Marines 156, 157, 219
Regimental Command Post, 11th Marines 71, 73, 75, 96, 103, 118, 120, 221–223, 227, 228
Regimental Commander, 11th Marines 170, 186, 188, 191, 192, 236
Regimental Communications Officer, 11th Marines 217
Regimental Memo, 11th Marines 126
Regimental Officers Mess, 11th Marines 185, 186
Regimental Operations dugout, 11th Marines 185, 186, 193
Regimental Paymaster, 11th Marines 222

Regimental Reconnaissance Officer, 11th Marines 217
Regimental SgtMajor, 11th Marines 84
Regimental Surgeon, 11th Marines 228
Reick, PFC Edward C. 92
Rekata, Solomon Islands 226–228
Relief, Guadalcanal 140, 149
Renfrow, Pvt. Paul A., Jr. 109
Reno, Nev. 52
Rifle Range, Parris Island, N.C. 42
Rifles, American: .30 caliber, 22, 32, 34, 37, 61, 73, 100, 109, 219; M-1 Garand 128, 205
Rifles, Japanese: .25 caliber 99, 103, 128
Rikko bombers 219, 226–228, 232
Road conditions: Cape Gloucester 175, 176, 179, 182, 184, 187, 188; Guadalcanal 107
Roanoke, Va. 32
Roll Call 50
Roosevelt, President Franklin D. 26–28, 40, 41, 46, 52, 53, 201, 202, 215
Roosevelt, Major James 138
Routon, PFC Lloyd A. 93, 95, 124, 228
RSOP (Reconnaissance, Selection, Occupation of Position) 19, 20, 46, 47
Rumors 18, 19, 43, 78, 84, 85, 87, 88, 103, 107, 109, 116, 119, 121, 125, 127, 131, 135, 139, 140, 149, 153–156, 161, 165, 171, 193, 203, 229, 231, 234
Rupertus, MajGen William A. *170*
Russell, GySgt Frank H. 168
Russell Islands 197, 224, 225, 237, 238
Russia 205
Russians 150, 201

Sailors 31, 74
St. Kilda, Victoria, Australia 168
St. Martha, Victoria, Australia 166
St. Martin, PFC Lawrence F., Jr. 108
Samoa 104, 217
Sampson, Pharmacists Mate 3rd Class Edward M. 106
San Diego, Calif. 198–200
San Francisco, Calif. 8, 10, 50–52, 197, 216
Sandman, PlSgt Daniel P. 79, 83, 84
Santa Barbara 215
Santa Cruz Islands 217

Saunders, Col. Laverne 233
Savannah, Ga. 27, 28, 41, 44
Savo Island *117*, 219, 233
Scalcione, Sgt. Alfred 106
Schnee, Olga 26, 29, 210
Sealark Channel 70, 222
Searchlight 110, 124, 130, 138, 157
"Second Matanikau" 70, 224
Second World War 208
Secretary of the Navy 152
Section Chiefs, 11th Marines 195
Semler (Simler), PFC Richard C. 112, 125
Sentries 12, 14, 15, 22, 45, 71, 74, 76, 78, 97, 98, 101, 109, 111, 117, 120–123
Sentry post 96, 97
Separation center, Marine Corps 208
Sergeant Major 165, 188, 191
Sergeant of the Guard 12–15, 17, 76
Seven Seas (restaurant), Miami Beach, Fla. 24, 210
Sewart, Major Allen J. 233
Sheldon 191
"Shellbacks" 53–55, *55*
Ships, English 85, 86
Shortland Islands, Solomon Islands 222, 232, 233
Sick bay 139
Sideman (Siderman), Cpl. Henry C. 83, 106
Siegler, Cpl. 116
Silberfeld, Rabbi 209, 210
Silver Meteor (train) 24, 26
Singing Bar, Miami 210
Skupien, Paymaster Sgt. 196
Sladovich, Sgt. Gregory G. 84, 123, 124
Sloan-Kettering Memorial Hospital 200
Smack, Cpl. 33
Smart, Capt. 112
Smith, MajGen Holland M. 6
Snipers, Japanese 98, 100, 101, 128, 142, 173, 174, 190
Solomon Islands 65–68, 84, 197, 217, 221
South Island, New Zealand 60
Southern Cross 12
Souvenirs, Japanese 74, 103, 106, 114, 115, 126, 128, 130, 190, *190*
Spain 150
Sparrows Point, Md. 61
Special Money Request 147, 148
Speed Graphic camera 186
"Spot warrant " 112

Stack, Lt. Col. Vincent E. 93, 222
Stalin, Joseph 201
Stalingrad 115, 150
Station Hospital, Newark, N.J. 197
Stevenson, Robert Louis 67
Strength, Japanese, Guadalcanal 65, 125, 218, 227, 228
Stuart, Marine Gunner Charles E. 64, 218
Studley 39
Submachine guns, American: Reising 100, 112, 125, 147, 148, 233, 234; Thompson 233
Submarines: American 13; German 41, 48; Japanese 61, 76, 81, *82*, 139, 155, 164, 220, 222, 231, 234, 235
"Suicide Creek," Cape Gloucester 237
Summary Court Martial 17, 58, 114
Superintendent of Vehicle Service 166
Supply runs, Japanese 234, 235
Surrender, Japan 206
Swedish-American Line 52
Sweidels 26
Swords, Japanese 103, 115, 128
Sydney, Australia 161

Taivu Point, Guadalcanal 219, 221, 222
Tank lighters 30, 35, 38
Tanks, Guadalcanal: American 35, 41, 122, 136, 237; Japanese 125–127, 132, *134*, 229
Tare Beach, New Guinea 9
Target Hill, Cape Gloucester 189
Tasimboko Raid 70
Task Commander, Guadalcanal 67
Tassafaronga, Guadalcanal 227, 231–234
Tatsch, Lt. James H. 59, 64, 67, 217, 218
Tee, PFC Cornelius C. 119, 123
Tenaru River, Guadalcanal 73, 78, 139, 219
"Tent City," New River, N.C. 216
Tents 162, 185, 187, 192–194
Texas Street, San Diego 198
Thefts, Cape Gloucester 186
Third Battle of the Matanikau River 70, 226
Tijuana, Mexico 198
"Time Fire" 135, 136
Tobruk 163, 167
"Tokyo Express" 221, 222, 225, 226, 231

Tonolei Harbor 233
Torpedo bombers: American 139, 144;
  Grumman Avengers 223–225, 227,
  231–233, 235
Torpedoes: American 139, 144, 232;
  Japanese 81, 139, 140, 151, 155, 219,
  220, 231, 234, 235
Torrey, MajGen Philip H. 217
Townsville, Australia 9
Tracer bullets 78, 99–101
Training Battalions 203
Tregaskis, Richard 220, 222
Trocadero (dance hall), Brisbane 163
Troop training 198, 203, 205
Troop transports: American 31, 62,
  134, 135, 143, 164, 215, 216, 230, 232;
  Japanese 120, 121, 127, 144–147, 152,
  227, 231–234
Troxler, Gus 22
Truckee, Ca. 52
Tulagi Island 103, 156, 217, 227
Turner, Rear Admiral Richard Kelly
  218
Turrentine 190, 191

Unlimited national emergency 215

Vandegrift, MajGen Alexander A. 53,
  84, 126, 217, 218, 220–224, 232, 234,
  235
Verona, N.C. 8, 162
Very pistol 132
Veterans Administration 40
Viall, Capt. Robert S. 49, 59, 101, 106,
  128
Victoria, Australia 165–169, *170*

Victory Medal 208
Virginia 28

Waggenheim, Charles 207
Walker 15
War Department 216
War Manpower Commission 197
War Shipping Administration 216
Warrant Officer 171, 191, 192, 201, 202,
  213
Washington Avenue, Miami Beach, Fla.
  25
Washington, D. C. 147, 173, 203, 207, 208
Way, Cpl. William B. 38, 106
Weequahic Park, N. J. 197
Wellington, New Zealand 8, *54, 55,*
  56–60, 62, 101, 107, 154, 162, 217
Wentworth Restaurant, Melbourne,
  Australia 168
West Virginia Pulp and Paper Company
  32, 33
Western Hemisphere Defense 41
White, Sgt. Austen G. 113, 119, 120
White House 215
"White poppy" 111
Williams, Lt. Lloyd O. 82
Wilmington, N.C. 18, 30, 51, 83
Wilson, N.C. *25*
Wire cutters, Japanese 79
Working parties 86, 161, 165, 182, 183,
  185, 187, 189, 193–196

Yarra River, Melbourne, Australia 168
Yemmassee, S.C. 43
YMCA 24, 33